Praise for
Good Girls Don't Get Fat

"*Good Girls Don't Get Fat* is not only immensely compelling, packed with valuable tips, resources and the latest research, but it offers sane solutions to help our girls thrive. Don't miss this must-read book."

—Dr. Michele Borba, author of *The Big Book of Parenting Solutions* and regular parenting expert on the *Today* show

"Raw, real, reassuring, and a must-read for anyone who has ever felt alone while dealing with diet drama!"

—Nancy Redd, author of *Body Drama* and *Diet Drama*

"*Good Girls Don't Get Fat* offers another deeply important layer to the conversation about body image and self-esteem. It is a vital and delicious read for anyone wanting to further explore the connection between our self-worth and appetite for life. She illuminates complex relationships with an ease and effortlessness that will further empower readers to take a look at their own value systems and begin creating a lifestyle that is informed, empowered and lacking in fear of your own power!"

—Jess Weiner, author of *Life Doesn't Begin 5 Pounds From Now* and global ambassador for the Dove Self-Esteem Fund

"As national president of the largest girl-serving organization in the country, I believe that every girl deserves a place, a process and a plan that will allow her to discover her inner power and to celebrate her inner beauty. I'm pleased to have contributed to a book that commemorates the magnificence inside each and every girl. Thank you, Dr. Robyn, for giving girls the confidence to embrace their bodies and love their true selves."

—**Connie L. Lindsey, national president, Girl Scouts of the USA**

"Now is the right time to help our daughters feel good about themselves, and Dr. Robyn can tell you how. Not ten pounds less or ten pounds more. Without a true connection to our uniqueness, we will continue to body bash, sink further into a culture of unsatisfied girls and women and live a life without true meaning. This book will be a must-read for every parent."

—**Emme, celebrity plus-size model, television host, author**

Good Girls Don't Get Fat

Good Girls Don't Get Fat

HOW WEIGHT OBSESSION IS SCREWING UP OUR GIRLS AND WHAT WE CAN DO TO HELP THEM THRIVE DESPITE IT

ROBYN J. A. SILVERMAN, PHD
WITH DINA SANTORELLI

A Stonesong Press Book

S

HARLEQUIN™

Good Girls Don't Get Fat

ISBN-13: 978-0-373-89220-4

A Stonesong Press Book

The names and identifying details of some characters in this book have been changed.

LIBRARY OF CONGRESS CATALOGING-IN-PUBLICATION DATA
Silverman, Robyn J. A.
Good girls don't get fat : how weight obsession is messing up our girls and what we can do to help them thrive despite it / Robyn J. A. Silverman with Dina Santorelli.
p. cm.
ISBN 978-0-373-89220-4 (pbk.)
1. Weight loss—Psychological aspects. 2. Body size. 3. Self-esteem. 4. Girls—Health and hygiene. I. Santorelli, Dina. II. Title.
RM222.2.S5433 2010
613'.0433—dc22
2010004612

www.eHarlequin.com

Printed in U.S.A.

For my dad, who believed in me,
and
my husband, Jason, who still does

Acknowledgments

When I finally handed in my dissertation on the ability of some girls to thrive in a "thin is in" world, I was elated, but there was an admitted letdown. Could all those years of backbreaking research really just be thrown into a drawer, never to see the light of day? And if so, how could it help all those girls, women and families who inspired the work in the first place? My advisor, Dr. Richard Lerner, suggested that I turn my dissertation into a book—a thrilling and truly terrifying proposition. I knew a book would be an amazing, challenging and demanding undertaking, and I was right—but, as it turns out, not just for the author.

If it was not for my husband, Jason—who took up more slack that any one man should ever have to—this book would not have been possible. His consistent patience, unwavering support and constant love during the many hills and valleys of this process have not gone unnoticed and will never be forgotten. Thank you for reminding me that the light at the end of the tunnel was actually daylight—not an oncoming train.

To Dina Santorelli, whose devotion to helping me with this project is apparent on every page of this book, I thank you for waking up early, going to bed late and treating my words as if they were your own. Your assistance was invaluable; your friendship, priceless. Thank you for urging me forward and helping me to realize that I was indeed bigger than this book, not the other way around.

I would like to thank Judy Linden and everyone at Stonesong Press for seeing the potential in this book and for pushing me to make it "great," even on days when I wasn't sure I had anything left. I know you share in the joy of its completion. A sincere thank-you as well to Deb Brody and the whole team at Harlequin, who, from the very beginning, supported this book. I could always sense your excitement, which made me feel that mine was not just another book in the crowd.

To the many girls and women in both my original research and the countless subsequent interviews conducted—my actual and honorary Sassy Girls—who candidly shared their stories and insights, I am eternally grateful and promise to keep working hard on your behalf.

It's a privilege to be in the company of so many phenomenal men and women who are working hard to improve the lives of children and families. To those dynamic go-getters who not only shared their insights with me but whose books I kept beside me to silently urge me forward—Rachel Simmons, Rosalind Wiseman, Dara Chadwick and Michele Borba—I found myself nodding in agreement as I read your words. A sincere thank-you to those men and women who are doing such commendable work and who graciously provided me with real answers to real questions in real time: Julia V. Taylor, Linda Nielsen, Jess Weiner, Kate Thomsen, Christina McGhee, Jean Kilbourne, Connie Lindsey, Joe Kelly, Bill Klatte, Toccara Jones and Thea Politis, among the many others whose contributions you will benefit from throughout this book. And to the incredibly connected and selfless Amy Jussel of Shaping Youth, I am so thankful for your vast media literacy knowledge and your passion for bridging great minds. Your assistance with compiling the Asset Girl resources found in Chapter 9 was immeasurable.

I'd also like to thank Dr. Richard Lerner and Ann Easterbrooks of Tufts University and Peter Scales and colleagues from Search Institute who grounded me in inspiring research and a new way of looking at youth. To me, young people will always be assets to be developed, not deficits to be managed.

A double clap and a "You rock!" to all those who cheered me on, from my Powerful Words family to my Facebook fans and to my Tweepies to my Girl Advocate community and the beautiful plus-size modeling community, who made sure to tell me that this work was needed and valuable. Thank you also to those who have provided me with a venue to help others, including *The Tyra Show, Bay State Parent* magazine, Education.com, *U.S. News and World Report,* LX.TV, ABC's *Nightline* and Fox News. Knowledge and experience are so much better when they're shared.

Thank you, Mom, for always telling me how proud you are of me and helping me through the rough spots with your words of encouragement. It is an honor to be your daughter, and, believe me, I know that my work with girls is better and more effective because of the mother you were, and still are. And to the Abeles, the Silvermans, the Barons and the Towler-Murrays—my family through blood, through marriage and through destiny—for checking in and cheering from the sidelines; it's always good to have you in my corner.

I will always be appreciative for my friends who were there in a flash when I needed them, especially Dena Shade Monuteaux, whose sisterhood is a gift beyond measure. I know if we made it through Tufts, we can make it through anything! To Randi Goldstein, Jennifer Jacobus, Joanie Pimentel, Dehra Glueck, Kathleen Hassan, Rob Berkley and Debbie Phillips for your years of friendship and Darelle Walsh, Megan Sommer and Antonia Fiddner for the weekly relief and fun. Yes, even adults need their own Sassy Sisters.

To my daughter, Tallie Paige, and the baby on the way, you inspire me to see life through new eyes, sparking my passion and giving me even more of a reason to work my hardest to make this world a better place. It is a privilege to be your mommy, and I am constantly amazed and humbled that out of all the children in all the world, we were blessed with you—a fate that fulfills and fuels me in every way. And of course, thank you to my dog, Casey, who curled up under the table on those late nights so that I didn't have to go it alone.

Contents

Introduction

Skinny or Else!

Two summers ago, it got personal.

I was sitting at the hair salon, my infant daughter, Tallie, gurgling beside me in her stroller, when a middle-aged woman with wavy blond hair ambled over, peered into the stroller and, with wrinkles creasing around her eyes, exclaimed, "Oh, look at her!"

I've always been used to people—strangers—making a fuss over Tallie. Even at five months old, she was quite engaging. But before I could smile or utter a proud "Thank you," the woman continued effusively, "Look at those fat thighs! Me, oh my! Enjoy it now, honey. It's the only time fat is cute." Then she laughed, and a woman nearby nodded in agreement.

I was thinking, of course, that the woman was an idiot. Not malicious. Just clueless. As far as I was concerned, she may as well have said, "Fat is bad, bad little girl, and you'd better learn it now!"

Taken aback, I simply responded, "She's a really healthy baby and doing well! We're so glad." I wish I had said more before she smiled and continued on her way, with absolutely no recognition that what she had said was the least bit offensive. Fat-bashing in all its varied forms—criticism, exclusion, shaming, fat talk, self-deprecation, jokes, gossip, bullying—is one of the last acceptable forms of prejudice. From a very young age, before they can walk away or defend themselves, women are taught that they are how they look, not what they do or what they know. Drawing attention to a woman's "assets" is usually the stuff of tabloid fodder, accompanied with a compulsory snicker or "wink, wink." Butt. Boobs. Legs. Think Betty Grable famously insuring her legs for a cool million, or the more current Mariah Carey upping the ante to a whopping $1 billion. The message is clear: A girl's body, stripped down to its "perfect" parts, slapped with price tags, carries a higher value than anything else she possesses.

Our daughters—with their beautiful, developing selves—watch closely from the sidelines and peer into their mirrors with derision, wondering, "Am I acceptable the way I am?" A November 2009 poll conducted by Girlguiding, a scouting association in the United Kingdom, found that an alarming 95 percent of girls ages sixteen to twenty-one want to change their bodies in some way, with portions of the group already expressing interest in cosmetic procedures. (A similar poll conducted by the Girl Scouts of America in 2006 reported that two-thirds of girls were not very satisfied with their weight.)

When girls believe that "fat" is bad, they internalize that message and think, "If I'm fat—if I have fat—I must be bad, too." And they'll do whatever they can to be "good." Plastic surgery. Extreme dieting. Overexercising. It's not an idea they grow out of. On the contrary, they grow into it.

But it's not just the physicality of being overweight. Ask almost any girl to do a word association for the word *fat,* and she'll likely give you a deplorable laundry list of connotative insults: ugly, lazy, gross, stupid, nasty, unpopular, smelly, blameworthy and, of course, bad. Play the same game with *thin,* and you'll get its virginal opposites: beautiful, successful, sexy, smart, sophisticated, controlled, well-liked and good.

In 2003, I created the Sassy Sisterhood Girls Circle for girls ages nine to fourteen, an ongoing workshop/coaching series that explores issues affecting body esteem and self-image, and the girls tell me that these hidden definitions color every aspect of their lives. Every year, on one of the first days of group, I ask them to close their eyes and raise their hand if they sometimes feel "too fat" or "not thin enough." And every year, after shifting for a few moments in their seats, they all raise their hands.

At first, the exercise alarmed me. The enemy—regardless of weight or body type—felt so undefined and omnipresent. But with the help of my Sassy Girls, I compiled a "flawed" belief system, a fixed and coherent set of erroneous guiding principles, based on the commonality of their experiences in order to fully understand the harmful messages they'd picked up and what we were up against. I now use this as a launching pad for discussions whenever I work with girls. I call it "The Good Girls' Weight Rules":

1. I believe thin is good, and fat is bad.

2. I believe my power comes from without, not within.

3. I will take unhealthy risks if I want to be thin and beautiful.

4. I strive for size 0.

5. My emotions should depend on how fat I feel.

6. My goals should focus on how I look.

7. I believe the media tells me the truth about how I should look, how thin and beautiful I can be if I just try hard enough.

8. My friends and family love me more when I'm thin and respect me less when I'm fat.

9. My values are to be disciplined enough to eat as little as possible, courageous enough to do whatever it takes and driven enough to strive for what perfect looks like.

10. I believe that I'm worth more when I weigh less.

The elephant in the room had finally been revealed in all its lackluster splendor. How was I to teach girls to follow their passions and embrace their most "extreme dreams" when their sense of purpose and personal power were tied up in a number sewn into the back of their jeans?

At the same time I started working with my Sassy Girls, I was knee-deep in my dissertation research at Tufts University, where I was hoping to find some clues that would help them. I set out to compare typical women's perceived sense of competence and body satisfaction with working and aspiring plus-size models. Why plus-size models? Because, in my view, they beat the odds.

They not only embrace a larger body type, citing a 13 or 14 as an ideal clothing size (my comparison groups cite a size 4 or 5), but they put themselves out there as examples of beautiful, confident women who don't strive to be "thin." I thought, Let's identify and harness these character traits. Let's expose the influences that drive plus-size models and other successful girls and women to feel proud of their bodies, their skills, their "assets," so that other girls, plus-size or not, can learn to be proud of theirs, too.

I have a firm conviction in the self-fulfilling feedback loop: You get what you give—and you give what you get. Girls will project the saturated messages they absorb from the many influences around them. So, if you're concerned about your daughter's weight and wondering whether you should be the one to tell her that she is "getting fat" or "putting on too much weight" or "needs to watch it" or "go on a diet," let me tell you now: Don't. Take a good look through this book and you will see who has already beaten you to it: friends, frenemies, acquaintances, advertisers, models, actresses and strangers, all of whom tell her and show her every day and every hour that she needs to be thinner. So many of our girls project grossly distorted images that lead to disordered thinking, disordered eating and disordered behaviors. To figure out how we can go from disordered to fulfilled, we must begin with young girls themselves.

I've structured this book from the "inside out," unveiling the ugly things going on in our girls' beautiful heads, and then following the ripple effect those ugly things have on the people around them. Each layer that we expose—from the self to mothers, fathers, family members, teachers and peers—provides us with an opportunity to address the overarching issues corrupting our daughters' sense of self and move them closer to becoming "Asset Girls," girls who own their strengths and use their power to do amazing things. Chapter 1, "The Body Bully Within: Her Own Worst Enemy," offers an illustrative reflection of the girl who believes she is fat, whether society would affirm that or not. A girl's inner body bully can be the meanest of all.

The next three chapters, "The Secret Impact of Mothers: I Love My Mom, But…," "Father Figure: Daddy's Not-So-Little Girl" and

"Hitting Home: The Butt of Family Jokes," tackle the sometimes paralyzing family dynamics that rule supreme in girls' lives. While our homes are supposed to be safe havens, sometimes families set up destructive codependencies that make our homes a battleground with direct or indirect hits about weight, pressures to diet, comparisons with siblings and bartering for pounds.

Chapter 5, "The School Fool, Part I: Teachers," exposes the difficulties educators have in combating body bullying within their school, as well as the insidious ways they may sabotage the future opportunities of girls who don't fit the thin ideal. Chapter 6, "The School Fool, Part II: Friends, Foes and Beaus," lays bare the powerful impact of the student population—peers, bullies, clubs, the dating scene—on our girls' self-image.

Chapter 7, "Kiss My Assets: The Secrets of Girls Who Thrive at Every Size," is a celebration of womanhood at any size. Here we trade in our self-limiting "Good Girls' Weight Rules" for the "Asset Girls' Ten Commandments," an affirmation of our daughters' abilities to pursue their dreams at any size, rather than wait for a moment of perfection that will never come. You'll read stories of happy, healthy and powerful girls who, having overcome body image struggles and other hardships, inspire with what they say and do.

At the end of Chapters 1 through 7, I've included a Body Image Quotient (BIQ): a brief questionnaire that will help you determine how your daughter is faring in this "thin is in" world. Your answers, which will take into account your perception of her views as well as the influences around her, will be awarded points. Your scores will be tallied and evaluated in Chapter 8, "Your Daughter's BIQ (Body Image Quotient): What's Her Total?" which provides a synopsis of where your daughter stands and tips on how to maintain or strengthen her BIQ. And, finally, Chapter 9, "Goodbye, Good Girl. Hello, Asset Girl!" is a resounding battle cry for finding health and happiness at any size, along with a list of asset-building resources, clubs, curricula and websites that provide ways to help girls become their best and be happy with who they are.

This book is not just an exposé and call to action, but a pointed and prescriptive guide for parents, guardians, families, teachers, counselors and anyone else who works with or cares about our young women. You are the ones who can make a difference. You are the ones who can counter these superficial messages. They listen to you. How do I know? They tell me they do.

My Sassy Girls have opened my eyes by opening their hearts. And then there are my friends, daughters of friends, friends of friends and the countless others who contact me through social networking sites and my Kiss My Assets blog, who shyly approach me after personal appearances or strike up conversations in the local coffee shop, bookstore or airport. My honorary Sassy sisters. You'll find lots of personal anecdotes; wisdom from physicians, educators, psychologists and other experts; and scientific research. But the stories of these girls and women who openly expressed their very personal experiences and deepest concerns are what have made this book possible. To all of them (in some cases, names, ages and other descriptive information have been changed, but never the sentiment), I am truly indebted.

I hope and pray that one day, when my daughter stares into the mirror and asks, "Am I acceptable the way I am?" she will confidently say yes. But I know that the real triumph will come when girls of all sizes and every age don't even have to ask. They'll just know.

Chapter 1

The Body Bully Within:
Her Own Worst Enemy

It's nearly 2:00 p.m. on a hot Wednesday in July, and my Sassy Sisterhood Girls Circle is winding down for the day. The girls hand in their "Real Me" diaries, which contain the answer to today's question: "What do you see when you look in the mirror?"

From one to the next, I see the same responses:

"I think I look fat."

"My belly is too big."

"I can't stand my legs."

Ashley, age fourteen, decides to read her entry to the group. She tells them that she looks in the mirror and squeezes the fat on her size-8 thighs. "You're disgusting," she admits to scowling at herself. She rolls her eyes and shakes her head when she recalls the triple chocolate sundae—made with frozen yogurt instead of the real thing—she ate the night before, during a family outing. "I try to be good…and I keep telling myself that I have to have more willpower, or I'll never be a size 0."

The other girls nod, twist their mouths or raise their eyebrows in empathy, their own encouragement coming in the form of self-loathing:

"I wish I had your thighs, Ashley! Mine are all squishy!"

"Yeah, and you have the flattest stomach. I'm like a beached whale."

"You guys are crazy. I'm the biggest one here!"

"I never eat ice cream. If I do, I feel huge. And I hate it."

"I'm getting depressed."

As girls—and, later, women—we're informally schooled to be critical of ourselves in order to fit in; we're taught to bring ourselves down in order to cheer someone else up. That's part of the way girls help each other reestablish their "goodness of fit"—their ability to interlock like puzzle pieces, to the best of their efforts, and claim their place within their immediate group or community. This often means scripting out a predictable exchange that denigrates the self while affirming the other—a pattern that is then picked up by the other girl as if it were a baton. As the girls say, "You can't be, like, 'I'm all that.' People like you better if you complain about how you look." The problem, though, is that somewhere along the line, we started believing our own criticisms.

Mirror, Mirror on the Wall, Who's the Fattest of Them All?

If it's true, as Mary Pipher, author of *Reviving Ophelia,* says, that in their teens, "Girls become 'female impersonators' who fit their whole selves into small, crowded spaces," I believe they get their practice in front of the mirror.

While the common perception is that "body bullying" or "body bashing"—which I define as the teasing, ostracizing or threatening of a person because of how she looks, specifically with regard to weight—is committed by external sources, such as teachers, family members, friends or strangers, more often than not, it begins with an even harsher critic: the girl herself.

The inner body bully tells a girl she's not good enough the way she is. It tells her to diet. She listens. She skips meals and pats herself on the back. Or she berates herself when she fails to stick to the diet plan, making her vulnerable to eating disorders, or worse. Being overweight—or simply believing they are overweight—might predispose some teenage girls to suicide attempts, according to a 2009 study that appeared in the *Journal of Adolescent Health,* which looked at more than fourteen thousand American high school students. The girl in the mirror never measures up.

What happened? Mirrors used to be so much fun. As young girls, my friends and I would slather on truckloads of my mother's old makeup, put on her high heels and jewelry and, replete with hairbrush microphones, dance in front of the mirror to Madonna's "Dress You Up." Our reflections would smile back, urging us on and telling us how amazing we were. We'd laugh. We'd cheer. We felt good. Not just good. Beautiful. Remember?

Fast-forward to Kasey, age eighteen, a size-10 girl with a sweet smile and a soft voice, who told me recently, "If my brother and I are joking around, and he calls me a name like 'Fattie,' I can shrug it off until I look in the mirror. I'm, like, 'He's just teasing.' Then I look at myself and say, 'Maybe you are, ya know, a Fattie. If you weren't, he would have chosen another name.'"

Mirrors have become this bizarre dichotomy: They symbolize both what we see and what we want. How did we come to expect so much from a simple piece of coated glass? Perhaps the ugliest truth about the mirror may be our willingness to imbue it with the ultimate power over our sense of worth, to be able to stare at a beautifully detailed reflection and see only flaws.

It would seem that the best solution would be to cover up all our mirrors or refuse to look at any reflective surface, as Oprah so famously did a few years back or as the University of California does annually to raise awareness of eating disorders. But the truth is that the critic doesn't really live in the mirror. Most of the time, she burrows deep into our daughter's head and spends the day whispering in her ear like her own personal demon—what I call a "sour" voice, as opposed to a "power" voice—rehashing what other people said at school, playing back the dismissive look someone gave her that made her feel insecure, awkward and ugly. A 2008 study conducted by the Children's National Medical Center in Washington, D.C., and the University of Miami found that what influences weight-control behavior is a girl's own definition of "normal" body weight and her perception of what others consider "normal."

Mirrors, Mirrors, Everywhere

If a girl tells herself she's fat, whether she is or not, she then goes out into the world conveying this self-assessment to everyone around her, who, in turn, become a metaphorical "mirror" of her own insecurities: Every look, every word, even a shrug of the shoulders, can intensify her lack of confidence. Ironically, while girls put themselves down to cheer someone else up, they look to others to pull them back up again. They crave feedback, but then are critical of that feedback. I've asked girls across the country how they know, for sure, if other people agree with all the things they believe—and say—about themselves, and they tell me some variant of "You just know":

→ "They don't say it's not true."
→ "They're, like, 'Oh, you're fine,' but then they turn around and talk about your fat butt behind your back."
→ "You can just tell from their face and how they act that they think it, too."
→ "I don't need them to tell me anything. I know I'm too fat."
→ "I walk around and feel like they're looking at me and whispering. It makes me feel worse."

And such disparagement isn't waiting for the teenage years to come around. The aversion toward chubbiness has been shown to begin at a very young age. According to research conducted in 2009 by the University of Central Florida and reported in the *British Journal of Developmental Psychology*, nearly half of three- to six-year-old girls worry about being fat. Similarly, a 2007 study of Australian preschoolers revealed that

> ## "Overheard"
>
> *"If you don't fit into a small size, it's like you just don't fit. I feel like I'm supposed to get into one of those Play-Doh plastic cutter molds my little brother has — the one in the shape of a girl."*
>
> Samantha, age 13

young children pick up potentially dangerous messages that "fat is bad" and "skinny is good" before they even start school. One of my good friends from college, now living in a suburb of St. Louis, confided in me that her daughter, Jordan, got out of the bath, looked in the mirror, her little face and body still dripping wet, and with a long face and quivering lip asked her mom if she was fat. "She's four!" my friend told me with exasperation.

What Do I Want to "Be" When I Grow Up?

Educator and coach Rachel Simmons, author of the landmark book about bullying, *Odd Girl Out,* reminds us in her latest book, *The Curse of the Good Girl,* that being "good" means being "unerringly nice, polite, modest and selfless." But I also would add, "not fat." These descriptors give girls a steadfast, yet (hopelessly) limiting target to aim for as they grow into women. Each year in my Sassy group, I like to do an exercise called "What to Be." On the top of a large piece of paper, I draw three columns:

- Be a Man
- Be a Woman
- Be Ladylike

I ask the girls to come up with adjectives to describe each column heading. For "Be a Man," the answers are free-flowing and easy.

- Strong
- Aggressive
- In charge
- Tough
- Assertive
- Confident

What about "Be Ladylike"?

- Dainty
- Small
- Thin
- Weak
- Doesn't eat much
- Agreeing
- Quiet
- Pretty
- Good

For "Be a Woman," the girls look at each other in confusion. Every year.

"I've heard of 'be a man,' but I've never heard of 'be a woman.'"

"You always hear 'Be a man' in things like sports, but you don't hear the same thing about being a woman."

"Sometimes my dad tells me to 'be a man,' even though I'm a girl. I know what he means, though. He wants me to be strong."

Nobody's ever told these girls what it means to be a woman, except that they get their periods, their bodies change and they get married and have children. So I challenge them. What do they *think* it should mean to "be a woman"? After some thought, suddenly there's a surge:

Wow.

- Be strong
- It doesn't matter what anyone says
- Or what you weigh

- Sure of yourself
- Don't care what other people think so much

- Assertive
- You can be whatever you want to be

At a mother-daughter conference at Woodward School in Quincy, Massachusetts, I asked that very same question. Abby, age thirteen, stood up and came to the microphone. "If 'be a woman' meant all those things, I would want to be all those things. Like I wouldn't care that other people were looking at me or thinking I should look different. Because I'd be confident with being... me. Just as I am. What I think and in my body, no matter what everyone else had to say about it."

"So what's the holdup, do you think?" I asked.

"It's hard. You'd think it would be good to be all 'I don't care what other people think' and all confident with your body no matter what. But people would probably just say you were full of yourself."

"Being confident means you're full of yourself?"

"Not all the time," she corrected. "Just for a girl."

Zero to Fat in No Time Flat

Ah, girls. It's no secret that puberty does a number on them. In a matter of a few years (sometimes it seems like days) their bodies change so much: breasts, pubic hair, underarm hair, menstruation. They grow considerably in height and weight. It's very normal—and healthy—for girls to gain twenty-five to forty pounds of fat during puberty, but in a weight-conscious world where every pound feels like a ton, every loosened belt or bra strap can spell social or societal doom.

It may be natural for teenagers to feel uncomfortable in their changing bodies and insecure about themselves in general during puberty, but these customary transitional feelings are a far cry from the all-consuming, self-effacing weight obsession that now affects, by many accounts, more than half the adolescent girls in this country.

The problem is that in our society, and in our girls' minds, developing curves is too often associated with getting fat. A 2009 survey by Pangea Media, a leader in online quizzes and surveys, tracked the body attitudes and preferences of tweens and teens, and this is what came out of it:

"Overheard"

"My mother tells me that girls are supposed to gain weight at my age. She should tell that to the girls at my school. I gained seven pounds over the summer, and I feel like a freak."

Hallie, age 13

→ 60% said they weighed too much.
→ 59% said they compare their bodies to those of celebrities.
→ More than 50% said they're inspired to improve their physical appearance when they see pictures of themselves and can pick out the "flaws."

When I ask girls about puberty, they get all weird and quiet. They giggle. They avert their eyes.

It was particularly telling when I asked Leana, a girl who was in my Sassy Sisterhood group two years in a row, about puberty. The first year, at twelve years old, with a long ponytail and flowered jeans, she told me, "I can't wait! I'll be a grown-up!"

Spoken just like a girl who has never been a grown-up. The second year, looking quite different, her hair now cut and styled, and a big soccer shirt draped over her new curves, she said, "I wish it didn't happen."

"Why's that?" I asked.

"I feel weird. I look down, and I'm, like, this isn't me. It's hard to explain."

"You feel like your body isn't supposed to look the way it does?"

"Right. I hate it. I feel like people stare. I thought I'd feel all grown-up, but I don't. I feel like a freak. I guess I must have eaten too much, because my clothes don't fit anymore, and I'm bigger than all my friends."

"Remember, we talked about how it's normal for girls to gain weight at your age?" I said.

"Yeah, I remember. But I didn't think you meant that we got fat."

Clearly, there's a disconnect between the truth about a girl's body and the fantasy of the perfect body making its home inside a girl's head. Girls are growing up believing that there is a certain mold they must conform to, and if they don't fit the mold, they don't fit into the world. Across virtually all socioeconomic and ethnic groups, young girls are trying to fit their bodies into increasingly smaller prefab molds.

A girl who is unhappy with herself and her body will turn to all sorts of things in order to change that body. I had a friend, Danni, during my college year abroad at Oxford University, who was effervescent, with blondish-red hair, tiny facial features and a hysterical laugh that sounded a lot like a honking hyena. Adorable. Danni, though, was acutely aware of her body. She told me that she was always the "fattest one" in her class, which is strange because Danni wasn't exactly plump, probably a size 8, if that. Well, that is until she got "elective" jaw surgery—for what she said was "TMJ" (temporomandibular joint and muscle disorder). But there was a side truth Danni hadn't admitted: She wanted to lose weight. By the end of summer, just a few months after her surgery, she visited my home for a fun day of swimming, and the change in her appearance was staggering. Her healthy roundness was gone, replaced by prepubescent curves. She was skin and bones. It was actually hard to look at her. And the worst part? She was thrilled.

"The jaw surgery was kind of my 'in,'" she told me.

"What do you mean?" I asked.

"Well, I didn't really need the surgery, but I wanted it. I mean, look at my tummy—it's almost completely flat!" She patted her nonexistent belly bulge. "That's seven hundred calories per day. I've never looked like this before, and I want to make sure I keep myself like this. I feel like people notice me now."

Elective surgery is just one of many things girls will do to lose weight. Because plastic surgery—procedures like tummy tucks and liposuction—requires parental permission for teens younger than eighteen, it makes much more sense to push for something elective, reveling in the fact that you won't be able to eat real food for a while and can get the side benefit of losing weight.

Unfortunately, though, more and more parents are giving permission—and their blessing—for surgical procedures that are purely cosmetic. The American Society for Aesthetic Plastic Surgery reported that the number of such procedures performed on youths 18 or younger more than tripled over a 10-year period—from 59,890 in 1997 to 205,119 in 2007. Liposuctions rose to 9,295 from 2,504, and breast augmentations increased nearly sixfold, from 1,326 to 7,882. While the latest figures show that spending on major plastic surgery procedures has decreased by 17 percent in the last year, don't break out the party hats. This change is likely due to the recent economic downturn rather than a renewed acceptance of a woman's body. In fact, the number of noninvasive cosmetic procedures—Botox injections, chemical peels, SmartLipo, etc.—continues to rise, as they are more readily accessible and financially feasible. All told, Americans still spent almost 10.5 billion dollars on cosmetic surgery last year.

And it gets worse. Whether or not their parents will grant permission for cosmetic surgeries or they can finagle their way onto an operating room table, girls are turning to plenty of other extreme—and dangerous—weight-loss measures out there to try.

Starving to Be Perfect

As if skipping meals isn't bad enough...starvation diets have skyrocketed. It's no longer about shedding a few pounds before a beach vacation: These diets have become a way of life for far too many teens. A nation-wide study of children in the United Kingdom showed that a whopping 40 percent of fourteen- and fifteen-year-old girls had either nothing or just a drink for breakfast. Many also went without lunch, and more than half believed they needed to slim down, even though only 12 percent were overweight, according to their body mass index (BMI). (I'm not the biggest fan of BMI testing, but more on that later.)

> ## "Overheard"
>
> *"A while back I was anorexic and totally depressed. I got better for a few years in high school but then became a binger as a senior, gained tons of weight, and I just couldn't take it anymore. Now, I'm bulimic and depressed."*
>
> Tami, age 19

I remember talking to Macie—her name stuck in my mind because she confided in me that her classmates called her "E-macie" as in "emaciated." Macie was eighteen, an age when young women are supposed to have a vitality about them, as they get ready to take on the world, but Macie's eyes were sunken, her skin somewhat ashen. She looked like she hadn't eaten in days. Turns out, she hadn't.

"I have this picture in my locker of this really big fat girl, and there's a quote under it that says, 'Have you ever noticed that most of the people you see eating are fat? You should remember that, because if you eat like those people, you are going to be fat like them, too.' I tacked it up in my locker. It's like my mantra... you know, you are what you eat, and all of that."

"So what are you eating?"

"Not much. I'm trying to cleanse from the last food I ate. Not to be gross, but my poop was green."

"Excuse me?"

"It was all the Jell-O. It's a Hollywood celeb trick. I started eating bowls and bowls of it to fill myself up—not the sweet stuff, the ones without sugar. I ate that and veggie broth. Very low cal. I felt full. Like, really, really full, but I was only eating Jell-O. It would have been a great diet if it wasn't for the green poop situation."

"How long were you just eating Jell-O?"

"Six weeks. I lost fifteen pounds. Pretty good, huh?"

Conversely, the Body Bully Within will also go in the other direction, going on a wild food binge and then purging it all up before her body has a chance to utilize all those important nutrients. An average bulimic binge, defined as the rapid consumption of a large amount of high-calorie food in a short amount of time, may consist of about three thousand calories, although some have reported eating up to tens of thousands of calories in only a few hours. You can imagine all the guilt, anxiety and self-loathing that follows an intake of that many calories, which then leads to purging, either self-induced—girls sticking their fingers down their throats—or by abusing laxatives.

"Have Your Brownie and Eat It, Too"

I met Adriana the summer of 2009, after she had come home from college in Rhode Island. She was tall and thin with dark hair and freckles, which made her look both grown-up and childlike at the same time. Sitting in Starbucks, she looked like any other eighteen-year-old slurping down iced coffee.

"My friends drink this stuff like crazy. It's part of the New England weight-loss solution. Not to be disgusting, but coffee is a great diuretic, and it's better than, say, eating a plate of brownies— although those can be a great diuretic, too, if made correctly."

"I'm afraid to ask…. What's in those brownies?"

"Well, this girl in my dorm made these brownies with all these chocolate laxatives as a joke to get back at this guy and some of his friends for being jerks. But some of the girls tried them, too, and, well, you can imagine what happened. So now the brownies are made that way on purpose—you can have your brownie and eat it, too, so to speak."

14 SIGNS THAT YOUR DAUGHTER MAY HAVE AN EATING DISORDER

1. **ERRATIC FOOD HABITS:** Eating large amounts of food and then disappearing from the table.

2. **PLAYING WITH FOOD.**

3. **RESTRICTING FOOD INTAKE.**

4. **MAJOR CHANGES IN WEIGHT IN A SHORT AMOUNT OF TIME:** Considering teen bodies are changing and getting heavier, dramatic weight loss for age and height can be a warning sign.

5. **HIDING HER BODY EVEN AFTER WEIGHT LOSS:** May be an indication that your daughter believes her body is very large even when it is not.

6. **HIDING FOOD:** Finding large amounts of food stashed in her bedroom, hidden under her bed or in her closet; disappearance of food from the refrigerator or pantry.

7. **REFUSAL TO EAT WHEN OTHERS ARE PRESENT:** You'll hear things like "I've already eaten" or "I have a stomachache" simply to avoid eating.

8. **COMPULSIVE EXERCISING:** Exercising to take off as many calories as were consumed. Exercising several times daily or exercising until she can't exercise anymore. Hyperfocused on how many calories she's burned, her weight, inches, etc.

9. **SKIPPING MEALS CONSISTENTLY.**

10. **MEASURING SELF-WORTH BASED ON WEIGHT:** Calling oneself "good" for not eating and "bad" for giving in to eating. Bashing self for eating more than the allotted calories.

11. **COMPLAINING ABOUT BEING OVERWEIGHT AND FAT WHEN SHE IS CLEARLY UNDERWEIGHT.**

12. **MISSING SEVERAL PERIODS IN A ROW:** Periods can stop when girls lose too much weight.

13. **OVERALL POOR BODY IMAGE:** Poor attitude when it comes to weight and appearance.

14. **SPENDING A LOT OF TIME IN THE BATHROOM:** Could be a sign of purging or laxative use.

"Don't people get sick from that?"

"Yeah, sometimes. My friend and I did it once, and we cut up the laxatives really small—ya know, like chocolate chips. We didn't use too many, because we didn't want projectile—well, ya know."

"And what happened?"

"We were totally fine at first. I mean, we were in the bathroom a lot, but we felt fine, and we thought it would help us have flat stomachs for the party we were going to that night. But then, we actually both wound up in the hospital. We got totally dehydrated. Scary stuff."

"My goodness. That's awful."

"Yeah. I guess the recipe needs to be tweaked."

Girls like Adriana know that what they're doing to their bodies is unhealthy. Yet, they justify it by arguing that being "fat" is unhealthy, too. Another teenage girl told me that she lost close to fifty pounds by eating "practically nothing" and taking laxatives to make sure nothing stayed in her system. "I knew the laxatives weren't good for me—I'm not stupid," she told me, "but I just wanted the food out as soon as it went in. I didn't want to get fat again. Fat isn't good for my mind or my body."

She also started smoking—a lot. "Chain smoking keeps me from eating," she told me, "and I am committed to a strict diet." Used to be that girls started smoking just to look cool. Now one in five women between the ages of eighteen and twenty-four smokes, and most say "they keep lighting up for fear of gaining weight," according to a 2009 study by Temple University. (Research, however, from the University of Montreal, funded by the Canadian Cancer Society, shows that teenage girls who smoke cigarettes are no more likely to lose weight than girls who don't smoke.) This is just another grim example of how badly teenage girls want to be thin—so much so that they are willing to risk dying of lung cancer or heart disease rather than be fat. Could a poor body image become the leading cause of death among women, rather than heart disease?

Bitter Pills to Swallow

In addition to downing laxatives or engaging in unhealthy nutrition or bad habits, girls are using pills, such as steroids or diet capsules, to slim down and tone up. Some girls, as young as nine years old, have found that steroids can help them get the physique they believe they should have. Lower weight. Less fat.

Think it's one in a million? Nope. One in twenty high school girls and one in fourteen middle school girls have admitted to trying anabolic steroids at least once, with their use rising steadily since 1991, various government and university studies have shown. And according to the Centers for Disease Control and Prevention's 2003 Youth Risk Behavior Surveillance System, 5 percent of high school girls are taking steroids to decrease body fat and get closer to the thin, toned body ideal. Just ask Lisa, age twenty-three, whose desire to look slim, buff and "Beyoncé-like" led her to take steroids twice a week when she was fifteen. "I didn't want to look waif-y," she told me. "I wanted to look strong and sexy. I found out from a friend of mine that if you take steroids you can lose weight fast and look awesome. I couldn't do it on my own. This is what worked, and I look great."

Alicia, age eighteen, definitely didn't seem like a girl who was hiding anything. When we met in the Fort Lauderdale airport while waiting for our flights to take off, we started talking. Alicia had wavy blondish-brown hair, light brown eyes. I guess she stood about 5-foot-5, probably about a size 6 or maybe even smaller. As she talked, she fingered her hair and twirled it around and around the pen that she had been using to write a letter—yes, an actual letter—to her friend Kathleen, who was staying in Brazil with her family for the summer. She missed her, but at the same time didn't want her to move back since Kathleen had been sending her some really great diet pills that were "actually working," as opposed to this "crappy American stuff."

"I had been taking straight caffeine pills for a while, since they were so available," Alicia said. "My mom made it clear that she didn't think it was a good idea for a young girl to be drinking coffee, but I heard that coffee and caffeine could up your metabolism, so I tried this. I feel bad, but it worked for a while. Then I moved on to diet pills—Dexatrim and a few others. It was just so easy."

Diet pills do seem really easy: You just go to the store, pop them into your cart and then pop them into your mouth. A 2006 study by the University of Minnesota's Project EAT (Eating Among Teens) found that high-school-aged females' use of diet pills nearly doubled from 7.5 percent to 14.2 percent over a five-year period. By the ages of nineteen and twenty, 20 percent of females surveyed used diet pills.

"I felt so full after eating practically nothing," Alicia said. "It was great. And then there are the antacids. One thing parents don't realize is that we can get whatever we want just like they can from the drugstore or even from Publix or Wal-Mart. I don't even have to wait until I'm eighteen, because I can just have one of my friends or my older sister get it for me…. And, of course, I can get it myself from, like, a million different sites off the Internet."

"Were you at all worried about how the pills would affect you?" I asked.

"Not really. Although the stuff my friend Kathleen is getting me from Brazil is pretty strong stuff. It's been banned in the U.S. I hate to get off it, but I actually might have to. It looks like there might be something wrong with my heart. I didn't tell my doctor about the pills, but I think she could guess. But I mean, being overweight is bad for your heart, too…so I see it as a bit of a toss-up."

Pain, No Gain?

I met Meryl at the local Hearth 'n Kettle, a restaurant chain in Massachusetts whose "fun-house huge tables always make me feel extra thin," Meryl said. I had asked her out for coffee "or whatever" because another girl told me that Meryl was willing to talk about how she "beat herself thin."

"I did it just today," she told me coolly. "I was in calculus class, and my stomach started making all these embarrassing noises. So I hit it."

"What do you mean by 'hit it'?"

"I just do. I hit it to make the sound go away. Sometimes I'll stick the corner of my book or the eraser end of my pencil or something into my stomach, and that helps, too. I do things like that."

"Doesn't that hurt?"

Meryl smirked. "That's kind of the point. Since your stomach hurts so bad you don't feel like eating. I've lost twelve pounds that way. Well, so far."

I couldn't help thinking that perhaps this was a rare occurrence, but I was wrong. Very wrong. When I asked other girls about pain for pounds, to my surprise—and dismay—they had lots of other ideas:

"My friend would wear a rubber band around her wrist and snap it anytime she thought about food. She had a welt for months."

"My sister would put her fingernail under her other nail or pluck one of those little hairs out of her chin or under her nose when she got hungry."

"I didn't really mean to start doing it, but I would kind of bite down on the skin on my lips, and my mouth hurt so bad that I didn't want to eat."

And then there was Stefanie.

"People thought I was such a rebel," she told me. "I got my tongue pierced, and they were like, 'Stefie's turning Goth' or 'Stef wants the guys to think she's into some crazy shit.' I'm sorry. Can I say that?"

"You can say whatever you want."

"Yeah, people thought I was into all this crazy shit, but I totally wasn't. Not really."

"What was the real reason for the piercing?"

"Well, I think it looks cool, but truthfully? I was keeping myself from eating too much. I didn't want to be the 'fat girl,' and it was getting toward summer. I had this total crush on this guy, Doug. My big sister had this bathing suit from last year that she gave me for motivation. I tried it on and was, like, 'Oh God, I'm friggin' huge.' Dieting never worked for me, so I had to try something else."

"How did the piercing help you to lose weight?"

"It got a little infected. It hurt too bad to eat. You can say I didn't exactly take good care of it. I didn't really want it to get infected. I just wanted to be aware of it. I figured that it would remind me not to eat. It turned out I couldn't eat."

"So it turned out not the way you hoped."

"Actually, better. I lost twenty-five pounds! And the scar I got from the infection is like my 'war wound,' telling me not to eat if I want to stay thin."

How do you help those who continue to hurt themselves? There's no magic cure, and ignoring it simply as a "phase" won't make it go away. Take notice. Be supportive. Be available. Don't let your daughter's body bully find support elsewhere. Because she will.

They say misery loves company. Many girls who feel "not good enough" and "not thin enough" let it all hang out in cyberspace. They blog; they tweet; they chat. They find each other. Some of the more popular weight-loss blogs and websites are simply known as "ana" and "mia" sites—code for anorexia and bulimia. These are sites started by and populated by anorexic and/or bulimic girls who are encouraging and "supporting" one another in their quest to become underweight.

Type "pro-anorexia" or "pro-ana/pro-mia" into Google and you will come across websites with titles like Pretty Thin, Bone Thin, Ana's Angel and Ana for the Fat People. These sites provide what most girls seem to want—a sense of belonging and status, a forum to read and exchange stories, ideas and tips about their dieting and clinical eating disorders. They are a medium to feed and justify the desire to be incredibly thin, offering "thinspiration" through images of ultraskinny models and actresses or by using negative imagery, pointing out overweight women with captions that read: "Don't Look Like THIS!" (Studies have shown that diet-impulse behavior is triggered as much by images of fat women as flattering ones of thin women.) A girl who's in the "club" doesn't feel so alone; she's given constant reinforcement, advice and encouragement, even in the middle of the night, when she may be wavering about whether to eat or to purge. Most likely, the advice she'll get is this: Purge.

Love Me Slender

Is your daughter talking to cyber strangers about feeling fat, losing weight and every single morsel she puts into her mouth? These blog titles tell the story that you don't know. It should be noted that during the six-month period in which I wrote this book, the memberships of nearly all these blogs tripled or, in some cases, quadrupled.

→ No Thanks, I'm Not Hungry (20,824 members)

→ peace. love. skinny. (17,487 members)

→ Fragile (thin and beautiful) (10,778 members)

→ because skinny jeans aren't meant for fat people (9,902 members)

→ -all i want is to be thin…to be happy- (2,498 members)

→ bye, bye fat, hello bones :) (377 members)

→ just water, thanks (6,901 members)

→ because nobody likes a fat girl (3,460 members)

→ Alice in Hungerland (7,808 members)

→ I want to be the best little girl in the world (1,376 members)

In November 2008, *Newsweek* reported that after meeting for years on anonymous and secret websites, pro-anorexia groups were moving to more public forums, such as Facebook. Parents view Facebook as one of the "safer places" on the Internet, since you actually need to "approve" the people you connect with, eliminating the "creepy old men" factor associated with other social networking sites. Facebook has hundreds of groups devoted to shutting down pro-anorexia websites and, yes, pro-ana Facebook groups as well. Some of them are legitimate, such as Stop Pro Ana (more than 4,000 members) and Real Women Have a Bottom and Thighs and a Tummy and Wobbly Bits (more than 32,000 members). The secret, though, is that many of these Facebook groups are now getting tricky—they're saying they're not pro-ana outright, and just with hints and pro-ana bread crumbs, they're gathering up their pro-ana members and are being overlooked by Facebook authorities.

Code Read

As a parent, you may be clued in to your daughter's social or school life but not her Internet life. Online, girls freely express exactly what they're feeling to anonymous people and receive guidance from those who provide medically unsound advice: "Repeat after me: I do not need food...I do not need food..." is just one of the many thinspiration tips out there. One mother wrote me recently: "My fourteen-year-old daughter had five friends over the other day, and they were playing around on the computer. I overheard one of the girls announce, 'There's a site that says you can eat anything you want and not get fat. All you have to do is not swallow.' Two days later, I caught my daughter eating a piece of cake and spitting it in the sink."

And that's just the tip of the iceberg. It took me just one click of a mouse to get to more than 19 million results for "pro-ana websites." Here's a sampling of the sort of advice that's at your daughter's fingertips. As seventeen-year-old Becka, a recovering anorexic and once devout pro-ana rule follower, told me, "Whoever starves the most, whoever can be more controlled, wins."

THE WORD ON THE STREET

In a teen's world, words have tremendous power. Here are thirteen terms that have become a part of the daily body-bashing lexicon.

MUFFIN TOP: The bulge of skin or fat that oozes out like the top of a muffin over the waistband of a pair of low-rise, hip-hugging, tight-fitting jeans and through the bottom of a too-short, too-tight top.

TEACHER'S ELBOW: The flab or atrophied skin that hangs down on the back of the arms where the triceps are, partially covering the elbow, and jiggles when moved, such as when a teacher is writing on the board in a short-sleeved shirt. Also called "water wings" or "grandma arms." Often associated with those who've lost weight quickly or lap-band patients.

POOCH: Lower stomach area that appears rounded on girls and women of varying sizes. Can be considered cute by some, but hated by others who will settle for nothing less than a flat tummy.

BRA BULGE: The bulges that result when a tight bra band digs into a girl's back and causes lumpy lines seen through a T-shirt.

CANKLES: When the leg meets the foot in an abrupt, amorphous manner, so you can't see where the leg ends and the foot begins. Calf + Ankles = Cankles.

BACK FAT: Either another name for "bra bulge" or the fat that sticks out of the back of the waistband of jeans that are too tight; the back half of "muffin top."

STICK CHICK: 1. A very skinny girl who is as flat as a plank with no curves or bumps; 2. A girl who could be on the cover of *Vogue*. Also called a "toothpick chick."

TITS ON A STICK: A stick chick with big boobs. Also called a "lollipop."

FIT CHICK: 1. A female, size 0–6, who works out four to seven days per week; 2. A girl who looks like a fitness magazine cover model; 3. A woman of any size who works out often and stays fit. Either a "stick chick" or a "fat chick" can be a "fit chick."

CURVY CHICK: 1. A woman with ample bust and bottom and a distinct waistline; 2. A plus-size girl who is fit and curvaceous; 3. A euphemism for a bigger woman who is body-proud and prefers the positive term *curvy* to the negative term *fat.*

FAT CHICKS (ALSO CALLED THICK CHICKS): Anyone over a size 16.

MIDSIZED FAT CHICKS: "Fat chicks" who are size 16 to 24.

SUPERSIZED FAT CHICKS: 1. "Fat chicks" who are size 26 and up; 2. Women, size 28-plus, at least 290 pounds and usually portrayed in the media wearing muumuus and kaftans; 3. Women labeled "morbidly obese" by the medical and media world.

How Not to Eat

- Pick one food for the day, like an apple. Cut it into eight slices. Eat two slices at breakfast, two at lunch, two at dinner, and you'll have two left for a snack. This way, your body thinks it's eating four times that day, but in reality you've only had one apple.

- Wear sticky lip gloss or ChapStick. It keeps you very aware of what goes in your mouth and makes you think twice about eating anything, because you'll have to carefully reapply.

- If you are really craving food, brush your teeth with a strong mint toothpaste. This helps to put you off food because of the taste it leaves behind.

- If you love a certain food, save the wrappers even after you've eaten it. Smell it when you're hungry.

- Drink two tablespoons of vinegar before a meal, which will help suck the fat out of it.

- One day on, two days off. Eat three hundred calories one day, and then fast for two days. Fasting cleanses your body and soul and makes you feel strong and empowered—like Superwoman!

- Eat paper. Maximum chewing. Minimum calories—if any.

- Watch pro-ana videos while you eat. The images will keep you from wanting seconds, and maybe even firsts.

How to Inspire Yourself

- Carry pictures of your favorite models around with you. When you're hungry, pull out one of the pictures.

- If you have a terrible craving, turn on the TV. Most likely, some sort of show will be on with skinny, gorgeous actresses/models. It's a definite way to curb an appetite.

- Get a piece of ribbon, and cut it to the measurement that you want your waist to become after you lose weight. Then tie this around your wrist like a bracelet. The idea is that each time you see the ribbon you remember your goal, and hopefully it stops you from eating. And whenever you need a motivation boost, take the ribbon off and see if it fits around your waist.

- Clean something gross in the bathroom, or if you have cats, clean the litter box when you want to eat.

How to Fake Out Parents and Friends

- If you're being watched, try the opaque cup trick. This one's a classic: Pretend you're eating, and spit the food in the cup while you pretend to be drinking. Don't forget to get rid of what's in the cup, though!

- Hide a plate or Ziploc bag near your computer. Right before supper, go to your room, and when supper is ready, tell your parents that you're doing your homework and want them to bring your meal to you. When you get it, just put it on the other plate or in the Ziploc bag, and bring the empty dish back in fifteen minutes. Just make sure you dispose of the food later on.

- Buy lunches of canned foods, then hide them in your room or locker as if you were going to eat them, and instead walk/drive them once a week to your local homeless shelter. This also helps those of you who feel guilty about wasting food.

- If you're talking about celebrities with other people, make sure to mention how you think Calista Flockhart is too thin and that Kate Winslet is gorgeous. Praise fat, and people will never guess that you're starving yourself into thinness.

- When you have to get weighed at the doctor's office, and you want to weigh more, obviously, put coins in a piece of paper towel or paper, wrap them up and put the bundle in a bun in your hair. Wear as much jewelry as possible. Right before you go to the doctor, chug a gallon of water.

Banish the Bully

While we always hope that girls will follow more healthy measures to change their bodies—or better yet, love the one they're in—can we blame them for wanting to alter themselves when other people's comments are so destructive and demeaning? Their little self-assurance shields are still developing; their armor is still filled with lots of cracks. If we want our girls to change their reactive behavior, we can help. We can change our attitudes. We can be their supporters, not their critics. Here are some ways for girls to practice a little self-respect:

1. Have your daughter say her "I am's" every day. Have her come up with a list of positive attributes, such as "I am

beautiful," "I am smart" and "I am powerful," and repeat them while looking in the mirror.

2. Decide on a family code word—a word or sound that is made when someone says something negative about themselves. This exercise can help bring disempowering language to the forefront.

3. Encourage your daughter to choose at least one thing she likes about herself and to express gratitude for it. For example, "I'm thankful for the curve of my hips." Sounds corny, but it works.

4. Play a game of "What I love about you" with the girls and women in your life. Sometimes just knowing the special things others see in them is enough to counteract some of the negative things they see in themselves.

5. If you catch your daughter making negative comments about herself, have her counteract them with three positive statements. And try to keep track of these negative comments so you can see how many go through her mind on a daily basis.

The hope is that the positive feedback will rub off, and our girls will learn to become their own cheerleaders, their own best friends, and they can go out into the world fully armed.

But is that enough?

In some ways, Micki's story is perhaps the most horrific of all—a reminder that body bullying is not a problem of absolutes, but one that is so pervasive that virtually all girls fall somewhere on its continuum.

Micki's Story

When I met Micki, age twenty-one, at a Greek diner near her home, she gave the menu on the table a cursory glance and handed it back to the waitress with a sweet, wide smile. "I'll have a club sandwich, fries and a soda," she said sweetly, without hesitation. A full-figured girl, about a size 12, with shoulder-length brown hair and sparkling eyes, Micki smiled a lot—at the gentleman who held the door for us on the way in, at the elderly couple at the next table, at anyone, really, who'd meet her eyes.

"I guess I should offer full disclosure," she said, turning her paper straw cover into an accordion, fold by fold.

"OK, what do you mean?"

"Well, I'm actually a very happy, normal person," she said. "Most days, anyway. I have high self-esteem. I'm driven. I'm studying to be a reporter, like the ones on the news. I would never really hurt myself in order to lose weight—you know, take drugs I wasn't supposed to, or do anything like that. I'm a good girl—I call my grandma all the time, don't get into trouble. But I'm one of the lucky ones."

I watched Micki closely. She seemed awfully genuine. "Then why did you want to chat?"

"Well, I wanted you to know. For your book. That it's not just the crazies or the insecure girls. This thing hits everybody."

"What thing?"

The waitress came with our order, and Micki squeezed a pool of ketchup on the side of her plate and started eating her fries. "Like, for instance, I come here with my friends all the time. And they watch what I eat—all the time. Make comments. 'Do you know how much fat mayonnaise has? Do you know how many calories are in those fries?' Jesus! Leave me alone. Can't I just eat a freakin' meal in peace?"

Micki's smile faded.

"And I do. I eat what I want—I probably do it to make a point as much as to eat. I go out of my way to order dessert. Like it's nothing: 'I'll have the vanilla milk shake. Oh, and make it a large.' I mean, I don't go crazy, but I enjoy myself. And the funny thing is, once I do, everyone orders dessert. It's like I gave them permission. 'Well, if Micki is going to have it, I might as well, too.'"

Dessert is a very big deal among girls. Many believe that it's very naughty and should only be taken with an "extra fork" off someone else's. It takes a lot for girls to break out and do something that carries so much societal shame and yet is so readily available.

"I do try to keep it balanced," Micki said. "I eat cereal for breakfast with low-fat milk, instead of a doughnut, try to eat vegetables, keep my portions under control. I think of it like my credit card—you're only hurting yourself if you go over your limit. But everyone else is eating what they're 'supposed' to. Who's eating hamburgers without bread—isn't that sacrilegious? Who's ordering grilled vegetables when they really want the grilled cheese? So many girls are not having what they want. Sometimes I feel like I'm liberating them, showing them that it doesn't have to be that way, and it makes me feel good."

"It sounds like you've got everything under control," I said.

Micki laughed. "That's the point. I look like I do, but I so don't. I totally look like the girl who doesn't give a crap. But I'm also that other girl." She paused thoughtfully. "You know, the one who obsesses about her weight. Truthfully, it's on my mind from the moment I wake up in the morning. Will this be a good eating day? Or a bad eating day? Mind you, my idea of an eating day is probably a thousand calories more than most girls' eating days, but still." Micki took a large bite out of her sandwich. I have to admit, it was nice to be with a girl who liked to eat and did so seemingly with reckless abandon. It had been a long time. Most just order water or a Diet Coke.

"Mmm, that's good. What would the world be without bacon, you know?" Micki said with a laugh, wiping her mouth. "Anyway, when I wake up in the morning, I can't eat anything until I weigh myself. Sometimes I'll put off weighing myself as long as possible, thinking that will make a huge difference when I finally get on that scale. And then it's a ritual."

Micki put down her sandwich, chewing purposefully, and took a sip of her soda. "First, I must use the bathroom—every little bit helps. Then I get totally naked, even brush my hair to get the stray hairs off my head and onto my brush." Micki paused to look at me, but I urged her to continue. "When I finally get on the actual scale, the first weight doesn't count. It's, like, just a tease. It's never really right, because your scale is just 'warming up.' I get on a few more times, and each time the weight is off by a few ounces: 173.5. 173.9. 173.4. How can you weigh yourself three times within ten seconds and get three completely different weights?

"Then I try to get the lowest weight. I try stepping on the edge of the scale. Top edge. Bottom edge. Feet on the left and right sides. See if it makes a difference. I stand perfectly straight. Try to do that yoga thing where you imagine that invisible string at the top of your head going to the ceiling, straightening my spine—that's bound to shave off a few ounces, isn't it? My personal rule is this: I have to get the same weight two times in a row for it to count. And then I enter that weight into my little chart that I've got stashed in the bathroom."

"Why do you think you do that?" I asked.

"I don't know." Micki shrugged her shoulders. "It's always on my mind. I want to think that I can be this girl who eats whatever she wants and still lose weight. Defy the odds. But that can't be. So I eat what I want and then agonize about it quietly, in the safety of my apartment. My roommate doesn't even know. It all takes place inside my head. The little games. I'll eat lunch in the café on campus and tell myself, 'Well, that was a great lunch. I am so full,' when I know that I'm not. Then I obsess about whatever it is I want at that moment—a cookie, a piece of cake, whatever's around. First I'll be in denial about it. 'I'm not hungry. I'm not hungry.' Then the next stage is, like, defiance. I convince myself that I deserve that cookie. Deserve to reward myself. And then I eat it, and for one glorious moment, I am completely at peace. But it doesn't last. Then the dreaded guilt and disappointment arrive. I think, 'How terribly weak and disgusting I am! Couldn't even win out over a damn cookie. I'm pathetic.'"

Micki looked down at her meal and rubbed her forehead, her self-talk revealed in one long purging of a secret. I assured her that she was certainly not alone in this struggle and that it actually was considered more normal than not to struggle with body image—there's even a term for it: *normative discontent*.

"Wow, this is clearly very tough on you," I said.

"Yeah, it can be annoying. I must weigh myself, like, twenty times a day. It's like a game. How much weight did I put on after breakfast? Lunch? If I do twenty jumping jacks, will I weigh the same as five minutes ago? I went through a Slim-Fast stage to lose some weight. It's supposed to be a meal supplement, but I convinced myself that I would drink them as a snack, because it would be a healthier snack than, say, a bowl of ice cream. So, essentially, I was having a meal and then having a meal-replacement meal. Obviously, it didn't work."

"Do you want to lose weight?"

"Of course! Who doesn't, right?" Micki said. "I know I'm pretty and that people think I'm pretty. I'm sweet and nice and all that. But I've always been chubby. Went through the usual torturous things as a kid, like being called 'Tubby the Tuba'—I made like it didn't bother me, but it ate me up inside. You carry that with you your whole life. My friend calls it 'fat head'—it doesn't matter how thin you get as you get older, you still feel like a fat kid, worry that you'll be fat again."

"So how do you control it? How do you keep it from making you stop eating and things like that?"

"I guess the difference between me and some of the other girls is that I don't let it consume me. I'm too strong for that. But it's the undercurrent of my life, no doubt about it. I remind myself of the guy from the movie *A Beautiful Mind*—the brilliant guy who walks around with these people in his head, talking to him, trying to influence him. And I think I've learned, like he did, not to listen. But it's a constant battle. Especially for a bacon lover like me."

The BIQs (Body Image Quotient) are a way to determine how your daughter is faring in a world that often stresses thinness at all costs. Is she on her way to becoming a body-confident girl? Or does she need some guidance and encouragement? Your daughter's scores will be tabulated in Chapter 8.

BIQ:
What Would She Say About Herself?

1. When your daughter talks to herself about her body, she says:

A. "Go on a diet! Do whatever it takes! You disgust me!"

B. "I should probably lose a few pounds, but I look all right."

C. "You look pretty darn good today."

2. Your daughter thinks that most of her friends find her attractive.

A. No way. She says she is one of the least good-looking among her friends.

B. She says some of them think she's pretty, but probably not as pretty as they are.

C. She definitely agrees. She tells me most of her friends think she's "pretty hot"!

3. Your daughter says her thighs (butt, stomach, etc.) are too big.

A. That's true. She looks in the mirror and says things like, "I can't stand my thighs."

B. There are times when she feels that way, but not always.

C. She thinks her thighs are fine just the way they are.

4. When it comes to laxatives, picking up smoking, taking diet pills or going on some crazy new diet, your daughter...

A. Has tried them all! She's open to anything that will make the number on the scale go down.

B. Has done a few things, but she isn't one to do them for long.

C. Stays away from any of those over-the-counter drugs or new fad diets.

5. In your opinion, is your daughter a Body Bully? Why?

A. Yes. She picks on herself and her body every day.

B. Not sure. She says insulting comments about her body every once in a while, but don't we all?

C. No. She almost never says anything negative about her body. She usually compliments herself.

Total number of:

As 1 point each	Bs 2 points each	Cs 3 points each	Total BIQ score for Chapter 1

Chapter 2

The Secret Impact of Mothers:
I Love My Mom, But...

I know my mom didn't mean it. I hate even saying this, since she has always been one of my greatest supporters, but when I came home from sleepaway camp the summer after eighth grade, she told me that she had never seen my thighs "so big." That's how I remember it anyway. Perhaps it was just me coming into my athletic body frame or my Eastern European roots catching up with me. Perhaps she was simply making an innocent, albeit poorly worded, observation of how her baby girl was filling out. Either way, all I heard was, "You're so fat!"

If words have power, a mother's words rule supreme. The way you talk to your daughter about food and weight can have an enormous impact on her self-image and her eating habits. Without exception, moms are the single most influential factor when it comes to their children's eating habits. Studies continually reveal that teen girls' desires to be thin are tied, at least in part, to what they think their mothers want for them. In other words, they want to please Mom. A 2009 poll by top-selling UK teen magazine *Sugar* surveyed 512 teenage girls and found that 6 percent had eating disorders, but when you look specifically at the girls whose mothers diet, that number goes up to 10 percent. Although many mothers like to tell me that "Nobody really listens to them anyway" or "It goes in one ear and out the other," the truth is that our daughters take in what we say—and do—all the time.

"I remember spending the summer with my grandmother when I was five years old," said Sage, age nineteen. "I was really skinny, and my grandmother thought I needed a little more meat on my bones. She was, like, 'What is your mother doing to you?'

Even though I had a great time, I was excited to go home and see my mom. It had been two months! We pulled into my driveway, and when my mom opened the car door, she pulled me out of the car and said, 'How did you get so fat? What have you been eating?' From then on, I've always been worried."

Who Has the Problem: Your Daughter or You?

As the parent, first, be honest with yourself. You need to determine if your daughter's weight—whether "too much" or "too little"—is a legitimate medical concern. *Fat* and *unhealthy* are not synonymous, just as *skinny* and *healthy* aren't always the same. Before looking further, ask yourself: Is your daughter's weight a real problem or simply a problem for others around her, including you? These key ten questions will help you find out:

1. Is my daughter healthy?

2. Is my daughter happy?

3. Is my daughter successful in school and extracurricular activities?

4. Does my daughter have good friends?

5. Does my daughter have a good work ethic and solid values?

6. Is my daughter embarrassed about her weight, or am I?

7. Does my daughter feel ridiculed, teased or discriminated against due to her weight, or do I fear that she will be ridiculed, teased or discriminated against?

8. If my daughter lost weight, would she be a lot happier, or would I?

9. Does my daughter complain about being fat?

10. Is my daughter's weight an issue for her, or is it an issue for me?

If her weight is your own issue, you have to make some changes, beginning with how you talk (or don't talk) about food and weight. Reality check: You don't need to teach your daughter the difference between a Ho-Ho and a piece of fruit. She already knows that. And she probably has a pretty good idea about the shape and weight of her own body. Pointing out the obvious is rarely helpful.

When Carol, mother of Brittany, age thirteen, told me, "I don't want my daughter to be fat," it was probably the hundredth time I'd heard such a statement since I'd begun my research. She went on to say, "She's only a few pounds overweight now, but what if she keeps gaining? I'm afraid people will tease her and that she'll have health problems. Whenever I say something to her about getting fat, or suggest going out for a run, she gets upset. I don't know what I'm supposed to do."

My advice? *Keep your comments and criticisms about the size of her jeans or the number on the scale to yourself.*

If your daughter feels great, typically makes good food choices and is strong, skillful and talented, why dwell on her weight? As Jess Weiner, author and global ambassador for the Dove Self-Esteem Fund, told me, "Girls long to hear from their parents, 'You're beautiful just the way you are. There is nothing to be fixed.'" When I asked a large sampling of women what they recall most in terms of weight and body image about their childhood or teen years, I heard pretty much the same answer across the board. They remembered whether their close family members supported them or shamed them.

Look How Big You've Grown!

When our daughters are born, they are just perfect in our eyes. We don't want anything to hurt them, and no one dare try. As girls grow, moms become their human security blanket and comfort them in ways that only they can—something in their touch, their smell, their calm voice that shows them that everything will be OK as long as "I have Mommy." When she nears adolescence, your daughter may gain weight in ways you find surprising or that are unexpected. Perhaps you're embarrassed for her. Or for yourself. But nothing makes a daughter feel worse than having her mother pile guilt and shame on top of her weight gain. Imagine what happens to that girl when the one person she relies on the most—the one person who makes her feel that she is most precious and valuable—turns on her. My Sassy Girls blurt out their moms' critical comments with both sadness and resentment:

→ "You have to be thin."
→ "Should you really be eating that?"
→ "You don't want to be fat, do you?"
→ "How come you're so much bigger than your friends?"
→ "Look, my thighs are thinner than yours."

All the girls and women I've interviewed about this topic tell me that comments like these make them feel angry, alone, frustrated, alienated or, worse, worthless. You might be trying to say, "I think you are worth giving yourself a better quality of life by eating healthier and making healthier choices," but it comes out, "You are worth more when you weigh less."

For Juliet, age thirty-two, a former straight-size model, and now a plus-size woman living in the ultra-weight-conscious world of Beverly Hills, California, the message was clear: "You're fat." A healthy child who had "always loved sports," Juliet never had a problem with weight, because she always burned off calories by running up and down the soccer field. Her mother, however, a former model, didn't see it that way. "From the age of fourteen on, she monitored what I ate," Juliet told me. "She entered me into beauty pageants and, in order to win, you had to have the right look—and the right look meant thin. 'Have a bran muffin, or a side salad, or a shrimp cocktail without the sauce,' she'd say. She would come down too hard—'You can't eat that, you're getting fat.'"

Juliet thought, "Oh, my gosh, maybe I am," and turned to "other means" to cope: Drugs. She became a model at age fifteen, was on a full modeling contract at age eighteen, and by that time was using cocaine every day. She was never thin enough and said, "Not one day would go by that I didn't think I wasn't fat."

"Does your mom know the connection between the drugs and her comments about your weight when you were younger?" I asked.

"Oh, no," Juliet said, defensively. "I think that would kill her."

As a parent, you want to protect your child from the criticism she may hear, the hurt she may feel, in our thin-obsessed environment. Maybe you just want her to lose a little weight so she seems more "normal." You take preemptive strikes by nagging and watching over her food, exercise and clothing choices. But while you believe your comments are constructive, they could actually be sowing seeds of self-doubt in an otherwise perfectly healthy girl. Instead of building on her assets, skills and strengths, you tear down her self-respect and make a mockery of her self-concept. The person who's left is the shell of a girl who is starved for acceptance—especially from the one person who she never thought would join the chorus of voices in her head that tell her she's not good enough. That person is you.

"My mom told me that when I was eighteen she would pay for a boob job and lipo," Kristin, sixteen, told me once. "I didn't know I needed plastic surgery until she made that comment. Now I can't look in the mirror without thinking about it."

A study conducted by researchers at Stanford University, published in the August 2006 issue of *Pediatrics,* showed that out of 455 college women with significant weight concerns, more than 80 percent said a parent had made negative comments to them about their bodies during childhood. And research from Harvard University in 2008 reports that many parents are saying negative things about their children's body development: Of the children surveyed, 23 percent reported that their parents made a comment to them about their weight, and 25 percent said that their parents encouraged them to diet (30 percent dieted themselves).

"When I was ten, I was at my softball game and actually hit a triple," says Ellen, age eighteen, a thoughtful blue-eyed girl who was preparing for college. "I was so excited and was on a total high until after the game, when I saw my mom. She said to me, 'Honey, we really need to do something about your gut. I mean, it must bother you that people laugh at you when you run around the bases with that big tummy of yours.' I didn't even know people were laughing. What I did know was that was the last time I was going to play softball."

Every day, a mother's words are stored and later repeated, or circle around her daughter's head for years to come, a collection of home movies that often are more vivid and impactful than anything she's seen on-screen or online. Think about it: What would the transcript inside your daughter's head say today?

Damned If You Do...

I know what you're thinking...the same as what Grace, the mother of three girls, was thinking: "Oh, that's just perfect," she told me. "As a mom, there are just so many rules that I need to follow so I don't screw up my child. Don't get fat, but don't get upset if you gain a few pounds. Eat healthy, but not all the time—you have to treat yourself! Teach your children to love exercise, but don't say too much—they might think you're saying that they're fat. Give me a break. I could be perfect, and I'd still mess up. After all, it's always Mom's fault anyway."

Yes, I know: It's a lose-lose situation. If you let your daughter eat whatever she wants, you're the bad guy. If you try to help her, you're the bad guy. Moms walk a fine line. So many moms tell me that they feel it is "their place" to say something, it's in their job description: "How could I not?" they ask me. But if studies—and our girls—are telling us that we should bite our tongues when our daughters down another cupcake or put on a pair of pants that are too tight and unflattering, what about the countless studies that are now telling us that obesity, a rising "epidemic," is linked with more cancers than cigarettes (not to mention heart disease and diabetes)? What about the reports that

> ## "Overheard"
>
> *"We were at a barbecue when I was about thirteen and everyone was asked if they wanted another burger. When they looked at me, my mom chimed in, 'She doesn't need another burger.' When I told her I was still a little hungry and that I really hadn't eaten that much, she pulled up my shirt and slapped me on the belly and said, 'Oh, yes you have.'"*
>
> Fiona, age 19

tell us that kids' foods are full of additives and that kiddie meals are portioned for a full-grown male rather than a young child? It's enough to make any mother scream and cry—and, yes, say the wrong thing—because we don't know if there is a right thing to say about food.

It's obvious why mothers are so confused. It's as if they need to pick between damaging their child's physical body by shutting up or screwing up their child's psychological well-being by saying something that may potentially be the wrong thing. But every statement comes with baggage—both good and bad—from every previous conversation or interaction you've had with your daughter her entire life, since she was born. That's just the way it is. So a casual remark about a shirt being too small may be linked, perhaps unfairly or inaccurately, with a statement you made three years ago, or even with something said by someone else entirely. Aargh!

"Overheard"

"I was picked on about my weight when I was younger, and I don't want my twelve-year-old daughter to go through the same thing. I see her gaining weight, maybe she's five or ten pounds more than her friends, and it makes me nervous. So I told her that we should go walking, so that she could feel comfortable wearing a bathing suit this summer. Now I'm wondering if I should have said anything at all, because she seems obsessed with how much she eats and what she looks like."

Kimberly, age 32

Imagine: You spend eighteen years sacrificing for your daughter, giving her everything you can, and what she remembers is a comment you made nearly ten years ago. For my Sassy Girls, it's often not about long, drawn-out stories or years of torment that challenge their body image and change the way they think; it's a moment, a phrase that was uttered once and never vaporized. Georgia, age seventeen, told me she was in the seventh grade when she performed in her first choral concert. "The whole chorus was standing in a line for this one number, and after the concert my mom said, 'I can't believe how much bigger you are than the other girls in your grade!' I was already self-conscious because I got my period before all my friends, so I guess I was particularly sensitive. She probably didn't mean anything by it—I wasn't a chubby kid—but that day I felt like an elephant." Did Georgia's mom really mean *taller,* but used the word *bigger*? Who knows? But Georgia heard *fat,* just like I did when I got home from camp.

When I've spoken to moms at conferences or in coaching groups, they say the same things every time: "I didn't mean anything by it" and "Why is she soooo sensitive?!" Mom says, "I think your jeans ride too low," and daughter hears, "I think your butt's too big." Mom says, "Don't you think that outfit would look better with a longer shirt?" And daughter hears, "Your stomach looks fat." Mom says, "My daughter is very smart!" and daughter hears, "She's not very pretty."

Yes, even compliments can end up conjuring up insecurities in girls who have a wavering sense of self-worth and confidence. "People used to comment on my legs a lot," Taylor, age nineteen, told me. "I was always very tall and lean, but every time someone would say, 'Wow, your daughter has such long legs!' or 'I wish I had those legs!' my mom would say, 'More importantly, she's smart, funny and kind.' I swear I used to think she thought I was ugly or that my legs were weird-looking or something." About a year ago, Taylor's mother asked her why she always wore long skirts. "She said they were covering my beautiful legs. It was the first time she said anything positive about my body. I mentioned that, and she was shocked. She had no idea how her words affected me, and I had no idea that whole time that she thought I was beautiful."

Teen daughters are dealing with two separate and opposing desires during adolescence: They desperately want to become individuals, but, at the same time, they want their mother's approval. So you need to give it, but also teach your daughter to develop her own.

In order to avoid the communication chasm that can exist between moms and daughters, moms need to speak directly with their daughters about body image. There doesn't need to be any special or formal time. Whenever the opportunity presents itself, seize it! For example, "What do you think about what that girl said on *Glee*?" or "Look at this magazine ad for face cream. What do you think about it?" Feel free to blame this book to get a dialogue started: "So I'm reading this story about a girl who only ate Jell-O for every meal to try to lose weight. What do you think about that? Would you like to read it?"

Mother, May I? Overcontrolling, Overbearing and Overdone

Overcontrolling mothers can make a girl so confused about food, she doesn't know whether to eat it, throw it up or throw it out. Eliana, a girl who had been put in pageants throughout her childhood and adolescence, found herself eating only what her mother told her to eat and then purging as a way to take some control back. "I was being told, 'Don't eat the bread. Don't eat dinner,'" she said. "I remember my mom saying, 'Just have a salad for lunch, and then have a salad when everyone else is eating dinner.' She never let me eat what the rest of the family was eating. It was so confusing, and horrible."

Say What?

Your daughter is wearing a shirt that is obviously too small for her and borders on indecent.

WHAT NOT TO SAY:
"Your belly is really sticking out. You should change your shirt."

WHAT TO SAY:
"Wow, you are growing so beautifully! But this shirt is for when you were a little girl. What about that great new shirt we got for you last week?"

Then there's Colleen, now in her thirties, who, ironically, works in the appearance-conscious magazine industry. She remembers how, when she was thirteen, her mother, a caterer, tried to control her food intake, which only led to more sneaking. "When my mother was catering an event, and I was helping her, I would be starving afterward, and she would say, 'No, don't eat the meatballs. Eat the salad.' I would think to myself, 'But I want the meatballs.' So I would eat the salad in front of her and then go back and eat the meatballs when she wasn't looking. I wound up eating double."

According to Rachel Simmons, in order for girls to exert more control over their bodies they need to be more in control of their eating. "They need to know the difference between being 'hungry' and being 'angry.' Or 'hungry' and 'lonely' or 'sad,'" she said in an interview. "If they don't have a vocabulary for their emotions or the skills to express them, then they may displace those feelings into their eating habits."

To compound the issue, by taking away a girl's ability to listen to her own body and figure out when she's hungry—

> ## "Overheard"
>
> *"I always felt like I was being graded by my mom on what I ate each day. When I got it right, it was like getting an A, and she would whisper that she was proud of me. When I got it wrong, like if I ate chips or ice cream or a cookie or something, it was like getting a big fat F."*
>
> Noelle, age 16

and if she's hungry—mothers teach their daughters that they don't have faith in their decision making about food. They tell them that this fundamental, natural thing called eating is not to be enjoyed but is a constant battle with grave effects if they get it wrong. They teach them that food is the enemy, but probably even worse, they teach them that they are a disappointment if the food makes them "fat."

Many moms believe in their hearts that when they approach their daughters about weight, they are doing it for their daughter's health—which many children actually believe is code for *weight*. But health is much more than what you see with the physical eye. It's what's going on inside your daughter. How does she view herself? How stressed out is she about her body? How does she value herself? When we teach our daughters that food is in control or that Mom has to be in control, she is cut off at the knees. She gets confused. She may start to overeat—always at the mercy of someone else telling her when to stop. Or she may undereat, afraid to consume too much, or she may just override the eating process by eating whatever she wants and then throwing it up. It may seem ironic, but when you control what your daughter eats, she feels out of control and may look for ways to gain that control back—eating disorders, overeating, binging, purging or overexercising. When you make food about weight, there is nothing healthy that can be gained.

Say What?

Your daughter has eaten an ice cream cone and wants another, but you think she's had enough.

WHAT NOT TO SAY:
"Sure, have another one and get fat."

WHAT TO SAY:
"It's great to treat ourselves once in a while. I love ice cream, too. But having more than one at a time isn't healthy for our bodies. How about we make another ice cream date for this weekend?"

"Bad" Girls

Many foods are labeled as "bad," and children then leap to the conclusion that if they eat these foods, they are bad, too, and the punishment is fat, which is also "bad." One time, I was on a plane and was sitting next to a tall, thin girl, Kerry, age nineteen, who was on her way back to college, and we got into a conversation about this book. She said she had a very controlling mother who was obsessed about weight. When I asked her about how food was treated in her teen years, she said to me, "If I heard one more thing about calories, I thought I might kill someone. Everything was weighed and measured—the food, the fat grams, the calories and *me*." She said that last part with a weak smile. "It was so stressful around mealtimes, so I often just skipped meals altogether. It was just easier that way. Now that I'm in college I don't know what to do. I was just at the doctor's for a checkup, and he joked that instead of gaining the Freshman 15, I lost it."

It's a big dilemma: On the one hand, if we simply let our children eat whatever they want, whenever they want, it's likely that they won't make the healthiest of choices. But if we restrict what they eat, "ban" certain foods, make disappointed faces, talk about counting calories and cutting out all fats, we create feelings of confusion, shame, guilt, fear and frustration associated with food.

A WAKE-UP CALL

→ If we push a daughter in such a way that she is always trying to please us, we cut her off from her body. It becomes your property, not hers. One very precocious thirteen-year-old wrote to me this one-liner that says it all: "Sometimes I think my mom thinks my body belongs to her and not me, and I hate it."

→ We need to teach our girls that they are in control and that we have faith in their judgment about their bodies. That will serve them well when we are not there to police them, whether they are at a friend's house, away at college or out on their own. We don't want them thinking to themselves, "Would Mom say this is healthy and right for me?" but rather, "Do I think this is healthy and right for me?" If you are doing your job right, they will know the correct answer.

As parents, we need to help our daughters realize their own power, help them to listen to their own bodies, and forge their own positive relationship with food. "Am I really supposed to stay silent when my fifteen-year-old daughter is drinking one of those triple mocha caramel 'makemefattos' from Starbucks that, in my opinion, are just a delivery system for who knows how many grams of fat, because it might hurt her feelings?" a mom named Marcia recently asked me. "I'm more concerned with death by chocolate and obesity than a few slammed doors and a pouty lip."

I say, yes, you should stay silent. Then, look at the big picture when it comes to Marcia's point about nutrition. Dara Chadwick, author of *You'd Be So Pretty If...*, and I discussed this topic recently and agreed that if the dessert coffee is just a once-in-a-while thing or the way this child chooses to treat herself, then forget about it. If this is part of a lifestyle, it may be time for you to gently step in with a conversation about better eating habits and a mocha caramel's place within a framework of healthy choices. The focus should always be on health, power and strength.

Annie's Story

When Annie was thirteen years old, she would go to bed each night and make a wish that she could wake up and look more like her mom. "My sister is the spitting image of my mother—you know, skinny and petite," said Annie, age nineteen, a 5-foot-8 beauty with a rather serene presence. "I, on the other hand, was huskier, like my dad. My mom wasn't happy about it. She'd say, 'Tall and big-boned isn't really flattering for a girl.'"

Annie's mother put her on "a million" diets: Atkins. Zone. Grapefruit. Weight Watchers. South Beach. "My mom was always eager to find out if this one would be the one," Annie told me. "She would always say, 'I was never your size when I was your age.' She made me feel like I was abnormal, because I didn't look like her."

> ### "Overheard"
>
> "My mom took great pleasure in telling everyone that I outweighed her by twelve pounds. I was fourteen years old. Of course, she never mentioned the fact that I was also four inches taller than she was. Even though anyone could see that, it really had an impact on me."
>
> Erin, age 19

Although Annie's mom told her that she loved Annie no matter what she weighed, Annie suspected that "this statement gave her permission to say or do whatever she needed to do to get me to go from a size 12/14 to a size 4/6." Her mother would say, "I think 135 would be the best weight for you," or "You would look and feel so much better if you lost thirty pounds"—statements that always seemed to be more about her mother's well-being than Annie's. Her mother would tell her that she wanted her to "be healthy," but "Then she put me on one more diet or one more exercise plan," Annie said. "She never did anything like this with my sister, and when I would ask her about that, she said, 'Life isn't always fair,' and 'This is for your own good.'"

Her mother's friend suggested that Annie try to "envision her goal" by posting "inspirational" pictures of actresses and models around her room or on "vision boards" so they would be the first things she saw when she woke up in the morning ("to start the day off right") and the last thing she saw when she went to bed ("to have productive dreams"). "In retrospect, those photos just taunted me and reminded me at all times that I couldn't measure up," Annie said.

Her mother also made her keep a journal of everything she ate. "She would weigh me every Monday, so I would start my week off 'in the know,' and she would chart my weight loss and make the tsk-tsk noise if it wasn't what she thought was acceptable. I hated to disappoint her, because I knew how important it was to her."

Still, Annie was hungry and angry. She started to sneak food and hide it around her room. "I would sneak in full boxes of cereal, eat the entire box and then hide it in my backpack to throw out at school."

One time, Annie's mother caught her eating a bag of Doritos she'd stashed. "She couldn't hide her intense disapproval," Annie said. "I still remember her face today. Shame. Disgust. Frustration. Anger. So I went into the bathroom and threw up. She came in and said, 'See what happens when you eat the wrong thing? That should teach you. Well, I guess it's better out than in.' So I started to throw up sometimes when I knew I ate something that she wouldn't like."

When the direct approach didn't work, Annie's mom started pretending that "she" needed to lose weight. "She would announce that she was going on a diet or doing a new exercise plan and ask me to join her since she 'wanted to do it with me.' Whatever. I did it." Annie's goal was to make her mother happy—even at the expense of herself. But, she said, "It never worked."

When Annie went to college last year, and was away from her mother, she began to lose weight. Without trying. "I think it was because nobody was watching me," she said. "I didn't really think much about it." When Annie came home for spring break, she and her mom were shopping and bumped into an old friend of her mother's. "She patted my mom on the arm and said, 'Wow, Janice, your Annie has started to look like your clone—just taller!' My mom beamed. She finally got her wish. To be honest, I felt kind of dead inside."

Monkey See, Monkey Do: How Your Body Image Impacts Your Daughter's

Even if you don't nag your daughter about what she eats and how much, she watches you. All the time. And if you, yourself, have a rocky relationship with food and weight, she'll know. "Food made my mom unhappy," says Hailey, age eighteen. "I would see her eating it, cursing at it, throwing it out in big piles to get it out of the house. I would hear her repeating under her breath things like, 'You're full, you're full, you're full' or 'Don't eat it. Throw it out.' She just never seemed happy when she was eating." Hailey, though, was naturally thin and told me she wasn't sure if she was part of the problem. "She would brag about my body to other people—like, if we were outside during the summer by the pool. She would tell me how lucky I was that I never had to deal with the 'hell' she was going through and that her body was a disappointment to her."

A mother's influence over her daughter is not just in what she says, but also in what she does—how she relates to food, diet and exercise, if she makes derogatory comments about herself. Rosemary, now thirty-two, had been dieting since she was twelve years old—all the big ones, Atkins, Zone, Jenny Craig, even fasting. They would work for a time, but then she would gain the weight back. "My on-again, off-again relationship with weight and dieting has been labeled my 'body war,'" she told me. "It was my own little joke, and I would say that eating salads was like 'ammunition' and skipping meals was like 'starving the enemy.'" Recently, her husband told her to stop dieting. "He said, 'What you do to yourself is your own business, but have you seen how your "body war" is affecting Jolene?'" Jolene is Rosemary's seven-year-old daughter. "He said, 'I was in the supermarket with Jolene today, and when I picked up the granola bars she likes, she told me she was going on a no-carb diet.' She told him that she wants to be skinny so she can keep a husband. I guess you can say I had an epiphany. It's not like you have to be a genius to see where she got that from."

Think about it: What's your food attitude? Your weight attitude? What are your eating patterns? Do you pick at your food? Criticize yourself when you're eating or after you eat? Talk about weight while you're eating? How moms regard their own food intake, their weight and their bodies plays a major role in how their daughters perceive food and diet. "My mom was always overweight," Jacqueline, age fourteen, told me. "She hates her body. She says things like, 'You don't want to look like Mommy. You should never look like Mommy.' I gained ten pounds last year, and even though the doctor says it's normal, I'm scared."

Antonia, age fifteen, noticed that her mother always was trying to avoid full-length mirrors—everywhere they went. "I asked my mother why, and she said, 'When you don't want to see an ugly picture, you put it away, right?' People tell me all the time I look like my mom. I used to think it was a compliment, but now I cringe when somebody says that."

Studies strongly indicate that mothers who are more concerned with (or fearful about) their own bodies are more likely to raise daughters who are more concerned with their bodies, even in children as young as three to five years old. In addition, mothers who are preoccupied with weight and try to influence their daughters' eating habits may be putting their daughters at greater risk for becoming overly concerned with weight.

Lily, age sixteen, a self-described "buxom brainiac," told me, "My mom never told me I was fat. Not to my face. But she was always looking in the mirror and saying that she needed to lose weight. So it made me feel fat, too."

"If she didn't actually tell you that you needed to lose weight, why did her comment about herself make such an impact on you?" I asked.

"Because I was bigger than her."

A mother's dissatisfaction with her own body can affect her daughter's attitude, even if she is careful to stay neutral about her daughter's weight. When I asked a group of girls and women on Facebook what their moms did, perhaps without their knowledge, that helped to shape their body image, I received these interesting replies:

→ "My mom was always complaining about how fat she was. She's a size 8, and I'm a size 12, so she's obviously thinner than me," said Alison, age seventeen. "When I asked her how she thinks it makes me feel when she goes on and on about how fat she is when I'm bigger than she is, she said, 'I'm talking about me, not you.' She just doesn't get it."

→ "The one thing that comes to mind is that I remember my mother looking in the mirror, sucking in her gut and flattening her stomach with her hand," said Kate, age twenty-one. "She would turn to me and say, 'See how much better I would look if I got lipo?' Then she would laugh. She would also pinch her thighs, so that some of the 'fat' was behind her so her thighs would look thinner in the mirror. Now I find myself looking in the mirror every day, sucking in my gut and pulling the fat back on my thighs. I wish she had never shown me that."

→ "My mom would always cook for us but she never would eat what she made," said Sidney, age fifteen. "You start to figure out that you shouldn't be eating it, either."

I recently spoke to a vibrant young speed-talker named Zoe, and when I mentioned this book, she launched into the story of when she baked a special cake for her mom's birthday when she was fourteen. "The cake came out great! I decorated the top and crushed Oreos into the icing. I stuck candles in it and hid it in the pantry and waited for dinner to be over," she said, smiling at the memory. "We cleared the table after dinner, and I presented my mom with the cake. She was so surprised, because I had never done anything like that before. Then she blew out the candles, cut the cake and handed everyone a piece—but herself. I was, like, 'Mom, what about you?' And she said, 'Honey, you know I can't eat cake! It goes right to my thighs!' And then she said, 'But you guys enjoy, and make sure you eat it all!' Yeah, right. Like I wanted fat thighs..."

Banning foods is not balanced; we need to teach our daughters not to be afraid of food and to enjoy it. Women have way too many guilt issues when it comes to food: We'll say things like "I really shouldn't have this cookie" or "I'm going on a diet on Monday," and these statements can affect our daughters. "Instead, they need to see us enjoying ourselves," journalist and author Dara Chadwick said. "If you've decided to have a piece of cake, then have it without a single comment about how you shouldn't be eating it or will somehow need to make up for eating it later. Make the conscious decision to have the cake and then simply enjoy it—and let her see you enjoy it." After all, what is cake? Flour, butter, sugar and flavoring? What's so scary about that? Girls need to see that we are able to be healthy, and we are able to eat a piece of cake. One does not negate the other.

Say What?	**WHAT NOT TO SAY:**
Your daughter turns down a piece of cake after dinner, after you do, but you can tell that she really wants one.	*"Good for you!"*
	WHAT TO SAY:
	"This cake looks so good. I'm not all that hungry now, but maybe I'll save a piece for myself for another time. Should I save one for you, too, or would you like to have yours now? Or how about we share a piece?"

The Mother–Daughter Club

The bond between a mother and daughter is one of the most intimate bonds there is—so much can be said simply with a look or a smile or a hug. And girls often feel even closer to their moms when they talk about food and weight, because they sense that these topics are important to them. It's their "special thing." "Whenever my mom and I go out for lunch, we eat salads and talk about how we need to lose weight," said Felice, age sixteen. "I don't do that with anyone else but her. It's just part of our relationship." More often than not, a mother's desire to share her weight struggles with her daughter is intertwined with her desire to connect with her. Unfortunately, though, the mother may be setting up a destructive codependency. I call this the "Mother–Daughter Club."

Think about it this way: If a daughter's relationship with her mother has always revolved around food, weight, size or shape, it's hard for her to extricate herself from the negativity without feeling as if she's extricating herself from the relationship itself. She doesn't want to offend; she wants to connect. But mothers and daughters need to be careful that they aren't bringing out the worst in each other. If you find that when you're together your conversations turn critical toward yourself or each other, especially when it comes to body and weight, you are likely a card-carrying member of the Mother–Daughter Club.

Alicia, age twenty-two, an aspiring New York City stage actress, found herself enmeshed in a mutually supportive/destructive relationship with her mother starting in her early teens. "Whenever I was with my mom, I was never embarrassed to try to squeeze my ass into a size 12 pair of Mudd jeans," she told me one afternoon over a latte. "She was just as big as me. She would pull those things up over my butt while I gripped the wall and sucked my gut in with all my might as she tried to button them. After all, neither one of us would dare wear 'plus-size.' We shared those moments just as we shared the ones when we went to Weight Watchers and cried because we just couldn't lose the weight. We could understand each other."

While Alicia's mother was acting in a way that was supportive of her daughter, she was also perpetuating and passing on an attitude of negative self-esteem and a lifestyle of weight-loss struggles—a lifestyle that may have begun in her own adolescence. Studies over the last several decades have confirmed that mothers who have dieted or who are currently dieting are more likely to have daughters who also end up dieting and having issues with food. Research conducted at Penn State in 2000 first reported that five-year-old daughters of mothers who engage in unhealthy dieting behaviors had more significant weight concerns than daughters of mothers who didn't engage in these behaviors and were also twice as likely to be knowledgeable about dieting at this age.

"I realized that I wasn't dieting because I felt like I needed to lose weight," Alicia confided to me. "I was dieting because my mom was dieting. I also realized that I was constantly talking about how much weight I needed to lose every time I was with her. We would go out to dinner and talk about weight. We would go out for a walk and talk about weight. We would stay up late eating ice cream, and talk about weight. This wasn't good for anyone—definitely not for me. That's when I knew I needed to do something about it if we were going to have a healthy relationship."

When Mikayla, a petite girl with speckled-blue eyes, was going through puberty, she and her mom would get into lots of fights, never seeing eye to eye—unless they were talking about weight. "At first we were just talking about other people," she said. "We would talk about people we'd see on TV and how they lost or gained weight and how good or how awful they looked because of it. But then we started talking about ourselves. We would talk about how much weight we lost or gained and how much we ate each day. We would congratulate each other if we didn't eat much and give each other a pep talk if we didn't eat the right thing. I felt like I was getting closer to my mom."

What could be wrong with "getting closer to Mom," right? On the one hand, Mikayla and her mom were talking about eating well and exercising, but on the other, it became all they talked about. "One day I was out with my friend Kim and her mom, and they were laughing and talking about a show they had watched on TV together the night before," Mikayla said. "Not once did they mention weight. It was at that moment I realized that my mom and I were totally messed up. I talked to my mom about it, and we agreed to try to talk about other things. But it's weird…we didn't have that much to talk about and somehow wound up slipping back into the weight thing. Oh well."

It's easy to fall into unhealthy patterns when it comes to weight, size and food. While mothers and daughters might believe that these topics connect them or that they can be a vacation from fights and stress in the home, they cause other codependent problems with regard to body image and self-esteem. I find it hard to believe that moms and daughters who've known each other for decades can only bond during Weight Watchers meetings or over diet and exercise rants. The commonalities are there, buried under years of neglect. But they're there. Find them, revive them and you'll unearth a whole new aspect to the Mother–Daughter Club.

Stepmothers: Joining the Club

And moms thought they had it rough. Not only is the stepmother/stepdaughter relationship the most problematic "stepfamily" relationship, but research suggests that it is the most complex of all family dynamics. When a new maternal presence enters a household, girls often feel that it threatens their single most important influence: Mom. When that happens, comparisons, coupled with resentment, become inevitable.

"My stepmother is tall and thin, and my mom is 5-foot-1 and 140 pounds. You see where I'm going here," Sonya, age twenty-four, a petite brunette dynamo, explained, her hands moving in illustrative accompaniment. "It was like I was living in a bad movie—so predictable. I couldn't be around my stepmother without feeling rage. How dare she be the one my dad was with! How dare she be so thin! I hated her. And I hate admitting this," she said, her pointer finger frozen in the air, "but I wanted to be just like her, too."

A symbol of the new, a reminder of the loss of the old, a stepmother's presence can be a potent cocktail of confusion—jealousy, admiration, disgust. "My father was always touching her when he walked by," Kinsley, age fifteen, told me. "Right on her waist. It made me feel weird and self-conscious."

Stepmoms who are walking into already established families with a teenage girl have to cope with a variety of converging stressors due to preexisting issues, such as parental animosity, custody and even puberty, that have nothing to do with them, but they may end up bearing the brunt of them. "I feel like a stranger is walking around in my own house," Nia told me. "My stepmother is always walking around in my dad's shirts with her bony legs sticking out. It makes me want to puke."

"She walks around in nothing but a shirt?" I asked, surprised.

"She has shorts on," Nia corrected.

"Are they very short shorts?" I asked.

"Not really. But my mother never wore shorts."

Nia obviously doesn't really have a problem with her stepmother's legs. Sometimes stepparents are put into the position of "offender" simply for being the outsider or "role model" without having asked for it. According to Christina McGhee, author of

Parenting Apart, "Especially in the beginning, stepdaughters represent another part of their spouse's life that the stepmother isn't connected to." That lack of connection can build scrutiny, animosity and anxiety, and good intentions can come out bad. "My stepmom tried really hard," said Shawn, age eighteen. "But she'd say these things. She'd say to me and my sister, 'Oh, I wish I had your flat tummy' or 'Look at my enormous thighs. I'm so fat. I need to lose weight.'"

"And that made you feel...?" I asked.

"Well, we were still really young! I mean, I was, like, eight years old and my sister was almost seven, but you file that stuff away. I would tell my mom what she would say and then my mom would get annoyed, which only made things worse."

But it doesn't have to be this way. Stepmothers can be powerful, positive influences in a girl's life—another woman with whom she can connect, get support, ask questions and learn. As Ali, age nineteen, a nursing student, told me, "I just call my stepmother 'Mom.' She offers a different perspective than my 'real mom,' and I like that. I think of them as my 'yin and yang.' My stepmom is a marathon runner, which I always found inspirational, which got me into fitness. And my real mom is a chef and taught me never to be afraid of food—to love it. Between the two of them, I feel like I'm pretty balanced."

Here are some ways that stepmothers can bridge the divide:

→ Be aware that you are under the microscope. Whether fair or unfair, your stepdaughter is looking at every aspect of your life and character to see what to do, what not to do, how you are alike and different. Be mindful of what you say and how you treat your body.

→ Cover up: You don't need to be embarrassed of your body, but at a time when a girl is confused about her own, she doesn't need to be thinking about yours.

→ Connect at her pace. Be available, but allow her to invite you in. Remember, the body is very personal, so keep conversations light, ask questions about her hobbies and get to know her as a friend.

→ If possible, discuss the situation with the biological mother. Since Mom's influence is so powerful, she can help a stepmother "find her place" within the family. As Robin, age seventeen, told me: "If Mom says it's OK, then it must be OK."

The Mother of All Examples

There are plenty of moms out there who are getting it right. And I would be remiss if I didn't start with my own mother. The thing about having a fairly pleasant childhood and a healthy relationship with your mother is that you nitpick. I know, it's not fair, it's not right. It just...is. So when I think about body image and growing up, I think of the time my mom told me that I already had enough turkey (she didn't want me to get a bellyache) or the time, as I told you, that she commented on my thighs the summer of eighth grade. The good stuff is all rolled up tightly into a ball of generalities because, well, she was a good mom, and she just didn't make a big deal about thinness, weight and size.

I remember when I was shopping for new clothes for seventh grade. We went to a small store where there were all different long printed skirts (they were "in" that year). I slipped one on, and when I stepped in front of the mirror, my mom said to the saleslady and to me, "That's strange, the skirt seems defective. It's shorter in the back than it is in the front." To which the saleslady replied, "That's because your daughter has a 'shelf.'" A shelf? Can you believe saying that to a twelve-year-old? Anyway, my mom had to giggle. "A shelf? She looks like a girl! This clothing designer just forgot who they were designing for. This must belong in the boys' section." Ha!

My mom is the first to admit that she's not perfect. Never has been, although there was a time, like most daughters, when I thought she was. She doesn't even remember that day in the clothing store, because it wasn't a big deal to her. She was just saying exactly what she always has—to be proud of who you are.

Chenese Lewis, the very first Miss Plus America, also is blessed to have a mom who taught her at an early age that "beauty is a state of mind, not a number on the scale." Chenese's mother, who was always thin, dressed her daughter beautifully and encouraged her to find her voice in something she loved to do. "She never made me feel like I had to wait to get a nice outfit or take pride in my looks until after I lost weight," Chenese told me. "She was proud right then and there."

It's not surprising that Chenese was popular, made honor roll and was praised for her style and her glowing personality. Called a "leader in the plus-model revolution," Chenese is now the president of the Hollywood Chapter of NOW, the National Organization for Women, for which she creates events about positive body image and self-acceptance for girls and women, regardless of size, across America. She is also the creator and host of Hollywood NOW's Love Your Body Day, an annual self-acceptance day that promotes positive body image. Stunning, vivacious and proud of who she is, Chenese doesn't mind telling the world.

We need to get our girls (and ourselves) talking about how we affect others—how we can be caring and loving and helpful and valuable to other people, not because of how we look but because of who we are and what we choose to focus on. Remember Juliet, the former model with the mother who undermined her self-image and her healthy eating habits as a teenager? She is now a mother herself, of a boy and two girls, and with her own family she emphasizes healthy eating, working out and a positive outlook on life. She doesn't allow herself to say self-deprecating things like, "I look fat,"

"Overheard"

"My mom would tell me that I was beautiful and ask me how I positively affected another person each day. If I couldn't come up with anything, she would tell me how I positively affected her. I always feel valued and beautiful in part because my mom nurtured it within me."

Valerie, age 22

especially in front of her daughter, Brianna, a tall girl with solid thighs and size 10 feet. "My mom always tells me that being in great shape doesn't mean being skinny," Brianna told me. "She always eats really good stuff, and we get out and do a lot of fun things together. We run. Sometimes I show off and go faster than she can go and say, 'Come on, Mom, put those wheels on, and go for it!' So many of my friends' moms are on these crazy diets, but mine is always really healthy. She's a great role model."

Getting it right has lots to do with setting the right example, but also with defending it. A lovely young woman named Leigh, now in her early twenties, told me that she would "never forget" the day her mom stood up for her when she was twelve years old, on a day her aunt came to visit. "We were at lunch when my aunt said to me, 'You never had a belly before! Rae, you have to watch what your daughter eats!' I wanted to hide under the table, but my mom immediately said, 'Julie, let me remind you that Leigh is currently going through puberty. She is becoming a woman and is just the most beautiful thing I've ever seen.' She turned to me when she said that last part. She talked about how I got second place in my track meet and how proud she was of me. I never forgot that."

It's important for moms to convey this message to their daughters: *Don't ever give anyone permission to make you feel anything but the beautiful person you are.* Moms must be a source of positive power—not so that we can take over, but so that our daughters can learn from us, draw from our strength, magnify their assets and learn that the power to love their bodies was theirs all the time.

Say What?

Your eight-year-old daughter looks in the mirror and says she doesn't think she looks pretty naked.

WHAT NOT TO SAY:
"Don't be silly! Everyone is different."

WHAT TO SAY:
"I think you have a beautiful body that is going to take you places! On the dance floor. On your bike. On the basketball court. Our bodies are amazing things, and when I look at you, I see a body that is going to open up a whole world of exciting possibilities."

Angie's Story

"My mother is the kind of woman that people can't just walk by," Angie, age nineteen, told me. We were sitting in Dunkin' Donuts at a rest stop in northern New Jersey. "She's beautiful. People stop on the street or crane their heads in restaurants to stare. She has really dark, long hair and big brown eyes," which Angie emphasized by making "Os" with her fingers and placing them up by her face.

When Angie first contacted me, I knew she had a sense of humor. "I may be big, but had I been born two hundred years ago, I'd have been as popular as Kim Kardashian." With Italian roots, she was curvaceous and forward and didn't seem to let anyone push her around. Except her mother. "You would think I wanted to be just like her, but I didn't. My mom moved here from Italy with her family when she was nine, so she had enough time to pick up on the whole 'being thin' thing. She had a terrible body image and would criticize mine and hers every chance she got."

"What would she say?"

"Let me paint the picture for you," Angie said, leaning in. "Here is a woman who's like 'this tall.'" She patted the air about three feet high. "And half my size. Seriously, she looks like she's my daughter from far back!"

I liked Angie. She was warm and blunt. Her hair would flop in her face while she talked, because she was so expressive. "And she would bash herself?"

"She would call herself ugly, and she'd pick at her stomach and say 'Italian girls aren't supposed to be fat.' Once she said, 'No wonder why my tummy got so big, look at you!' and I, being a pissed-off teenager, would be like, 'Oh, so you wish I wasn't born?'"

"It got worse and worse. She actually threw her scale right out the window once. Seriously. And then one day, it stopped. Like…stopped."

"Do you know why?"

"Yes. She got cancer. I know it sounds awful, but it was actually the thing that turned everything around for us—in a really good way."

Angie's voice became quieter. "Well, she had these horrible, aggressive treatments. I mean, they were really bad. She lost all her hair. She had no energy. I mean, most people in that situation would, like, just fall apart. And who could blame them? But instead of falling to pieces, she pulled it together. I remember walking into the kitchen one day, and she was baking—she hadn't baked for as long as I can remember—and she was sitting down and saying, 'I've never sat on my butt so much in my life.' I knew she was feeling bad about it, and I didn't know what I could say to make her feel better, so I just said the first thing that popped into my head: 'Mom, God gave us an ass for a reason—we should use it.' And she actually started laughing.

"She laughed so hard she cried. I never realized how much I missed that sound until I heard her laugh at that moment. She was completely bald, covered in flour and completely exhausted, but she looked more beautiful to me than she ever did. We went out for a walk later on, and she told me something that I will never forget..."

Angie started to cry as she continued. "My mom said, 'I spent so much time worried about what I looked like that I didn't realize how amazing I was.' She took my hand and said, 'I feel beautiful. Right now. Taking a walk with my favorite person, my beautiful daughter.'"

Angie sat back in her seat and took a deep breath. "I didn't realize how much I needed to hear it from my mother—that I was beautiful. I thought I didn't care. But I did. A lot. My mother is now in remission. And we're taking it day by day. But, most importantly, valuing our time together. We take a lot of walks now and talk about all kinds of things. We never criticize. That's just who we are now. And it's the best I've ever felt."

Mother Muck-Up: I Messed Up... Now What?

After reading this chapter, you may have realized that you said something or did something that negatively affected your daughter. You may be cringing about a comment you made seven years ago that you can't take back or about your own hatred of your body and what your daughter may be drawing from that. You should know: It's OK. We all make mistakes and can learn from them. If you're an involved mom, the likelihood of a Mother Muck-Up is even more likely, but that doesn't mean that we can't clean up our messes when we realize we've done something hurtful. It doesn't mean we can't say we're sorry, or start over, or begin a brand new dialogue with our daughters today. Right now. Smile at her again. Be proud of her again. Tell her she's beautiful. All the time. Just the way she is.

Reality Check: 11 Tips on How to Get Wise and Help Your Daughter Thrive

1. Model a positive relationship with food and body. Love food for the energy it provides, how it makes you feel and, of course, how good it tastes! If you regard food as the enemy of thinness, your daughter will likely inherit your disdain. Marvel at what your body can do when it's fit, healthy and nourished—not when it's a particular size—and your daughter will follow suit.

2. Be the woman you want her to be. Admit your own mistakes if you mess up, and toot your horn when you do something that makes you feel good about yourself. You want your daughter to understand that no one is perfect, and no one needs to be, that we all are lonely and disappointed sometimes. A mother who can compliment herself and take a compliment well from others is showing her daughter an important skill that builds self-esteem, body esteem and positive self-worth. Let her know, so that when something calls for celebration, she doesn't assume others will criticize her for being "all that."

3. Fake it till you make it. Everyone can find something good about themselves. However, if you never have anything nice to say about your body or your daughter's, just lie. Your daughter needs to hear that you think you believe in yourself, your worth, your body and your mind. You are modeling the self-image that she will ab-

sorb! You may hate your butt or wish your stomach were flat, but criticizing yourself, as you've seen in all these stories, is damaging. Commit to saying one thing a day about something you like about your appearance. Even if you don't really believe it at first, do it anyway. It will help your daughter, and it may just help you, too.

4. Ask, What purpose does it serve? "I hate my thighs." "Her boobs are so small." "Those jeans make your butt look big." Stop yourself before you say something about your body, your daughter's body or someone else's body in the media or in the neighborhood. Ask yourself, What purpose does it serve? Think ahead about how the statement will impact your daughter. Is it worth it? Will it cause pain? Will it really help her at all? If not, keep it to yourself.

5. Arm her with the truth. Given the growing numbers of girls engaging in dieting and eating-disordered behavior, you should certainly have a conversation with your daughter about weight and weight loss. However, don't join the hysteria. Be ready with the truth. Kate Harding, author of the Shapely Prose blog, reminds readers that "poor nutrition and sedentary lifestyle do cause health problems, at any size," and that "weight itself is not a health problem except in the most extreme cases." Talk about the choices that people make when it comes to food and exercise, and link binging, purging, eating lots of junk food and watching TV all day to poor lifestyle choices for anyone of any weight, rather than to "fat." After all, you don't want your daughter to make choices based on fear, but rather because she truly wants to be healthy and strong regardless of what size jeans she wears. Discuss the problems with dieting, weight-loss drugs, laxatives and vomiting before someone else gives her false information about these activities.

6. Model a healthy lifestyle. Get out and get moving with your daughter! Regular exercise correlates with posi-

tive physical health. Spend quality time with her doing something that can promote both your physical health and your positive bonding. In addition, cook healthy foods together and eat healthy-sized portions of them.

7. Stay away from numbers, whether they're dress sizes or on the scale. It should be about feeling good and feeling healthy and strong.

8. Take pride in your daughter's and your appearance. Don't try to squeeze into clothes that are too small, or cover up with over-sized clothes that are sloppy and un-attractive. By wearing nice clothes and keeping up with good grooming, you send your daughter the message that we should be proud of who we are no matter what size we are.

9. Ensure that your relationship with your daughter is based on a variety of activities that do not include weight loss alone. Take a hard look at the time you spend with your daughter. Does it typically involve food, talk about weight or body bashing? Be sure that you do a variety of activities, so that your closeness is built on positive commonalities. Take a class together or make a list of things you've always wanted to do, and do them together! Create more important things to discuss than how much you ate for breakfast and what your scale told you today.

10. Don't compare your body to anyone else's: We all do it sometimes. We look at a celebrity or a friend and mutter, "If I had her legs…" or "I wish I had a flat stomach like hers." But each time we compare ourselves to someone else, we are encouraging our daughters to do the same thing. Is that really what you want?

11. Watch shows together that support all different types of bodies. Many of the style and makeover shows on cable television deal with real people with different body shapes, heights, weights and ages. They teach the

participants how to choose clothing that flatters their bodies and works with their tastes and lifestyles. Good examples include *What Not to Wear* on TLC (The Learning Channel), *How Do I Look?* on the Style Network and *How to Look Good Naked* on Lifetime Television. These shows can be fun to watch together, and they provide a springboard for discussion about likes and dislikes, without the negative message that style comes only after you lose weight. Even fictional programs like *Drop Dead Diva* and *Glee* show that plus-size girls can be successful, smart, interesting and attractive if they embrace who they are rather than a thinned-out vision of who they think they should be.

BIQ:

Attitude Adjustment

1. When I see my daughter take out a box of cookies, I think:

A. Where would she have gotten those? I didn't buy them! How many calories is that going to add to her daily intake? I'd better tell her to get rid of them.

B. They're not the best choice of snack. She'll have to watch her weight a little more closely over the next few days.

C. I trust her to know what is healthy for her body. It's OK to treat yourself every once in a while.

2. Dieting for me is:

A. A way of life. There isn't a diet I haven't tried!

B. Something I do when I have a special occasion or event coming up, and I want to make a good impression.

C. Something I don't do. I maintain a healthy, consistent diet every day. Of course, I still enjoy dessert every now and then.

3. I criticize my daughter about the way she looks:

A. Nearly every day. If I can't be honest with her, who will?

B. Sometimes. But if I do, I try not to say anything negative but rather suggest a different outfit that I think looks great on her.

C. Rarely, if ever. I think my daughter has a good sense of style.

4. When we're together, my daughter and I:

A. Spend most of our time talking about dieting, eating and everything that goes along with it. We share all the perils of weight loss!

B. Occasionally complain about our bodies to each other, but usually we are too busy with other mutual hobbies to think about that stuff.

C. Go for walks, play games, talk and just try to have fun.

5. I encourage my daughter to diet:

A. Often. People in this world base their decisions on looks, so we need to conform.

B. Sometimes, especially if summer is coming up or we are going to a special party.

C. Rarely. I encourage my daughter to eat healthily each day and leave it at that.

Total number of:

As	Bs	Cs	Total
1 point each	2 points each	3 points each	BIQ score for Chapter 2

Chapter 3

Father Figure:
Daddy's Not-So-Little Girl

I loved my dad so much. He died in 2006 from cancer, and there isn't a day that goes by that I don't miss him. On my desk, I keep a picture of him from my wedding. He's laughing with a big, goofy grin, and his eyes are closed. It's awesome.

He was an amazing listener. Gentle. Kind. Giving. I admired him, connected with him, wanted to be like him. But that doesn't mean he always got it right. Like many men of his generation, my father was swayed by the notion that beauty, for girls, got them where they needed to go—well, at least if they didn't have the brains to get them there. When I was little, he all but admitted that he didn't think I was very bright—or not as bright as my brothers. But that was OK, because I was "cute"—petite and thin, with blond hair, hazel-green eyes, pigtails and little shirts that said things like "Daddy's Assistant Manager" for my brothers' baseball teams, which he managed.

So during my formative years, I primped and obsessed. I squeezed myself into tight jeans. I made sure the boys noticed me, because that was my asset: cute, not smart. That label followed me for a long time, until one day in middle school I had had enough. My dad, as usual, was typing one of my term papers, but as I peered over his shoulder I noticed that he was changing my words around to make the paper "smarter." "That's not what I said, Dad," I told him. "Change it back. Or, actually, let me just do it myself." I sat down and took responsibility for my own work for the first time, and, as slow going as it was for me to type it myself, I did it.

He was taken aback. He was impressed. That was the day my dad realized that I could be more than "cute." It was the day I realized it, too. Since then I never put my work—or my self-esteem—in the hands of anyone else, and I began to expect more from the opposite sex than just mere admiration. I learned I was more than a sum of my body parts. And now with my dad on board, there was no stopping me.

Father → Figure

If you believe that a father's influence is any less powerful than a mother's, you are severely mistaken. Still, although traditional roles of parents have clearly changed from the time that Dad was the absolute and only breadwinner and Mom was the homemaker, many fathers aren't fully engaged in the parenting process, especially when it comes to their maturing girls. This, according to clinical psychologist Margo Maine, results in what's called "father hunger"—the "deep, persistent desire for emotional connection with the father that is experienced by all children." And for girls and women, Maine notes, this father hunger often "translates into conflicts about food and weight."

Sometimes dads forget just how important they are: A Roper Poll, commissioned in 2004 by the nonprofit advocacy group Dads and Daughters, reported that two-thirds of fathers surveyed didn't think their active involvement in their daughters' lives was vital to the daughters' health and well-being. Hogwash. Whether you get it right, get it wrong or get it *really* wrong, you matter. Linda Nielson, a professor at Wake Forest who has devoted much of her professional career to exploring the relationships of dads and daughters, has gone so far as to say that "throughout her lifetime, a daughter is profoundly affected by the kind of relationship she has with her father, often more so than by her relationship with her mother."

Similarly, in her book *Strong Dads, Strong Daughters,* Meg Meeker writes to dads, "If you fully understood just how profoundly you can influence your daughter's life, you would be terrified, overwhelmed, or both. Boyfriends, brothers, even husbands, can't shape her character the way you do." Indeed, more and more research suggests that girls who have comfortable, supportive relationships with their dads benefit in the following ways:

→ Increased self-confidence, self-reliance and assertiveness

→ Higher academic achievement (these girls are twice as likely to go to college and 80 percent less likely to go to jail!) and career advancement, most notably in the fields of science, math and technology

→ Better able to avoid teen pregnancy (75 percent less likely), early marriage and emotionally or physically abusive relationships

→ Better equipped to resist peer pressure regarding issues such as premature sex, smoking and eating disorders

→ More sociable and better able to work with people in authority, such as teachers or employers

→ Show more willingness and readiness to try new things and take on challenges

THE GOOD NEWS

On average, married, employed fathers spend a little over two hours each weekday and six hours on weekends with their children.

The more hours the mother works outside the home, the more hours the father generally spends with the kids.

Most fathers and daughters say they love one another and get along well most of the time. Even during the teenage years, fathers and daughters usually argue less than mothers and daughters and have a less competitive, more affectionate relationship than fathers and sons.

THE BAD NEWS

Fathers tend to spend more time with their sons than with their daughters.

Dads tend to talk more, share more and give more advice to their sons.

While bonds between mothers and children usually grow stronger over time, those between fathers and children usually do not.

Dads Are from Mars?

Striking that harmonic chord between dads and daughters can be difficult. I realize that sometimes fathers feel like they tucked their little girl into bed one night, and she woke up the next day as an alien who finds fault in everything they do. Some of the dad/daughter complexity, particularly as a girl matures, likely boils down to basic communication differences between men and women in general. According to the book *You Just Don't Understand: Women and Men in Conversation* by Deborah Tannen, a professor of linguistics at Georgetown University, a man tends to engage the world "as an individual in a hierarchical social order in which he was either one-up or one-down." In other words, conversations are viewed as negotiations, or as a game of one-upmanship, in which men try to maintain the upper hand and to protect themselves from being "pushed around." Women, on the other hand, Tannen says, approach the world as "an individual in a network of connections"; negotiations are for closeness, consensus and support and to protect themselves from being "pushed away." Conflicting goals. You can see why girls will do whatever they can to please their dads, who may not respond in ways daughters will understand. There are other gender communication differences as well.

"Information" versus "Feelings": According to Tannen, men view "talking" as a means of giving and receiving information, whereas women place more emotional weight on "talking," viewing it as an outlet, a way to vent or rant. And since men view body image issues as falling into the territory of "feelings" rather than "information," it makes sense that so many girls complain to me that their fathers remain silent on the topic and that they are quick to blame their body insecurity on their moms, who tend to be more vocal—Dad typically gets a pass because he hasn't really "said" anything. The problem, though, is that Dad's silence is really speaking volumes: Daughters view it as either endorsing what's being said when he's around—by Mom or friends or the media—or, worse, as Dad not caring one way or the other. It can be what fathers don't say. It can be their actions. It can be nothing about weight, but what she hears him say about "looks" and why they are so important, which may make her feel "not good enough" in Daddy's eyes.

"Advice" versus "Understanding": To many men, a complaint is a challenge to come up with a solution. Conversely, women see complaints as opportunities to console and comfort and understand. So when a girl comes home and says, "I'm fat," Mom and Dad respond differently—Dad is likely to flip into "information" mode, while Mom goes in for the hug.

"Conflict" versus "Compromise": As a general rule, men are not afraid of conflict, and women want to prevent it—one of the few gender holdouts from our hunter-and-gatherer days. Conflict is especially unsettling for girls who see it as synonymous with criticism—not of how they handle things, but of them personally. Therefore, they are much more apt to conform, meld and mold themselves to what their fathers want—even if they wholeheartedly disagree, as Tannen suggests. According to *The Supergirl Dilemma: Girls Grapple with the Mounting Pressure of Expectations,* a research report commissioned by Girls Inc. and conducted by Harris Interactive, 74 percent of girls say that they are under pressure to please everyone. This can be a great opportunity for dads to step in and model—and encourage—assertiveness, particularly if moms are unable to, even if it means ruffling a few feathers every now and then. These communication differences, coupled with fathers' profound influence on their daughters, help us to decipher how girls respond when they hear their dads expressing concerns about weight—their daughter's or their own.

Rebecca's Story

"My dad was a fat kid," Rebecca, age twenty-two, told me late one night, the only time she could talk on the phone. "He was eating-disordered, and so were my aunts. His mother had grown up during the Depression era and carried over the hoarding and binging behaviors common for that time—my grandmother was feeding him malted milk shakes to make sure her kids 'survived.'"

I had met Rebecca seven years earlier, while visiting a private prep school in New Jersey. With a smile like the *Mona Lisa,* long, straight auburn hair and nearly poreless skin, she seemed more "still life" than teen in perpetual motion. "He became bulimic," Rebecca said. "I'm fairly certain even though we wouldn't talk about it. He wouldn't eat anything all day, and then he would down a box of Oreos or Chips Ahoy! and go into the bathroom, and I'm pretty sure he would throw it up."

Of the estimated 8 million people in the United States who are suffering from an eating disorder, 10 percent are men. Men experience the same shame and guilt that come with having bulimia as women, but even more so because it's considered a "women's" disease, which may be why Rebecca's father is secretive about his eating disorder. Rebecca said that her father always knew where the restrooms were in restaurants, excused himself often, and was very conscious of calories and fat grams way before it became hip to count them. But as severe as his suspected bulimia became, he never addressed the problem professionally—a detriment to both him and his daughter. Research conducted at Stanford University and reported recently in the *Journal of the American Academy of Child and Adolescent Psychiatry* shows that daughters are influenced toward bulimia by their fathers, particularly when fathers are overweight and want to be thinner, and dads can unwittingly set their daughters on a lifetime battle with their bodies.

"Because of what he went through, he was always on us about getting fat," Rebecca said. "He would say to me, 'It looks like you've gained a couple of pounds.' He was so worried that I would suffer. It was out of fear and love, I know, but still!

"My mom was never on a diet, which makes it even stranger that she would let me be on one. I was on my first diet when I was eight or nine. When I would complain directly to her about my weight, she would be all, 'Pooh, pooh, what are you staring at your ass for? You have better things to do.'"

When I asked Rebecca about her current relationship with food and her body, she said, "People say I'm eating-disordered, but I just say that I'm picky about what I eat. I don't like how lots of foods make me feel, so I don't eat them." Rebecca admitted casually that she has trouble keeping on weight because of her issues with food, but doesn't see this as any kind of eating disorder; she sees her habits as quite normal.

Whether initiated by Mother or Father, an open discussion helps our children learn from our struggles and the consequences of rejecting food to cope with painful feelings about weight. We want to encourage our daughters, as they become adults, to seek help when they need it. While you may not have food issues as severe as Rebecca's father, whatever your relationship with food or weight is—positive or negative—it is transferable.

Dads Gone Wrong

You want to connect with your daughters when it comes to this whole weight, size and body image issue, but sometimes you fall short or fail completely. You're not alone. What follows are prototypes of fathers who share common missteps. The good news is that it's never too late to steer back to a more positive path.

THE JOKER

"My dad isn't proud of me."

Emma sat sullen beside her mother, Deana, a beautiful aspiring plus-size model, as if someone had broken her spirit. What should have been a vibrant fourteen-year-old girl, whose body already was beginning to mirror the vivacious curves of her mother's, was instead rigid and lifeless, her chocolate-brown hair hanging in her face like a veil.

"What makes you say that?" I asked.

"He calls me 'Petite Couchon.' I've always hated that nickname. Do you know what that means?"

"No, I don't."

"It means 'Little Piggy' in French."

Thud. The conversation stopped momentarily. "That must hurt your feelings," I managed to say, covering up my own anger.

"Yeah, he thinks he's being funny. He'll squeeze my thighs and say, 'You're getting awfully fat there.' He says it with a smile on his face, as if that's supposed to show he's kidding."

Enter the Joker: The dad who makes jokes at the expense of his daughter. He calls her names, pinches her thighs and pokes fun at her weight. He uses weight humor to try to connect with his daughter without realizing that he is treading on very thin ice: Several studies have shown that even lighthearted teasing about sensitive topics such as weight, size, shape and general physical appearance should be off-limits, because the teasing is linked to body dissatisfaction—even into adulthood. Ask Kiley, now in her twenties, who still remembers a remark her dad made during a pool party for her twelfth birthday. "When I came out in my bathing suit, my dad turned to my aunt and said, 'There's twenty pounds of jiggle in a five-pound bag!'" she told me. "He cracked himself up. Even though he knew I was mad, it wasn't the last time I heard that expression come out of his mouth."

> ## "Overheard"
>
> *"My dad thinks he's so funny. He and my mom were watching TV on the couch, and I sat down next to them, and my dad said, 'Zara! You're making the whole couch sag!' I skipped dinner that night and barely ate for two days."*
>
> Zara, age 14

According to Deborah Tannen, men use jokes to entertain or as a way to sidestep communication. Or perhaps making jabs is a way to connect without being too "touchy-feely." As one father in Roanoke, Virginia, told me, "Busting each others' chops is a guy's way of saying, 'You're my buddy.'" But this is not the way girls connect. Using this strategy to parent girls can make them feel inferior, unloved or undervalued when you have no intention of doing so. It can perpetuate body image issues, even if you think your daughter is thin. Remember, daughters of all sizes often worry that they are fat, whether you think they are or not.

THE CRITIC

Dads can provide valuable perspective and help cut through the emotions that weigh down problem issues, but sometimes the advice can be unwelcome. A Critic Dad just can't seem to leave his daughter alone when it comes to weight—her thighs are too

big, her hips are too wide and the way she dresses is messy and embarrassing. Often these verbal jabs are direct. Their impact is profound. Their effects are long-lasting. "When I was thirteen, my dad walked into the kitchen one night when I had just gotten home from studying over at a friend's house," Morgan, age twenty, wrote me. "It was around 7:30, and I had missed dinner, so I got out a bunch of different leftovers and was going to make myself a plate when my dad said, 'Whoa there, girl. Shouldn't you be eating salad at this hour? If you're
not careful, you'll wind up with your mother's big behind and your aunt Sally's guy-thighs.'" It's no wonder that Morgan is now a gym fanatic and doesn't wear anything that draws attention to her thighs, hips or butt. Then there's Nola, age seventeen, who brought home an English paper that had a B–. "My dad said to me, 'You can either be pretty and dumb or fat and smart—you, my girl, had better start hitting the books.' I think of that every time I am about to take a test or write a paper."

> ## "Overheard"
>
> *"I just wish my dad would ask me how I felt sometimes, or that he'd ask me for some ideas on how I could solve a problem. Then, at least, I would have been a part of the conversation. As it was—and still is—weight was the subject, and I was the object."*
>
> Leah, age 16

Other times, the Critic's advice is drawn-out and relentless, coming in the form of long lectures. Kelly, age twenty-seven, of Oklahoma wrote me: "My dad has berated my sister, my mom and me for being overweight for as long as I can remember. His lectures would always begin with 'Why did you let yourself get fat? We're short, we've got to watch our weight.' When I would tell him that I was walking for exercise every day, he would laugh at me and just keep saying in fifteen different ways, 'If you think that walking around the block a few times is actually helping, you're wrong.'"

That feeling of being trapped when someone is lecturing us makes us feel that we would never want to purposely put ourselves in that situation again. Your daughter won't seek you out when she has a problem regarding body image—when she wants advice—because she knows you have your own agenda. Kelly's dad's agenda ultimately became hers as an adult. "I equate my self-worth with my weight," she told me. "I know this is wrong and self-defeating, but I can't seem to stop thinking this way. I can't break out of the cycle."

Because many girls believe that they *are* their weight, any criticism in this realm feels like an attack on their value and a loss of love. Dads must realize that there is a great difference between critique of a daughter's actions and criticism of her body and mind—one feels changeable and the other doesn't. If they don't impress upon their daughters how beautiful or worthwhile they are today, not ten pounds from now, their daughters might spend their lives seeking that approval from other men. Becky, age eighteen, told me, "I did unspeakable things just to hear that I was attractive and that someone wanted me."

> ## "Overheard"
>
> *"The night before I was going into middle school, my dad told me to stand up and turn around. He turned to my mother and said, 'Well, at least we don't have to worry about her attracting any guys with that baby-fat body.' When my mother looked at him with a shocked face, he was like, 'What? You can't possibly think she's as pretty as her friends.'"*
>
> Rosie, age 17

I remember a conversation I overheard while in a restaurant in Livingston, New Jersey, the town next to the one where I grew up. A guy was talking his daughter's ear off without stopping for a breath: "You see how your mom looks really good and all her friends are fat? You don't want to be the fattest one in the group. That's never a good thing. You want to be the one who looks like she has it all together, even when you don't." His daughter listened as she moved the food around on her plate, likely wishing she were someplace else.

Although sometimes daughters speak up to their dads or tell them that "they know," many times daughters of Critics wave the white flag of surrender—they tune in and obsess, or tune out and withdraw. I asked my friend Sue, who was sitting with me that day in the restaurant and whose parents were big believers in the "long lecture," how she could stand it. She said to me, "Sometimes you have to let them talk. It's just easier." I leaned over and asked quietly, "Does your dad ever have any good advice?" She let out a quick laugh. "I don't really know. I stopped listening years ago."

THE CONTROLLER

Whenever these dads hear about a problem, they want to get out their trusty toolbox, give the quick-fix solution and move on.

Girls told me:

→ "I confided to my dad that I felt fat and that the girls at school teased me about my weight. He said, 'So? Go on a diet.'"

→ "My mom made a comment at the dinner table one night that I was looking kinda thin. She didn't know that I'd been purging for a few months. My dad looked up from his plate, looked at me and said, 'Eat.' So I did—and then threw it up fifteen minutes later."

→ "I told my father that I thought my belly was getting big. He told me, 'Just suck it in. That's what I do.'"

Some dads take it a step further and attempt to fix the problem for their daughters. They are determined. They become "Mr. Fix-It" on a mission. "When my dad heard that a girl called me a 'pig' in middle school, he went into commando mode," Brandy, age nineteen, wrote on my blog. "He called my school counselor and left a message. He e-mailed my teachers. He contacted the girl's parents and ratted her out. For a long time, people heard about what my dad would do, and they would tease me about being a daddy's girl and a baby and knew just how to push my buttons by saying something about me being fat or ugly...I didn't know what to do. I didn't even know where to start." Remember the feedback loop: Because Brandy doubted herself, she put out subliminal messages that she could easily be targeted, so kids continued to pick on her, she continued to expect to be picked on and she sent out the messages over and over again. It's not a recipe for success in middle school.

Then there are the hostile takeovers—Controller Dads get so caught up in fixing problems for their daughters that they start micromanaging their daughters' lives. "My dad made mealtimes at 6:00 a.m., 12:00 p.m. and 6:00 p.m. Snack was at 9:00 and 3:00," recalled NancyLynn, age twenty-three. "It was always the same. If we misbehaved, he would threaten to take one of our meals away. If we were really bad, he would take away two. And if we were 'unacceptably disrespectful,' he would take away whatever meals were left for the day, even if it was only breakfast time. Food was a major source of currency in our house."

Food as currency...it's a dangerous path for fathers to follow. When dads withhold food, they subliminally tell their daughters that they aren't worthy of sustenance, whether it's based on a particular action or how they look that day. When a dad gives food to make his daughter feel better or to reward her for good behavior, he sends the message that she needs nourishment from the outside to assuage or honor her feelings on the inside. NancyLynn's father believed that without his militant control of his daughter, she would be unable to succeed. But now that NancyLynn is on her own, she has adopted her father's pattern of punishment. "The other day I pigged out with my friends when we were on vacation in New York City," she said. "The next day, I didn't eat anything but three Triscuits and a Diet Coke."

Like most Dads Gone Wrong, the Controller's heart is in the right place. He wants his daughter to be happy, safe, worry-free. He doesn't realize that he disempowers his daughter when he solves the problem for her—he swoops in and takes the reins on her life, often leaving her embarrassed, broken down, insecure and likely a little worse for wear. Questions that plague the daughters of Controller/Mr. Fix-It types include *Is this problem really that easy to fix? Why couldn't I see the solution? Could I have dealt with it on my own? Do I really need Daddy to do it for me?* These questions, left unanswered, or answered through repeated "knight in shining armor" actions, can morph into a daughter's statements of perpetual need, uncertainty and mistrust of self. This "learned helplessness," a term coined by psychologist Martin Seligman, leaves these girls unable to care for and stand up for themselves when Daddy is no longer there to solve their problems.

Instead, Controller fathers should channel their "Mr. Fix-It" tendencies toward helping their daughters develop the tools they need to combat name-calling and teasing—or the self-confidence not to care. They must try to see their daughters' problems as opportunities to connect and develop, rather than correct and manage.

THE GIFT-GIVER (AKA THE NEGOTIATOR)

"You do know that this is blackmail, right, Dad?" Courtney, age seventeen, told her father when he told her that he wouldn't pay for her prom dress unless she lost the ten pounds that put her over into the "overweight" category on the medical chart. I e-mailed back and forth with Courtney right before the peak of prom season. She was furious. After we discussed some ways for her to approach her dad—calmly—and tell him how she was feeling, she marched right up to him and in her most mature voice said, "You always make me feel like such a heifer!" Well, so much for calm and nonaccusatory, but I hoped that maybe Courtney's dad would finally get the idea that promising gifts wasn't motivating her. Courtney later wrote to me, "Can you believe it? He apologized and said, 'What if I sweeten the deal and not only buy you the prom dress but also a few new outfits for the summer?'" Guess not.

With the popularity of weight-loss reality shows such as *The Biggest Loser,* it's not surprising that some dads are turning to money and gifts as rewards for their daughters to shed pounds. A study published in the *Journal of the American Medical*

Association found that people who had financial incentives to lose weight were much more successful at dieting than those who did not. (Conversely, a study published by the National Bureau of Economic Research in 2009 found that money had very little effect.) Still, it's a mistake to make your household a war zone for weight loss. The strategy doesn't get to the heart of the problem: why your daughter is unhappy with herself. And while "presents for pounds" can yield short-term results—"I wanted the iPod so badly that I lost the thirty pounds my dad wanted me to lose," said Regan, age seventeen, "and then, I gained it all back"—the last thing you want to do is set your daughter up for her first bounce of a lifetime of yo-yo dieting.

THE GHOST

The Ghost Dad, for one reason or another, is just not around for his daughter. Generally, he comes in three forms:

→ The absentee father who is either too busy to spend the time with his daughter or is simply out of the picture. He has a great impact on her, because his absenteeism tells her, in no uncertain terms, that she is unimportant and not a priority. Therefore, daughters of a Ghost Dad feel that they must do something—anything—to get his attention, and they turn to food, exercise or other issues of weight.

→ The "It's Not My Department" father, who is not necessarily absent but feels that he is not supposed to be the one who handles anything related to his daughter's body, puberty or frustrations with weight (the "feelings" territory). He leaves that to Mom. This Ghost simply disappears—shrugs, leaves the room—when the conversation veers off in the direction of body image.

→ The distant dad who is absent not because he is too busy or doesn't care but simply because of geography. As one commuter dad told me, "My daughter knows I'm working hard. I call every night and look through every paper, project and school notice when I get home, but I know, at the end of the day, it's not the same."

"The other day, I was eating some chips in the kitchen when my mom, dad and grandparents walked in," said Shae, age eighteen, an adorable blond-haired, blue-eyed girl who met me for coffee one morning just off the University of Massachusetts at Amherst campus. "My mom yelled, 'You shouldn't be eating that!' She kept telling me how when you eat at night you can get fat really easily. She kept going on and on about it, and finally I snapped and told her to leave me the 'F' alone."

"What did your dad say?" I asked.

"My dad? He told me to show more respect for my mom, and then he walked out of the room. He always does that when it comes to girl things."

A missed opportunity. When dads do speak up, their words have impact; their daughters hang on every word. But their daughters need—and want—more. "My mom and I had gone shopping for a gradua- tion dress," Chamein, a mocha-skinned, red- haired recent college graduate recalled when we spoke on a cold, snowy night in her hometown on Long Island, New York. "I tried on a size 14, and it fit perfectly. But when we got home, I noticed my mom had bought the size 12 without me knowing to 'inspire me to lose the weight.' I practically starved myself and rode our exercise

> ## "Overheard"
>
> *"I wasn't around for a lot of the drama. I only got called—and yelled at—when things really got out of hand. You miss a lot of what's going on in your daugh- ters' heads. I wanted to be there for the regular daily grind, but I just didn't know how to be when I wasn't seeing them day to day."*
>
> Mike, divorced, father of three daughters

bike every chance I got. When it came time for graduation, I fit into the 12. My dad looked at me and said, 'I want you to know you look beautiful, but more importantly, you would have looked just as beautiful in the 14.'" Chamein smiled as she recalled her father's words and then looked me square in the eye. "Every day mom would cry, beg and scream for me to lose weight. That was one of two times I remember him speaking up for me. Two times! And I recall every detail, but I shouldn't, because there should have been countless times like those." A couple of years later Chamein learned from her father that her mom—who never once told her that she was beautiful—had been teased as a girl because of her weight. "I wish my dad would have told me sooner," she said. "I could have understood that. I feel kinda left out. He just had to give me a chance."

Daughters of Ghost Dads often fear that they will turn into the Ghost Daughter—present, but not significant enough to be taken seriously. In response, they look for a way—any way—to get their father's attention. Drugs. Alcohol. Eating disorders. As Katherine, age twenty-two, told me, "I got tattoos that I knew my dad hated, piercings in five places on my body and wore clothes that no fifteen-year-old had any business wearing. I realized after a lot of introspection and four years in college psychology classes that I was doing it to get my dad to 'see' me. I dressed so that he couldn't miss me."

LIVE-AWAY DADS

Fathers who don't live with their daughters are Ghost Dads of circumstance. These "Live-Away Dads," a term coined by Bill Klatte, a Milwaukee psychotherapist, often have trouble connecting with their daughters simply because it's difficult to maintain a reliable continuity when you are apart for long periods. Divorce, deployment or frequent travel force parental relationships to be maintained through telephone calls, videoconferencing, brief visits—all of which can be poor substitutes for the kind of ongoing personal contact needed to nurture a growing child.

A "difficult" divorce adds an extra layer of complexity for Live-Away Dads. When there is latent anger as a result of an estrangement, these dads may misdirect the resentment they feel for their ex-wives toward their daughters, who get caught up in a power struggle—or, as Deborah Tannen calls it, "one-upmanship." For example, if a daughter is picking at her meal because her mother encourages restrained eating, Dad may be tempted to exercise his dominance and say, "You must eat this! This is my house!" Or, conversely, Dad might say, "If your mother is going to let you eat that fatty junk food, that may be her choice, but when you're in my house you are going to eat healthy." Remember, Live-Away Dads are also eager to make their mark in the short time they have with their daughters—maybe one or two days a week—so conversations turn into quick commands: Eat this! Don't wear that!

"Weekends with my dad were interesting," said Jamie, age twenty, a kind-eyed, self-identified "crazy blond" who is in a constant state of chasing her ideal body size. "He was tired, worn out and many times drunk. And when he was angry...boy, did he let it build up!

"I was called a 'bitch' once, and so was my sister," she said. "And a 'loser.' Was called that a few times... He was just so angry and fed up when we went to see him. Now when I visit him, I stay a short while, tell him I love him and go home."

Obviously, Jamie's dad's alcohol problem was a big impediment in their relationship, but Live-Away Dads have to let go of the resentment and frustration—if only for the weekend. According to Klatte, fathers must learn to open up communication, rather than demand control of it. "Before you

"Overheard"

"My daughters' relationship with their dad is sacred. I make that the standard, the guide, for my own interactions with him when we find ourselves needing to tweak our custody schedule in response to the girls' changing needs."

Deesha Philyaw, cocreator, CoParenting101.com

talk, think," Klatte told me. "Then, think again. Let them be who they are, not who you think they should be."

And be willing to talk—a lot, and about anything. "Sex, body image, dating. Being involved in your daughter's day-to-day thoughts lays the groundwork so that you can talk about anything, and it won't seem weird," said Christina McGhee, divorce and children expert and author of *Parenting Apart*.

This "any topic is approachable" mind-set becomes especially important if dads remarry, but dads also must be careful about how they speak and what they say in front of their daughters, even if what they say isn't a statement about them. "I've had daughters tell me that it really hurts their feelings when Dad has a new wife and says, 'I think she is the most beautiful woman I've ever known,' and she's got this tiny body and the mother does not," said McGhee. "And if the daughter looks more like Mom, the daughter also hears, 'I don't think you're pretty, either.'" This "new truth" created by daughters can then take on a life of its own and fuel grand emotional declarations, such as "You never thought I was pretty!" or "You always thought I was fat!" Dads must address this kind of "drama," however bizarre or "out there" they think it is, with sensitivity and awareness, rather than avoidance.

> ## "Overheard"
>
> *"It was like everything changed between my dad and me. We went from spending tons of time together to spending practically none. I think he thought we didn't have anything in common anymore once I started developing. It was like he was saying, 'You're not the girl I knew,' even though I felt like I was the same inside. It made me really resent my body for changing at all."*
>
> Shayna, age 13

Perhaps just as important, dads need to make sure that their new wives know that their relationship with their daughters will remain a top priority. McGhee, herself a stepmom, said that her husband schedules "dates" with his daughter, which he treats as special occasions. "He opens the door for her," she said. "He compliments her and gives her positive feedback on her appearance and her strengths. He shows her the level of respect she should come to expect."

MR. DENIAL

This father doesn't even want to acknowledge that his daughter is growing up. He wants to keep her young and himself in the dark. Similar to the Joker, Mr. Denial uses humor to relate to his daughter's changing body, saying things like, "You can't date until you're thirty" or "You're not really sixteen. You're still seven years old, right?" or "You'd better cover that stuff up." Without realizing it, his remarks and his inability to accept that his baby girl is becoming a woman can lead her to reject her own body. In extreme cases, she may go so far as to crash diet to effectively slow down or stop puberty and maintain a prepubescent body that is closer to what she believes is to her father's liking. As Margo Maine wrote in *Father Hunger*, "Girls need to have their rites of passage honored by their fathers. They want to feel attractive, womanly and acceptable to the most important man in their lives—their father."

I remember talking with Isabella, age twenty-three, a long-haired brunette with striking green eyes and an athletic body frame, about this topic in a hole-in-the-wall breakfast place in Las Vegas, where I was giving a seminar. Isabella had always been Daddy's little girl, and by that she meant "the son he never had."

"And the dieting and the athletics were a way of connecting with your father?" I asked her.

"Not *a* way...*the* way," she said as she played with her scrambled egg whites. During our entire chat, Isabella held a piece of multi-grain toast in her hand but never took a bite. "He always said when I was younger that he would 'mourn the day when I grew up.' He'd joke that his empty-nest syndrome would happen when I turned thirteen. I was determined to prove him wrong and started dieting and exercising like crazy."

"Did it work?"

"Actually, yes," she said with a laugh. "I'm sure you'd rather me say that it backfired, but it didn't. My dad and I remained pretty close during most of my teen years."

"And were you happy?"

"It's hard to say yes or no to that," Isabella said. "It's not an easy answer. On the one hand, I was thin, I was popular, I got to hang out with my dad and it was good. But on the other hand, I was hungry, had practically no real friends and was pretending to be something that I wasn't."

"So what about now? How are you with your dad?"

"Same as always," she said, part happy, part sad, part flippant. "But I still feel like a little girl when I go home for a visit. I can't believe half the things I say, like I'm still trying to prove myself. 'Hey, Dad, I'm going to the gym every day!' or 'Want to play a little one-on-one?' I don't even like basketball. It's like 'Isabella has left the building,' and someone else is there in my place."

"And the food? The dieting?" I asked.

"Oh, I eat." Isabella looked down at her plate. "Well, sometimes."

Isabella will never know, unless she lets go of this shadow self, if she and her father could enjoy a closer, healthier relationship. Without celebrating her transition into womanhood, she continues to compromise herself—in the way she eats and how she treats her body. It is a robbery of her womanhood, but also of her authenticity and identity.

SUPERMAN

Perfection. This dad wants it and expects it—from himself and everyone around him, including his daughter. No room for failure. He is incapable of it (or so he says), and he projects this perfectionism onto his daughter, who believes that she must not do wrong. She must be Supergirl, with a super body, super grades, super friends and a super attitude.

It's hard to be Superman's daughter. She must live up to what is expected of her, however unrealistic. In *Supergirls Speak*

Out, author and self-proclaimed overachiever and eating disorder victim Liz Funk tells us that in striving for perfection—to be the "It" girl who's "smart, popular, slender, beautiful and a great athlete"—food becomes a steadfast source of strength. "Nothing can guarantee admission to Harvard," Funk says. "Bosses can be demanding…*good* doesn't have a workable definition…but food can be Spackle to temporarily fill the emptiness and provide a sense of reliability." A recent Penn State study revealed that "personal perfectionism, reinforced by peer and parental expectations of perfection in combination with the allure of advertising, may cause many young people to feel that they are not in control of their own lives and bodies." Eating—as well as exercise—then becomes an area in which daughters do have a sense of personal control.

"Our family had a reputation of being the best," Catherine, age eighteen, told me one day when chatting online way past my bedtime. "My dad never pressured us directly, but by example. He knew everything. He did everything. And he did everything really well. Tennis. His job. Barbecue. He was even a fitness nut. And he was always so proud of me for being into sports and fitness, too."

"So that was good, right?" I asked.

"You'd think," she said, hesitating. "In many ways, yes. But then puberty hit, and my body went haywire and wasn't up to the family standards anymore. I couldn't *not* be great, though, so I exercised and dieted my butt off. But I wasn't myself. I was tired. I was shivering on warm days and drinking buckets of coffee. To his credit, my dad confronted me about it. He asked me where in the world I would get such a crazy notion that I needed to be so perfect all the time."

"Did you tell him?"

"I couldn't hurt him like that. I didn't want to see the disappointment on his face."

That's right, Superman. In your daughter's quest for perfection, she doesn't rock the boat and make a fuss. She doesn't want to hurt anyone, even if it means hurting herself. Fathers, therefore, must step in and help their daughters see that striving must happen on a continuum—doing our best while in action, taking a rest to recharge and gain traction, and admitting faults, needs and wants to gather strength and perspective along the way.

THE YES-MAN

This father wants his little girl to be happy, so he gives in to whatever she wants, even if it's to her detriment. If she is teetering on the brink of anorexia and Mom is concerned, he says she looks fine. If she is teetering on the brink of obesity and the doctor warns that her health has been compromised, he dismisses these claims. He showers his daughter with whatever might put a smile on her face, even temporarily: gifts, food, compliments, clothes. But what he's really doing is shunting aside the real issues in favor of what's easy. He doesn't want any confrontation—he just wants everyone to get along and be happy. In the Deborah Tannen model, the Yes-Man is functioning as the traditional female, as the pleaser.

Saying yes to everything is a bad setup to a lifetime of chasing happiness through food. Plus, it's poor behavior for daughters to model. Alexa, age twenty-four, told me, "My mom never seemed to say yes, and my dad never seemed to say no. People loved my dad—he was the kind of guy who let you hang on his back, watch TV for as long as you wanted and eat pizza on the sofa."

"How did you feel about your dad?" I asked.

"Are you kidding? I wanted to be like him. And at first it was really great. I was the one everyone wanted to play with, because I was game for anything. But as I got into middle school, being so adaptable actually made me do some pretty stupid things. When my friends started doing South Beach, I was on it, too. When my friends switched to Weight Watchers, that's where I went. And even when my friend got hold of her boyfriend's little ADD pills in college and said we should try them to see if those could help us lose weight (as she had read on some website), I did that, too. It's pretty ridiculous, but I didn't think about it as being a follower, but more like I was being agreeable, like my dad." On the flip side, sometimes daughters of Yes-Men become demanding girls who believe they are entitled. They expect everyone to give them what they want because Daddy set it up that way. Saying yes may be one of the perks of being a parent, but fathers also must teach their girls the importance of knowing when to say no, particularly when it comes to unhealthy eating practices or risky weight-loss methods. When we show them how—and encourage them to do so—we are teaching them to find their own voice and not only listen to it, but fight for it.

Stepdads: Stepping In

Like stepmoms, stepdads often enter the parental picture as latecomers, but they can offer lifelong love and support, just like biological dads. However, the stepdad/stepdaughter relationship poses some unique challenges.

THE NEW MAN

Stepdad represents Mom's new man, and daughters watch closely to see how Mom acts around him, how she preps herself (especially if it's different from before) and how they act as a couple—all of which reveals a lot about how men and women behave and what's important to men. "It was amazing," Miriam, age eighteen, told me. "My mom was miserable after the divorce, and then she went through this complete transformation. She joined a gym, ate organic and lost, like, thirty pounds. She looked great, but she didn't look like Mom. Guys definitely seemed to take notice. It said to me that if you want to hook a guy, you need to be thin and shiny if you want to get noticed." Now, there's nothing wrong with Miriam's mom wanting to look good and make healthy changes in her life, but her daughter's perception is that she must look good and thin to make a marriage work, since her marriage pre–weight loss fell apart. This is a perfect opportunity for a stepfather to remind his stepdaughter of the traits he values in her mother—her spunk, her quick wit, her kind heart—and to relate non-weight-related attributes to her as well: "You have such beautiful red hair, like your mom."

THE NEW REGIME

"My stepdad jumped right in and started criticizing me, saying he would never let his daughter dress like me and that I ate like a pig," Madison, age nineteen, told me one night over the phone. "We could never connect, because I always knew I didn't stack up to his daughter." Comparisons, in any form, are never good and wind up pitting one camp against another; instead, stepdads need to bridge the divide—not only must they refrain from comparing stepdaughter to daughter, but they must keep from trashing the stepdaughter's biological father. He is still your stepdaughter's father, no matter what you believe his shortcomings are, and he is part of what makes her who she is. Therefore, as with Live-Away Dads, sensitivity, in all aspects of the blended family, goes a long way in forging lasting relationships. Rather than imposing rules, stepdads should tread lightly and realize that their way of running things may not be the best way. There will be an adjustment to the new home environment for everyone.

THE NEW NORMAL

Stepdads bring a fresh perspective into the home that was not there before, since they're not tied to the family through lineage. While stepfathers may think this gives them less power in the household, it actually gives them a unique form of power— the power of neutrality: "I've never met this friend of yours, but if she is saying that about you, she doesn't seem like a friend at all." Stepdads should think of themselves as the blank slate and sounding board that their stepdaughter needs to help make sense of all the body image messages inundating her.

Becoming the Dad She Really Needs

Not sure of the kind of dad you should be? Ask your daughter. She knows. And the more aware a father is about what his daughter needs and how he impacts her sense of self-worth, the more willing he may be to modify his actions and the environment of the whole household for the better. Here are tips to get you back on track.

1. Show respect for all different types of women by talking to them with interest and about them with admiration. Show your daughter that there is much more to a woman than her looks, like what she contributes to the world, how she thinks about herself and how she affects others.

2. Never tie a compliment to weight. I have had girls tell me that they come home after their first semester of college and their fathers say to them, "Wow, you look great. You must have lost weight!" The daughter now thinks, "I must have been fat!"

3. Take an interest in what she cares about. What does your daughter like to do? Sports? Drama? Art? Your daughter is so much more than her looks—make sure she knows that you know that, too.

4. Encourage her to talk to you. Make sure she knows that she can talk to you about anything. That she can get emotional, and you won't freak out. That she can speak her mind, and you won't reprimand her for doing so. She needs to know that you're in her corner.

5. Teach her that she's worth protecting. Take a self-defense or martial arts class with her. Tell her how proud she makes you. Teach her how to stand up for herself—both literally and figuratively.

6. Become an expert in things that impact her world. Check out Facebook; brush up on your Beyoncé. Relate to your daughter on her terms.

7. Make parenting a priority. Being a dad needs to be your most important job—more important than watching

TV, talking on the phone, going out with the guys, even working. You will never get these times back. There are no do-overs. She needs you.

8. Deal with your own hang-ups, issues and concerns. We all come to parenthood with our own baggage. Some of it is good and positively prepares us for what's to come. Some of it is not so good and negatively affects how we cope, what we say and how we behave as a parent and as a spouse or partner. Deal with these things. If you have a problem with food, deal with it before handing down your baggage to your children. If you have a hang-up about how a woman is supposed to look, nip it in the bud before making your daughter feel undervalued or ugly. And if you have a problem with your own body image, seek help so that you don't pass on those insecurities to your daughter.

9. Be a respectful husband and partner: Your behavior toward her mom speaks volumes about how you respect women and girls. It tells your daughter how she should look at herself and what she needs to prepare herself for as she grows older and gets into relationships of her own.

10. Listen. Sometimes all your daughter needs is an open ear and a shoulder to cry on. Ask her, "Do you want my advice or do you just want me to listen?"

11. Don't be afraid to say nice things. Unfortunately, society makes it seem "sexualized" when Dad says something complimentary to his daughter about her appearance, such as "You look great in that outfit!" But not everything has a sexual context. Be brave enough to say those things. Your daughter needs to hear them.

12. Pull your weight. Don't push the teen years onto Mom or any other woman in your life. Girls don't need only their moms, just as boys don't need only their dads. Step up!

13. Let her know your flaws. It's OK. You don't need to be perfect to be a dad. Nobody is. Let her know that you've made mistakes, how you dealt with them, took responsibility for them and had the courage to move on.

14. See your daughter as a whole person. Yes, tell her that she's beautiful, but don't let that be all that you tell her. Point out her strengths, her power, her smarts, her focus and all the other amazing characteristics that make your daughter special and who she is.

15. Watch mixed messages! Don't tell her that looks don't matter and then buy the *Sports Illustrated* Swimsuit Issue and hoot and holler at the Dallas Cowboys cheerleaders on TV.

16. Get physical. Kick the ball around, play Frisbee, go for walks, hike, camp and bike-ride. Show your daughter that her body does amazing things.

17. Take a stand. If you don't like what the media is saying about and to your daughter, write to magazine editors, company CEOs and other people in charge. Don't take a backseat when it comes to these pressing issues. You might not get a response, but your daughter surely will be affected by your stance.

18. Don't criticize. There are so many messages out there telling your daughter that she isn't enough. She doesn't need to hear it from you, too—just because you think it's true doesn't mean you should say it out loud—so refrain from name-calling, body bashing, comparing and telling her she needs to lose weight or change her appearance. If you do this, you are helping her to buy into the cultural toxicity that says she will never be enough.

19. Work on your emotional IQ. Professor Linda Nielson, author of *Between Fathers and Daughters,* advises fathers to spend less time talking about the facts ("What's new lately?") and more time asking about her feelings ("What

made you happiest today?"). This advice can be applied to body image, weight and media messages. When your daughter comes to you with frustrations about someone who teased her about her weight, instead of grilling her on the exact circumstances, time of day and plan of attack, tune into her emotions and say, "Tell me how her words affected you." Ask how you can be most helpful.

20. Work on your tone, volume and word choice. Listen to yourself when you talk to your daughter about body issues and weight. Do you sound condescending or respectful? Do you speak in generalities, or do you stick with the current situation? Do you shout and get argumentative when she disagrees, or do you try to see her point? It's about what you say and how you say it. Be sure to be respectful, present, calm and responsive to her needs.

21. Set aside special father-daughter time. Go out. Stay in. Go biking. Eat popcorn. Whatever. Just be "there." I was discussing this book with former Arkansas governor and political commentator Mike Huckabee before an appearance on Fox News, and he told me, "I went out to lunch with my daughter Sarah every single week, and before she went off to college she said something I'll never forget: 'Thank you for making the time for me.' To which I replied, 'You mean going to lunch? That was my pleasure.' 'No,' she said, 'it wasn't just that. It was knowing that you were pushing off so many other important things just to be with me.'"

22. Live your life as if your daughter were by your side—always. Joe Kelly, author of *Dads and Daughters: How to Inspire, Understand and Support Your Daughter When She's Growing Up So Fast*, suggests that fathers should imagine their daughters are holding their hand when one of their coworkers says something derogatory about a woman's weight. What would your response be? Would you be ashamed? It's important to be the father your daughter needs, even when she's not around.

23. Start early! A father should be talking about these topics with his daughter in very age-appropriate ways way before she hits the preteen and teen years. If your daughter is used to hearing you say, "You've got such beautiful eyes" or "Wow, you've got powerful legs that make you run really fast!" it doesn't become taboo or strange when you broach appearance-related topics when she's older.

Just before my father died, I was sitting on his hospital bed, and his last words to me, aside from "I love you" and "I love my family," were "I could have been a better dad." Maybe he could have. Who knows? But it is his voice inside my head that tells me "I can do it" when I'm facing a challenge. It is his voice that tells me to "go for it" in those fleeting moments when I wonder if I am good enough. He may have thought he could have done better, but what I remember about our life together was quite wonderful. Not a laugh a minute. Not full of gifts or easy fixes. Not perfect. But pretty darn great. How will your daughter remember you?

BIQ:

Dads on Daughters

1. Do you encourage your daughter to "watch her weight"?

A. Yes. If she is going to be successful out there in the real world, she needs to look thin, beautiful and put together.

B. Sometimes, but I only want her to be at a healthy weight.

C. Almost never. I've always tried to show by example that we need to eat for energy and to feel good.

2. If and when the topic of weight, food, body image or fat is broached in your family:

A. I tend to leave the conversation to the women. If I do talk, I must admit, I can be somewhat negative.

B. I chime in every once in a while with some encouragement.

C. I'm an important part of the conversation. I make my stance clear that a healthy body is more important than a number on a scale.

3. Do you make comments about your daughter's weight and appearance?

A. Yes. If she is looking a bit chunky or I think she could look better if she lost a little more weight, I let her know it.

B. I will occasionally make comments; sometimes I'll tell her that she looks really nice, and sometimes I'll tell her that she might want to ease up on the chips.

C. I tend to make positive comments about how she looks, but I comment mostly on other things, like how hard she works and what a good friend she is.

4. If someone asked me how well I know my daughter, what my daughter's concerns are, who her closest friends are and if she even worries about her weight, I would say:

A. My daughter and I don't really have that kind of relationship.

B. I know some of the things she is into, but I'm not aware of her deep concerns, fears or wants.

C. My daughter and I have a very close relationship, which allows her to come to me with concerns about any topic—weight, friends or otherwise.

5. When it comes to conversation about weight and food at our dinner table:

A. It's usually about how much weight someone needs to lose or what someone should or shouldn't eat.

B. It may be about how someone's diet is going, but it could also be about how good something tastes.

C. Weight isn't something we discuss in our home. We will compliment the chef and then simply talk about how everyone's day went.

Total number of:

As 1 point each	**Bs** 2 points each	**Cs** 3 points each	**Total** BIQ score for Chapter 3

Chapter 4

Hitting Home:
The Butt of Family Jokes

It's not just about Mom and Dad, of course. Research shows that girls are at a greater risk for disordered eating and body image dissatisfaction when the family endorses the thin ideal. Depending on your family subculture, your daughter will live in a safe haven or a battleground.

For my friend Jessi, home was a combat zone. I met Jessi when we were nine years old, and by the time she and her three sisters were teenagers, each one of them had had cosmetic procedures *somewhere* on their growing bodies—nips here, tucks there. Given that the whole family was fit, it always seemed odd to me that so much attention and effort were placed on being thin, but there were constant complaints, especially among the four siblings, of "needing lipo" or "having saggy butts." It was there that Jessi learned that it was bad to be "fat"—a word they did not say in hushed tones, as many do, but, rather, loudly and with disgust, as if they were spitting it out on a plate. The body bullying wasn't always done maliciously (unless there was a fight, which could get ugly). Most of the time, it was subtle, performed with furtive looks, guttural sounds and shared giggles between family members—Jessi's sisters could topple her self-esteem with one cruel stare. This kind of *relational aggression*—a term first coined in 1995 by researchers Nicki Crick and Jennifer Grotpeter—is typically seen in peer-to-peer relationships, but siblings can bring these tactics home and use them to covertly fight or get the upper hand.

A 2009 study published in the *Journal of Early Adolescence* found that 50 percent of young girls said their siblings provided the most negative comments about their appearance among all members of a household. Of course, not all comments are personal attacks; yet sometimes, heard from a sister's mouth, the gravity of the statement becomes magnified in such a way that "Your nose is bigger than mine" easily becomes "I think you need a nose job." I still remember the day Jessi told me about her impending plastic surgery. Sitting on her bed, next to her worn out "Belle" stuffed animal, I pressed her: "But why?" She said, "I can't look in the mirror anymore without feeling like I need it. And even if I avoid the mirror," she smirked sarcastically, "don't worry, my sisters would remind me."

Female siblings are in a position of major impact—close in age, close in development, easy to compare. Some research even indicates that adolescent sisters, as modeling agents of weight concerns, can have influences as potent as mothers. In a household that boasts a positive, encouraging environment, this is great news. "My sister Beckah is beautiful," said Rachel, age eighteen. "She wears a size 12 and doesn't give a crap what size the celebrities wore to the Oscars. She has such presence. Watching her has helped me keep my head up, even though I've never been as tiny as

> ## "Overheard"
>
> *"Brutal honesty. That's what sisters are all about. Like when your sister tells you that the jeans you've been wearing all day make your butt look fat. Gee, thanks. Can I just die now?"*
>
> Tasha, age 19

my best friends." However, within a negative family culture, sister modeling may promote bulimic behaviors, dietary restriction and what Vicki Stark, author of *My Sister, My Self,* calls "contagious insecurity." "My sister was obsessed with her thighs," said Amber, age twenty-one. "She couldn't wear this or that, because it didn't 'look good.' Now, I'm the exact same way, even though people say we're built differently."

Like the "club" syndrome we discussed with regard to mothers and daughters, sisters form bonds of commiseration, with weight as the primary topic of discussion, regardless of their birth order. Those bonds, if not kept in check, can penetrate and undermine a girl's sense of identity. An aspiring artist, Jocelyn, age sixteen, wasn't "naturally petite and thin" like her older sister Janine, who "walked around the house in a sports bra and the tiniest shorts I've ever seen," Jocelyn told me. At a "round" 5-foot-7 and 135 pounds, Jocelyn felt like a "whale" next to her cheerleading sister who, at 5-foot-0, boasted 110 pounds of solid muscle. "My parents thought it would be important for us all to 'take our cue from Janine' and get into better shape," Jocelyn said. "We had to do whatever she said. Sit-ups. Push-ups. Laps. It was so hard. Janine would say things like 'I can't believe you can't do twenty push-ups!' or 'Pull your stomach in!' and my parents would just laugh it off and tell me to try harder."

Younger sisters already feel compelled to keep up with—and be like—their older siblings, without their parents outwardly telling them to do so. At the same time, they want to be seen as individuals and step out of their sisters' shadow. Add in weight concerns, and a sister may feel like she travels with a label—"I am fatter than my sister"—while the other sister becomes a "walking tape measure," a constant reminder of how she falls short.

Say What?

Your daughter is saying she feels fat in comparison to your older daughter.

WHAT NOT TO SAY:
"Well, maybe you should try being more active, honey."

WHAT TO SAY:
"What makes you say that? Your clothes fit so nicely and show off your beautiful curves and tall frame!"

The inverse is true as well. "My sister has always been bigger than me," said Abigail, age eighteen. "I never saw it as a big deal until I heard my dad—who rarely, if ever, compliments us—tell my sister, 'You should take your cue from Abigail and take it easy on the eating.' I totally latched on. If he thought eating less was worth a compliment, then eating nearly nothing had to be better. That was the real start of my anorexia and my sister's bulimia." Parents must help their daughters gain confidence in their own shape and size, independent of their sister's body type and appearance. This is about the brain—not the body. By permitting the comparisons between the sisters, parents intensify the already competitive nature between them.

Survival of the Thinnest

"My sister Kayla was the 'thin one,' as my relatives liked to say," Olivia, age twenty-six, told me on Facebook one evening. "I refused to be the fat sister, so I lost the weight, and then it was 'They're both so thin!' That was much better for my self-esteem." Within such a controlled, close environment, siblings are natural rivals. It can be like watching pawns on a board game: One sibling makes a move, and the other needs to keep up, surpass or go in a completely different direction. Sometimes this means falling into a system of opposites in order to stake out a particular "turf" or defining characteristic: If one sister is responsible, then the other will be unpredictable. If one is bookish, the other is social. That's fine. But parents must be careful that the friendly competition doesn't escalate into an all-out war. "When my sister, Naomi, was in high school, she started thinking she was 'all that' because she could squeeze herself into a pair of size 0 jeans," said Mandy, age twenty-three. "But being the thin one was my thing, so I made sure to take her down a few pegs at home—you know, called her 'Fatty' and 'Chubsy.' She never said a word, but I know it bothered her."

"Many women permit their sister an honesty that they reject from anyone else," Vicki Stark writes. "She's the one person who will tell you the truth when you ask, 'Do these pants make me look fat?' And from her, you can take it."

Having a sister is supposed to conjure up thoughts of deep connectivity that allows free-flowing honesty without the need for restraint—but only up to a point. Stark found that some of the healthiest and closest relationships among sisters included a very clear "No Trespassing!" sign. For example, Brenna, age twenty-one, said her sister, Laura, knows how sensitive she's always been about her weight "and she would just never go there." "She saw me at my most vulnerable, my most private moments, and she never used it against me, because it would be such a breach." However, some sisters don't tread so lightly on the line between empathy and honesty. Some butt right up to it—testing the boundaries—while others delve full throttle over it in an attempt to establish family rank or make themselves feel more powerful.

Kimmy's Story

"My sisters are openly vicious."

Kimmy, age twenty-one, is a very heavy girl. She knows it. She weighs close to three hundred pounds. Half Hispanic and half Irish, Kimmy is about 5-foot-7, dark-skinned, with shoulder-length curly hair, which was tied back in a short, tight ponytail on the day we met. She wore no makeup and hid under a baseball cap and baggy clothing. I wondered how she could be such a big girl but look as though someone had let the air out of her tires. She was painfully serious during our discussion. "Siblings have so much power," Kimmy told me. "You love them, respect them, look up to them. You want their approval so much, but if they don't respect you back, how can you expect the rest of the world to respect you?"

Kimmy is the youngest—and biggest—of her sisters; the eldest, Caroline, is seventeen months her senior and is the thinnest and "most beautiful physically," while Kimmy's twin, Maryann, older by only three minutes, falls somewhere in between. The girls have suffered hardships: Their mother collapsed and died suddenly when Kimmy was twelve. Vicki Stark talks about real-life events being pivotal in the lives of families and resulting in possible conflict among sisters. "Either the kids band together into a tight, cohesive team, or they scatter to the winds, each one trying desperately to protect herself," she writes. "Girls will be looking for substitutes in their sisters and become increasingly frustrated and angry when they cannot fill their mother's shoes."

For Kimmy and her sisters, who weren't all that close-knit to begin with, tensions flared after their mother died. "I looked the most like my mom, and they were jealous of that," Kimmy said. "Maryann and I fought all the time. It was intense. She threw me over a chair, punched me in the eye. Even though we were all we had, there was this underlying animosity, and it always came out against my weight. They would call me 'disgusting.' They would call me a 'monster.'" She said the words matter-of-factly, as if they were items on a shopping list.

"They don't still speak that way to you, do they?" I asked.

"Why wouldn't they?" She motioned to her body. "Words like *monster* still apply."

Kimmy's sisters are creating what Deborah Tannen would call an "asymmetry" within the family dynamic. In her book *You Just Don't Understand,* Tannen explains that symmetries of connection create communities, where everyone is on the same plane. Conversely, when individuals connect via status—in this case, the status of "weight"—they create unequal planes, asymmetries, and a hierarchy develops. The oldest sister is on top as the thinnest, the younger twin lies in the middle and Kimmy falls to the bottom—excluded and isolated. "One time, my sisters went shopping together and were like, 'It would be fun to have all of us in the same outfit,'" Kimmy said. "'It comes in both of our sizes, but not in Kimmy's, so Kimmy can't.'"

Kimmy has tried everything she could think of to be included by her sisters. "I won't lie. I've done some stupid things to try to lose weight," she said. "I played with eating disorders, threw up for a year, ate only apples and grapes for days. I just wanted to be one of 'those girls.' Like my sisters, the ones who get hit on by guys." She even allows her sisters to make attempts at reforming her. "Sometimes they would try to make me up. You know, fix me."

Fix me.

"They would do my hair and stuff, but I would look in the mirror, and I wouldn't like what I saw. It wasn't me. But I would try anyway. I would dress up, but it was never good enough. It was never 'Oh, that's ugly.' It was always, 'That's ugly on *you.*' Maryann would say, 'Your shirt doesn't hide you very well,' and Caroline would follow with, 'It's giving away how big you are.' And they would say this in front of my dad."

"What would your dad do?" I asked.

"Nothing. His philosophy was 'If it didn't bother him, it didn't bother him.' After Mom died, he grew more distant from me. I used to be his favorite, but I became independent. Because of my sisters. Because of my weight. My sisters would cling to him—they still do—and now they are his favorites. He sees me as a failure."

"Are you like your sisters in other ways? Do you have similar interests?" I asked, hoping to move away from "looks" and get Kimmy to think about ways in which she and her sisters were "on the same plane." Invariably, the conversation turned back to weight, as if all her memories were shrouded by it.

"My oldest sister, Caroline, and I shared some similar interests," Kimmy said. "We were both in marching band. I played the baritone horn. It's huge. My sister played the flute, of course. One day, we were lined up by instrument, and my sister made some snide remark about how we were matched up by size and, you know, ten flutes can fit inside a baritone horn. I knew she was talking about my weight. It hurt."

Caroline and Kimmy also loved drama, and one day Caroline surprised Kimmy by asking her to join a local theater company with her. "I guess she needed someone to join with, so I had to go," Kimmy said. At first, Kimmy was unhappy there; Caroline only brought her along to isolate her, to find new friends and then exclude her. But after Caroline got bored and left the company, Kimmy started to flourish.

"I made my own friends," Kimmy said. "I didn't have to worry that my sister was going to tell them what I did or said at home. She wasn't there to say I was fat and ugly. I could just be myself. And guess what? I found out people like me. The kids wanted to be around me. I don't always understand why, but I know that when I'm there I'm home."

Kimmy also met Faith, a fellow drama fan and "goofball." "Faith became one of my best friends, like the sister I never had." A jarring statement, given that she has two sisters, close in age, in her family. "Faith's mom, Debbie, invites me to dinner, has me over for holidays and takes me shopping. If I say that something looks good on Faith or her sisters, they take my advice. It's like—" she paused thoughtfully "—all of a sudden I had value."

At a time when Kimmy was struggling with the loss of a maternal figure, Faith's mom stepped in, treating her like another "daughter." "She helped me pick out this outfit for the opening of one of the shows that I helped to direct," Kimmy said. "She knew how important it was to me. She told me it was pretty on me, so I bought it and wore it on my big night, which Faith's whole family attended in support. When I got home from the play, I was on such a high. Then I saw my sister Maryann." Her voice drained of energy as she said her sister's name. "She was like, 'Why are you wearing that? It makes you look old and big. If you want to get clothes that look OK, I should have gone shopping with you, because I would have told you the truth.'"

> ### "Overheard"
>
> *"When I was in middle school, my older brother would bring these girls around who looked like pencils with boobs. I didn't look like that, but I knew I should. Whenever they were around, I thought, 'I should diet…and start stuffing my bra!'"*
>
> Jody, age 19

When home is a place of constant criticism, it's hard to go there, so on many nights, Kimmy simply doesn't—she hangs out at the theater company, sleeps over at Faith's. Yet she never cuts herself off completely; she remains mildly optimistic that perhaps one day things will be different. "Of course, they never are," she said. "But I have other places to go now. I finally mean something to someone. I finally can be me."

Rules of Engagement

The culture of some families proclaims that what's between siblings—sisters or brothers—should stay between siblings, as if allowing them to "fight it out" will help them learn how to negotiate, assert themselves and argue their points. While we want children to learn these important tactics, which are vital to becoming healthy adults, engagement among siblings cannot take place at the expense of a daughter's dignity and respect, as with Kimmy and her sisters.

The following ten Rules of Engagement provide a training ground for teaching children good conflict management.

1. Think before you speak. "What do I want to say? How do I feel? What is really bothering me? How can I say this to get my point across gently, but firmly?"

2. Approach and ground. Tell each other how you feel about the importance of the relationship: "I love you, and you mean the world to me"; "You're more than a brother to me. You're my closest friend."

3. Admit your hesitation. Many times, siblings are worried about saying something, because they don't want their brother or sister to be "mad" at them. I always tell girls, "Say the hesitation." For example, "I haven't talked to you about this, because I was worried about hurting your feelings."

4. Start with "I." When tough topics are broached, begin statements with "I feel" or "I want," instead of "You are" or "You did." For example, "I feel hurt when you tell me I look horrible in something I'm wearing after I've been wearing it all day" instead of "You make me feel like a fat whale."

5. Quash the name-calling. Teach your children to use words that convey how they are feeling rather than those that direct anger or sling mud, such as *bitch* or *fatso*.

6. Admit your mistakes. Conflicts are rarely one-sided. Teach your children to own up to their contribution to the argument or problem.

7. Be specific. Don't use generalizations, because they only serve to confuse or hurt. Statements such as "You always say things like that to me" or "You're never nice to me" don't get to the heart of the current squabble.

8. Apologize authentically. Saying "I'm sorry" when you don't really mean it is meaningless and counterproductive. It should be done only after some reflection and with sincerity.

9. Work on a solution as a team. Siblings are friends for life and must learn how to solve their problems together. Teach them to ask one another, "How can we make this fair for both of us? What can we do differently next time?"

10. Let it go. Once the conflict is resolved, don't hold a grudge. The next argument should not involve a rehashing of the previous one.

Understanding how to respectfully confront and collaboratively settle issues can even be a way to bridge the gender divide—the one between brothers and sisters, whose body differences become even more dramatic as they approach adolescence.

Oh, Brother

Growing up, my brother Marc always seemed to have a girlfriend. He was five years older, so his girlfriends were like goddesses to me. I watched how he looked at them, held them. Once, when one of his girlfriends was sitting on his lap, and he was stroking her legs and saying how beautiful they were, I decided to do something I hadn't done before. I shaved my legs. My brother, without saying a word to me, made it clear that guys liked that in a woman, so I did it. Didn't even tell my mom.

Like dads, brothers, particularly older ones, become a barometer for what guys like. They answer three important questions for girls:

→ **Will guys find me attractive?** Who they bring home, have crushes on and look at in magazines tell a sister what boys are looking for.

→ **How should guys treat me?** What a brother says about women tells her how she should be treated—what he gets mad about when his friends do something with a girl that he finds inappropriate, or what he laughs at when he thinks it's acceptable.

→ **Should I be embarrassed of my body?** Even indirect teasing about another girl's "thunder thighs" can affect a sister who is self-conscious about her own thighs.

POWERFUL WORDS

I write a monthly character education curriculum, called Powerful Words, that after-school programs around the world use to teach their students key principles, such as courage, discipline, kindness and confidence. Parents have embraced it as well. Time and time again, they tell me that they use these principles to set the tone in their own families, particularly when dealing with sensitive issues, such as a girl's appearance and weight. Powerful words help on several accounts:

1. **RESPECT-BASED WORDS**—kindness, courtesy, gratitude, charity, empathy—teach siblings to take a walk in their sister's shoes and imagine how they would like to be treated if they were in the same situation.

2. **DISCIPLINE-BASED WORDS**—impulse control, anger management, focus, responsibility, tolerance—help children learn to manage their frustration and anger in a productive way so that they don't do the first thing that pops into their heads and they take responsibility when they've said something harsh.

3. **CONFIDENCE-BASED WORDS**—courage, self-esteem, self-reliance, self-worth—remind children that they are valuable, that they should take healthy risks, that they should defend their beliefs and their values, even in the face of challenges and opposition.

By naming the words outright, connecting them to current behaviors and praising those behaviors, children become very clear about what is valued in the home and among family members.

Older brothers also are looked at as a source of protection. "My brother found out that a girl was calling me 'Expanda' at my bus stop," Amanda, age twenty-two, said. "He started standing with me at the bus stop, instead of talking to his friends. He had this way of not caring about what that girl was doing, even though I could feel her looking at me, and his attitude seemed to rub off on me. I started to laugh more and care less."

But boys don't always feel that they can speak up when the source of bullying is a parent. "I had a boy tell me, 'Whenever my sister is eating something or getting an extra helping, my mom says to her, "Do you really need to eat that?" It freezes the family,'" said Rosalind Wiseman, author of *Queen Bees & Wannabes,* in an interview. "The boy could see that this tactic was in no way helping his sister lose weight and was just incredibly irritating, but he felt that it was completely futile to say anything."

Other times, brothers take their cues from parents. When parents are supportive and complimentary, brothers follow suit. But when parents are accusatory, or their tone is condescending, they give brothers free license to be the same way. Remember Emma, the girl in Chapter 3 whose dad called her "Petite Couchon"? Her brothers picked up on their father's tone and would tease her and her mother, Deana, because of their weight. "After hearing my dad, my stupid brothers became 'Mini Me's' and started making fun of me, too," Emma told me. "They're skinny, so they like to call me 'fat.'"

However, not all teasing is torturous. Some is silly banter that both siblings enjoy. My brother Scott and I verbally sparred with each other in the car, in the den and, to my mom and dad's dismay (or entertainment, depending on their mood), at the dinner table. It was usually fun, and both of us laughed throughout our exchanges. However, when one sibling continually is on the attack, while the other remains frustrated and hurt on the sidelines, parents must step in.

Ideally, parents want to create a positive atmosphere that gets the entire family working together, facing one another instead of the TV or computer screen. Special family time can be carried out around the dinner table, a board game or a campfire. To foster a family environment where there is support, love and encouragement among siblings:

→ Think HEALS—Healthy, Energetic, Active, Lively, Strong. Instead of allowing them to sit on the couch hour after hour playing video games, encourage your kids to move their bodies and do something active together. It's recommended that children and teens engage in at least sixty minutes of vigorous activity on most or all days.

→ Declare your home a Fat Talk Free Zone (FTFZ). Remove commentary such as "Fat is bad" and "Thin is good" from the family lexicon, and ask guests to do the same when they're in your home. Research shows that it's more important to decrease negative communication about weight, size and food than it is to increase positive statements.

→ Join something together. As someone who loves participating in musical theater, I always like to see parents and their children engaging in this activity together. Sometimes both love the stage; other times one prefers to do set design or stage managing. The point is to share time in a constructive activity. Sports and other physical activities often offer family classes as well.

→ Encourage experimentation. Some facilities provide a trial membership, while others provide weeklong "camps." Birthday parties at gymnastic academies or swimming facilities can help whet a child's appetite.

→ Keep it light. When parents get overzealous, it places undo pressure on children's performance, whether it's competitive sports or a game of Scrabble. Remember to stay relaxed and cheer considerately.

→ Ask yourself: Who are we as a family? One of my friends, professional speaker/self-esteem coach Kathleen Hassan, had yearly family meetings to discuss "what it means to be a Hassan." Kathleen, her husband and her children, who are now grown, talked about their goals as a family and the characteristics that made up a Hassan—kind, helpful, works hard, whatever. "Looks" were never part of the discussion.

Relative Success

When the nuclear family sets the tone, others outside the family unit are quick to take the cue. That means that whatever precedent you set and enforce creates an atmosphere that is adopted by whoever else enters your home—close friends, neighbors and, of course, relatives.

These individuals, many of whom have known your daughter since birth, mean well. But sometimes their support is proffered in a negative and disturbing way that causes hurt and animosity. One Christmas, Jalissa, age nineteen, a 5-foot-10, dark-skinned girl who described her body type as "thick," watched her sister unwrap a gift from her grandparents—a beautiful cashmere sweater. "It was bright blue and gorgeous," she told me on the phone one day in between two of her college classes. "I was so excited. I figured if she got one, I would, too. Maybe in my favorite color. But I didn't. I got diet shakes. Can you believe? That's not a gift. That's an insult."

As much as you appreciate their love and support, things like books on weight loss and memberships to Weight Watchers—all actual gifts received by some of the girls I interviewed—are reminders that our daughters don't deserve to be treated and celebrated like others until they look a certain way. It's important to tell family members how much you appreciate their love and support and need them on your side—after all, fighting all of society takes muscle power. Here are three ways they can help you lean against the door when all those "thin is in" messages are trying to blow it down:

→ Let the compliments flow. When those who are closest to a girl can make statements about someone else in a way that shows appreciation rather than disapproval, they teach girls how to accept and give a genuine compliment.

→ Let the parent be the parent. Extended family and close friends should play supportive roles, but leave the disciplining and tough love to those who know their children best.

→ Let your daughter make the first move. When she does, a neighbor or a grandparent can be a wonderful source of perspective and objectivity in the wake of confusion or frustration. Research shows that the majority of adolescents have at least one important relationship with a nonparental adult—extended family members are among those most commonly named as mentors— and that these relationships can have a strong, positive effect on their development.

Molly, age seventeen, told me she feels her mom "gets too wrapped up and starts blaming herself" whenever Molly gets upset about her plus-size figure, so she often turns to her aunt Jen for some perspective. "She can be more objective than my mom and less judgmental than my friends, so it's the best of all worlds," Molly told me. When I asked Molly if her mom ever questioned why Jen was the go-to person instead of her, she told me matter-of-factly, "She just tells me that she's glad I can talk to Jen."

It takes a very strong parent to be able to step aside and watch someone else take a coveted position with a daughter. By allowing Molly to spend time with another trusted woman, she not only opens up connective opportunities for her, but she has made her own relationship with her daughter that much stronger. Failure to provide that kind of trust creates what Lyn Mikel Brown and Carol Gilligan, authors of *Meeting at the Crossroads,* call the "crisis of connection"—a lack of authentic, supportive relationships in a girl's life during adolescence, particularly when the mother herself is disconnected. Imagine the enormous emotional loss that a girl experiences when she has no one to turn to within as well as outside the family unit. She is all alone.

Rita's Story

As a young girl, Rita was starstruck by her smack-talking, trendy neighbor, Darla, who at 5-foot-7 wore designer duds and the coolest makeup, had the best body and straightened her highlighted hair. She even made freckles look good, since Rita had them and detested them. "I looked up to her like a big sister even though she was an adult, like, probably early thirties," said Rita, age thirty-two. "I was an only child."

The problem was that Darla treated Rita like crap. "When I was ten years old, she'd tease me about my chest until I cried, called me the 'Titless Wonder' and a slut. I'd never even kissed a boy!" said Rita. The abuse happened openly, in front of Rita's parents and their friends. "She would say, 'Look at you. You're gaining so much weight. You're going to be fat.' She would say these things until I cried, and then she was satisfied. I would run up into my room." Instead of defending her daughter, Rita's mom would ignore the jabs or laugh them off. "She'd say, 'Oh, Rita, stop being so sensitive.' I could engrave that on my forehead: too sensitive. I still hear it."

It was in tenth grade that Darla finally crossed the line, at least in Rita's mother's eyes. "During a house party, she was telling my mother in front of everyone, 'Rita will end up pregnant and fat and living off you.' And then she called me the 'C' word. That was the final straw. My mother was furious and stopped talking to her. Darla even moved away."

Darla was gone, but her impact remained. Rita still thought of her, wondered what she was up to. All through college, Rita took diet pills to get thinner on the off chance that she would one day see Darla again. She met a man who asked her to marry him and prayed that she would bump into Darla "out of the blue" and impress her with her thin figure and the fat rock on her left hand. Finally, the pressure was too great. Rita called her.

"I was a glutton for punishment," she told me. "I even asked her to be the maid of honor in my wedding." Things were "great for a while," but it wasn't long before the bullying resumed. "It started all over again," Rita said. "'You look fat. Ugly. Your marriage is never going to last. You're immature.' I said forget it, took back my maid-of-honor request and cut all ties with her."

Finally, I thought hopefully, Rita was going to start a new life. "We got divorced after two and a half years," she said.

After her marriage failed, Rita looked for a psychologist who could help her to interpret what had gone wrong. It didn't take long to discover that her unhappiness and her inability to value herself were rooted in her abusive relationship with her neighbor and the neglectful way her mother handled that relationship. "But even after learning all that and understanding the negative influences that Darla had on me, she was still on my mind," Rita admitted.

Rita recently had liposuction, after a guy she met on Match.com told her that her legs looked like "pumpkins." She continues to fad-diet. Right now, she's doing the no-carb thing, eating bacon for lunch and dinner. She claims that it's "finally working," that she's losing "tons" of weight and that "everyone at the office" tells her how great she looks. To me, she seems physically and emotionally exhausted. I needed to ask the inevitable, since the abused so often cycle back to their abuser. "So you don't talk to Darla now?"

"No. Well, I mean, not really. I 'friended' her on Facebook." Rita became louder, more emphatic. "I want to throw it in her face. I want her to see that I'm not all those things she called me, that I've done things! I want to say…" She grew thoughtful and quiet. "Look at me now."

Women know intuitively when they are being devalued. I believe that we must raise our daughters in a nurturing environment that teaches them to access their emotions and to express

> ## "Overheard"
>
> "Should *is a dangerous word that leads to unreasonable expectations. No one has the right to sit in judgment of another, and* should *means they already have.*"
>
> Mikelle, age 25

themselves—"I am worth something, and you can't talk to me that way, not now, not ever, and certainly not in my own home." In such a safe refuge, they learn to accept themselves as they are.

BIQ:

Attitude Adjustment

1. Your daughter comes out of her room and her sister tells her that the jeans she's wearing look too tight. Your daughter will likely:

A. Freak out and say, "Why do you always think I look fat?" and start an argument that can last all day.

B. Get a little huffy, regroup, put something else on and be on her way.

C. Speak her mind. If she thinks they look good, she'll keep them on, but if her sister confirmed what she was thinking in the first place, she'll fault the jeans and find something else to wear.

2. Your daughter tells you that she's sick of her brother making fun of her weight (no matter what it is) and calling her nicknames that make her feel self-conscious about her body, so you:

A. Tell her to get over it. "All brothers make fun of their sisters."

B. Tell her brother to stop it. "You're hurting your sister's feelings."

C. Have an open family discussion about the impact of weight and body teasing, get everyone to agree that such teasing is off-limits and make sure that her brother apologizes sincerely.

3. *Your daughter's grandparents tell you that they'd like to give your daughter a membership to Weight Watchers for her birthday. You tell them:*

A. "Perfect! I'll buy her the gym membership."

B. "I'm not sure how she'll feel about that. Why don't you ask her?"

C. "That's quite an offer. But weight is a sensitive topic for girls. Why don't you ask her what she wants for her birthday and go from there?"

4. *Every time your relatives are over for dinner, they talk about weight. You:*

A. Go along with it.

B. Try to change the subject, but are not always successful.

C. Make your home a Fat Talk Free Zone (FTFZ), and make sure everyone, including your relatives, knows it.

5. *Your friend makes comments about your daughter's body, both good and bad, every time she sees her. You:*

A. Usually agree with her. After all, good friends tell each other the truth.

B. Laugh it off and joke that she always says things like that.

C. Let her know before she comes over that while you know she means well, you'd like her to stop making comments about your daughter's body.

Total number of:

As	**Bs**	**Cs**	**Total**
1 point each	2 points each	3 points each	BIQ score for Chapter 4

Chapter 5

The School Fool, Part I:
Teachers

Kit had finally had enough.

While her fifth-grade classmates were all at lunch, she asked her teacher if she could talk to him. Privately. She had been taking notes for three months—to the day—in her *High School Musical* diary, and she was ready. "I finally got up the courage to tell him that some of the kids were calling me 'Big Fat Kit Kat'—you know, in that painful singsongy way," Kit, age nineteen, recalled wistfully. I imagined her freckled face, wide eyes and wispy brown flyaway hair on a determined eleven-year-old. "Do you know what he said? 'Well, if you lost some weight, people wouldn't make fun of you anymore, would they?' It was devastating. I threw out my diary when I got home."

Research consistently shows that effective teachers are the number-one factor in how students perform—the more positive children's interactions, the more enhanced their cognitive, socioemotional and language development. Great teachers know that education goes beyond core subjects. But even for great teachers, it's not always easy.

Problem #1: Teachers Are "Overstretched" and "Undertrained"

"Everyone is breathing down our necks," said Janet, a fifth-grade teacher. "Teach to the test, but also make sure there is outside enrichment—talk about bullying and respect and bring in speakers. And if we say there is no budget? Figure it out! Fund-raise! But where are we supposed to find the time?"

According to a recent study of more than 15,000 teachers, 13,000 principals and 40,000 teacher evaluation responses, released by the New Teacher Project, the best teachers aren't recognized for their achievements, the average teachers aren't getting the feedback and training they need to improve and the poorly performing teachers are rarely removed from the classroom, making them all seem "interchangeable." If teachers are feeling unsupported by their school administration, it is difficult for them, in turn, to support their students.

"Overheard"

"Teachers are so stupid. They think that an hour assembly on bullying will make us nice and a weeklong program on kindness will make us kind. It's such a joke. Kids are signing the 'kindness pledge' with one hand and texting about how stupid it all is with the other."

Shay, age 15

Problem #2: No Protocol or Established Curriculum

I recently posted the following on a teacher chat site: "What do you do when you see a girl being bullied about her weight?" Here's what I got:

→ "We don't have a bullying problem in our school."

→ "I would tell the kids to try to get along."

→ "I would call the girl's mother and get her involved."

→ "I would never get the parents involved. No mother wants to hear that her daughter has a weight problem."

→ "I would contact the school counselor to deal with it."

On another popular teacher chat board, a school counselor was posing the question to other school counselors about how to deal with a girl who was being bullied due to weight. Nobody seemed to have the same answer. Teachers feel like they have their hands tied.

Stephanie, age thirteen, told me that her friend started what I could only call a Grade Brigade—a gang of girls that rolls through the school like a tidal wave, pulling everyone in its wake—leveled against a girl named Erica who, at a size 14, was the biggest girl in her eighth-grade class. And it started with one word: "WOW." (I didn't know what it meant, either.)

"WOW stands for 'weird obese woman,'" Stephanie told me. "All the popular kids would walk past Erica and say, 'Wow!' and laugh. The teachers had no idea what was going on. And if they figured it out, what were they gonna do?" According to Rosalind Wiseman, author of *Queen Bees & Wannabes,* girls literally "strip" another girl of her identity by labeling and identifying her with the very thing that belittles her.

"Oh, that's awful," said Tonya, a high school music teacher, when I related Stephanie's story. "But she's right. What could we do? No one was really hurt—you know, *hurt.* It would be hard to complain and be taken seriously."

But relational aggression is a serious matter. There must be a culture within the classroom—and within the school—that does not accept humiliation and degradation, however subtle. This must be emphasized repeatedly, so that students see the seriousness of the subject. "Teachers don't need to show a documentary on people being nice to kids with larger body types," Wiseman told me. "They need to set the tone. And if they don't, the students will do it for them."

I know what she means. I remember crying every day. Her name was Janie, and she wore red high-top sneakers, a high ponytail and a flowered T-shirt. I can honestly say that, even as an adult and after four years of infertility and four painful miscarriages, I still peg fifth grade as one of the worst years of my life. I just remember feeling so alone. As if I wanted to disappear. Janie had successfully gotten the rest of the class, including my best friend, to turn against me. One day, when the teacher was out of the classroom, I returned from the bathroom, and all the kids turned around and simultaneously started singing the David

Lee Roth song "Just a Gigolo." They belted out, "IIIIIII ain't got nooooooobody! Nobody cares for me, nobody! IIIIIIIIIIIIIIIIIIIIIII'm so sad and looooooonely, sad and lonely, sad and lonely…" My heart was in my stomach. But it was exactly how I felt.

Even as the bullying continued, my teachers had no idea what to do with me. They watched me outside during recess, standing alone, pushing rocks with my feet while the rest of the class, barring some loners and stragglers, sat up on the cement stairs by the school—talking, whispering, laughing with Janie. To their credit, the teachers felt sorry for me, but that didn't do me a lick of good.

Problem #3: Breaking the Code of Silence

Many teachers don't know how to get their students to come to them and confide in them. Far too many girls say nothing and endure the torture of bullying silently. "Most of the time these situations are only addressed when the adult hears about or finds out about the bullying situation by accident," said Angela, a teacher in a Catholic elementary school. "The bully is very secretive, yes, but so is the victim." Heather, age nineteen, was a seventh grader in southwestern Ohio who "just wanted to get through the day without crying," she told me. "People called me 'Heifer' instead of 'Heather.' Yes, I hated it, but I knew if I complained about it, it would get worse, not better. My teachers just wouldn't get it." According to *The Supergirl Dilemma*, one in five high school girls says she does not know three adults to whom to turn if she has a problem. That has to change. A girl needs to know (1) how to approach someone who is bullying her at school, and (2) who to go to for help—discreetly—when she feels the problem is bigger than she can handle.

When the Teacher Is the Problem

While discrimination is expected from students, it is both surprising and despicable when it comes from teachers. Research on bias tends to focus more on students than it does on teachers and school staff, but there's enough evidence to show that educators aren't immune to linking weight with negative attributes. Research conducted at the University of Minnesota in the late 1990s revealed that one in four junior and senior high school teachers believed that "fat people are untidy," with teachers admitting that being obese was "one of the worst things" that could happen to a person. A 2007 study by researchers at the University of Otago, New

> ## "Overheard"
>
> *"Every kid has heard from her dance teacher that she needs to lose some weight. If any girl is telling you that she hasn't heard that, she's either anorexic or flat-out lying."*
>
> Sidrah, age 19

Zealand, found that students who were studying to become physical education (PE) teachers displayed the highest levels of antifat bias (associating "fat" with being "bad," "lazy" and "stupid") of any group of professionals studied at the university. This trend increased the longer these PE teachers–in–training studied at the university. (Similar research at the Cooper Institute in Dallas, Texas, in 2004 found that university exercise science majors felt strongly that being fat was the result of being "lazy.") And when this bias comes out in the form of humiliation or unfairness, a 2010 study out of the University of Alberta says, students can develop lifelong negative attitudes toward physical activity.

"I had a teacher in seventh grade who had a sarcastic sense of humor," Sophie, age twenty, told me on Facebook one morning. "I remember him picking on boys and girls who were overweight or awkward. He'd comment on their laziness and stupidity and would punish them by making them sit by the window for weeks or months, joking that the sunlight would make them smarter. The rest of us thought the only way to escape getting made fun of was to laugh along."

In a landmark survey conducted in 1989 by the National Association for the Advancement of Fat Acceptance (NAAFA), members reported being denied placement on honor rolls, sports teams, leadership/performing arts programs and cheerleading squads more so than average or thin students. They also reported a lack of teacher support for college admission, even though they believed that they achieved scores comparable to those of thinner students on tests and homework.

"I'm glad I steamed open my college recommendation letter before putting it in the package to send to Yale University," said Meri, age twenty-two. "My English teacher made a comment to me about college affording me 'a fresh start,' which was enough to make my antennae stand up. The letter went something like this: 'Meri is a talented student with an unfortunate appearance.' I remember her saying 'unfortunate,' because it was so horrible, like I was underprivileged for not being a twig. It went on to say, 'She will almost certainly never reach her potential until she loses at least fifty pounds.'"

> ## "Overheard"
> "Zero tolerance *is just code for 'Don't do it in front of the teacher.'*"
> Kenni, age 16

For the life of me, I don't know why a teacher would do this. By commenting on Meri's weight in her college recommendation letter, this teacher (1) automatically negates everything else she says before or after the statement (which could have been very complimentary) and (2) devalues all the work Meri has done up to this point, which serves as the real indicator of her future success. Research already suggests that a "heavy" high school girl has a third of the chance of getting into college as a "thin" girl. Some of this is attributed to the social stigma theory, which says that it is more likely for those with perceived negative traits, such as excess weight, to be put down and ostracized. Similarly, a 2007 study by researchers at the University of Texas at Austin reported that when obesity is rare at a particular school, those students who are obese—in addition to being more likely to skip school, fail or abuse drugs—are less likely to attend college.

Preacher Teacher

The obesity epidemic has gotten everyone so riled up and ready to fight the "war" that teachers are eager to impose their views on the subject. Sometimes the advice is just plain bad: A 2001 study conducted by researchers at the University of Sydney in Australia found that nearly 90 percent of trainee PE and home economics teachers promoted unsound weight-loss advice and demonstrated "a great deal of misinformation" relating to nutrition education, weight control, adolescent nutritional needs, eating disorders and fad diets. Most of the teachers in the study were "recommending strict calorie-controlled diets to their fat students, many of whom were in the middle of their adolescent growth spurt." (Ironically, a significant number of the trainee teachers themselves admitted to having dangerous eating disorders, many of which had gone untreated, and some had used potentially dangerous methods of weight loss, including laxative abuse and vomiting.)

More often, however, the weight advice is unwanted. "When I was fifteen, my home economics teacher gave me an hour lecture in front of my friends about how I needed to lose weight if I was ever going to experience 'life,'" said Ella, age twenty-one, who was on break from the Rhode Island School of Design when we met near her home in Connecticut. Ella had a great "artistic" look about her—sort of black goth mixed with hippie chic; she wore heavy eye makeup, a long black skirt and a black tank, with a colorful knitted scarf that looked like it came from her grandmother's closet. "I had just come out of the bathroom, and my teacher said she could see that I didn't look quite like myself for the last few days. It was nice how she sounded all concerned. But then she was saying this stuff about 'solidarity' and women needing to keep each other on track. My friends and I were just smiling and wondering where she was going with the whole thing. Then she said, 'As friends, you need to say something if you think someone is eating the wrong thing or is getting lazy about exercising, because that can make anyone feel out of sorts.'"

"How did you react?" I asked.

"I could feel my body getting stiff," Ella said. "She was saying it as if she was trying to be my friend, like all buddy-buddy with her arm around my shoulders. And it dawned on me that she was talking about my weight. I was kind of chunky, like a size 14, which, I guess, is big for a preppy suburban high school."

"How about your friends?"

"They all agreed with her! They were like, 'She was only doing it because she cares about us and wouldn't say anything if she wasn't really concerned.' I couldn't believe it. After that, every time I saw her in class, I couldn't pay attention. I just kept thinking, 'Who cares about these stupid oven mitts? People must think I'm fat!'"

I believe this teacher created the problem she was trying to fix. According to Julia V. Taylor, school counselor at Wake County Public Schools in Raleigh, North Carolina, "Teachers bring their own body image issues with them to class, and those attitudes, however subtle and 'hidden,' have a way of seeping into the classroom and impacting how our daughters view others, themselves, obesity, size, stereotyping and health."

"My Spanish teacher was also my cheerleading coach," said Jasmine, age nineteen, a brown-haired girl with a cherubic round face and round eyes. "One day, she asked me to stay after class. I figured she wanted to talk about my latest test grade—I had never gotten below a B before. But that wasn't it. She took out a whole packet of information that had a weight chart and food pyramid on the first page. She said, 'I'd like to go over this with you, OK?' What was I going to say? No? She told me she was doing it because she wanted all her girls to be healthy. But if that was true, why was I the only one sitting there?"

Divided They Fall

"Every September, I would be pulled out of my classroom—in front of all my classmates—to go to the nurse's office," said Jane, age twenty-four, a computer analyst who told me she believes all nurses should have to go through sensitivity training before getting hired at a middle school. "It was time for this heifer to get tagged, weighed and measured. BMI, the whole thing. I dreaded it. And it wasn't just me—it was any other chunky monkey that the teachers had 'cause for concern.' We'd sit on these hard, small chairs, which only seemed to underscore that we were 'too big,' and the nurse would tell us that 'school was a place to learn, and when we ate poorly and didn't exercise we wouldn't be able to learn as well.'"

I have a love/hate relationship with BMI scores. By definition, BMI is a measure of weight for height—calculated as weight in kilograms divided by the square of height in meters—not of "body fatness," as is commonly thought. Due to its ease of measurement and calculation, it is the most widely used diagnostic tool to identify weight problems; many schools compute each child's BMI and send it home as a part of an evaluation. While I understand the importance of monitoring our children's health and growth, BMI is not a good diagnostic health measure—and it wasn't originally meant to be. It doesn't differentiate fat from lean body mass and fails to predict fitness, blood pressure, body composition or health risk, according to the U.S. Preventative Services Task Force, which also reports that BMI screening should not be used as incentive for weight loss. The cutoffs are arbitrary—plenty of children can wind up with a high BMI who do not need to lose weight to be healthy.

"If we have a six-year-old girl who is 3 feet, 9 inches tall, she would be considered to be a 'healthy, normal weight' at 49 1/4 pounds (BMI 17.1)," according to registered nurse Sandy Szwarc, BSN, RN, CCP, author of the widely celebrated blog Junkfood Science. "If she gained 1/4 pound more, however, she becomes 'overweight' at 49 1/2 pounds. For untold numbers of children classified as 'overweight,' they are within a fraction of a pound or a few pounds from 'normal.' But just think: If this little girl grew a mere 1/8 inch, she'd be considered a 'healthy, normal weight' again." That fraction of a pound means little for a developing girl, whose weight will fluctuate dramatically over the course of her adolescence, but the *pronouncement* of her BMI score to a class of girls struggling with their body image means a lot.

Put Me In, Coach

Although body size, alone, is a poor indicator of a girl's athletic ability, a 2006 study by the Girl Scout Research Institute, titled "The New Normal? What Girls Say About Healthy Living," reported that 23 percent of girls don't participate in sports because they feel that their bodies "do not look good." (The study also showed that girls who are physically active are more satisfied with their weight and appearance than other girls—no matter their weight or size.) Appearance factors into the "line" of aesthetic athletes, such as figure skaters, dancers, gymnasts and even swimmers, and those who conform to the unwritten rules of femininity are often the most popular—the more they conform, the more popular they become.

"Cheerleading has its own weighted class system," said Sasha, age eighteen. "To be a flyer, you have to be the lightest—I was determined to be the lightest. It was one of the best days of my life when I went from getting stood on to being the one who got to stand on top of everyone else's shoulders. Our cheer coach said to the girl who had to switch with me, 'Shannon, you've eaten one too many doughnuts.' And I was in."

Coaches, among all educators, are particularly influential when it comes to a girl's athletic performance. They are seen as a mix of gods, heroes, parents and friends in the eyes of children or teens, because they wipe the tears, provide the shoulder to cry on and drive our girls to become their "best" during some of the most intense moments of their lives. "So when a coach makes offhand comments about weight or articulates a training philosophy that values weight loss more than getting stronger, the athlete's drive for perfection can become desperate," says Courtney Martin, author of *Perfect Girls, Starving Daughters*.

"I didn't just figure skate. I *was* a figure skater," said Jen, age twenty-two. "And I had to look the part. Thin. But I wanted to be me. I wanted to go to the mall after school and buy an Italian ice or have a pretzel. My coach told me that I needed to fight it. And if I was strong enough, I could do it, that I could help my team be number one. But the truth is, I wasn't strong enough to tell him I didn't want to."

"What happened?" I asked.

"I quit. It was too much pressure. I hated myself for quitting, and now I'm not doing something I love to do—and was really great at—all because I didn't look right. And to top it off, I started eating. A lot. Then I couldn't get the pounds off, and I felt worse. I tried everything—diet pills, those shakes. Nothing worked. See?" Jen grabbed a chunk of her thigh and, with downcast eyes, showed it to me. "Still weak."

Fighting Back

"When I was in the fourth grade, I was a good student who did my work, but I was a little chubby," admitted Joanie, now age twenty-three. "There were three boys in my class who thought it was hilarious to taunt me on the playground by yelling their new nickname for me, 'The Whaler,' and then run off," she said. Joanie had wild, curly brown hair, a thunderous laugh and an amazing way with words. "One day, we had recess indoors. They started to taunt me again, but this time they had nowhere to run. It was like I turned into the Hulk. I could feel the rage build up in me, and in a burst of strength, I grabbed the scruff of one of their shirts and hurled him over the table next to us." Joanie explained all this while "acting out" the scene for me, so I could see it unfold. "I filled my lungs as much as I could and let out a really loud roar: 'All right, who's next?!'"

"Did you get into trouble?" I asked.

"The recess monitor had witnessed the whole thing—she was a tough broad with a giant red beehive hairdo and a low tolerance for funny business. But she just looked at me and said, 'I didn't see anything...' and told me to go to the bathroom and cool off for a minute."

Although I root for girls to take action, a very important teaching moment had been missed here. This would have been a good time for an educator or a school counselor to take Joanie aside and say, "You were right to stand up for yourself. I applaud you for doing so. But let's discuss the way you did it. What were your other options? Let's talk about this now, so next time you'll act in a way that shows character and assertiveness rather than aggression."

"Two years ago I was in math class, and the teacher called me up to the board to do a problem," said Jade, age eighteen, an aspiring plus-size model with dark skin and a sassy attitude. "When I was done, he made what he thought was a funny joke: 'I can't tell you if it's right, because your big body is in the way!'"

Wow.

"I turned around and said, 'I don't appreciate you disrespecting me like that. All you need to say is please move, so I can see your answer.'"

Wow!

"The teacher was really surprised and apologized," Jade said, with a smile. "The whole school was buzzing with what I had done. Nobody picked on me again. I wasn't the easy target they thought I was. Believe it or not, I think they saw me as a badass."

"Why do you think you were able to stand up for yourself like that?" I asked.

"My parents," Jade said. "They always told me, 'If you don't say it, they won't know it.' It's not so much standing up, but speaking up."

Our daughters have a right to learn in an environment in which they feel comfortable and safe. Parents must know that inappropriate comments or discrimination should never be dismissed as insignificant and should keep a journal of any incident in which a teacher or staff member has made improper remarks or taken inappropriate action regarding their daughter's weight. The more specific you can be in your complaint, and the more evidence you can present, the more seriously the principal, school counselor, superintendent or school board will take it.

Rosalind Wiseman offers a terrific boilerplate conflict approach technique in her book *Queen Bees & Wannabes* called SEAL—Stop, Explain, Affirm, Lock In (Lock Out)—that could be used to help teachers confront colleagues whom they suspect of bullying.

→ **Stop.** Politely approach the teacher and say exactly what you need to do: "I'd like to talk to you about something that is uncomfortable, but I know you would want me to tell you."

→ **Explain.** Say exactly what it is: "I've noticed that you've been particularly hard on 'Mary' about her weight, because she can't do as many jumping jacks as the other kids. She always comes back from gym very upset and can't pay attention to what we're learning in class." At this point, the other teacher might get angry, gossipy, defensive and/or dismissive.

→ **Affirm/Acknowledge.** Acknowledge that this has been hard for you to say and that it is something you've been sitting on for a while but felt it was important to bring to the other teacher's attention.

→ **Lock In the Relationship.** "Our working relationship is really important to me, and the best way to keep our relationship healthy is by being honest with each other."

I'd like to add one last piece to SEAL for our purposes, making the word *SEALER*: the *ER* would be for "Evaluation and Reflection."

→ **Evaluation and Reflection.** Ask yourself, "How did that go?" "How did I feel doing it?" "How did I feel after it was over?" "What would I have changed—or kept the same—about the experience?" It's not enough for adults to tell children how to handle themselves when relationships get uncomfortable; they must be able to live these directives out in their own lives, or their words will end up being impractical—and meaningless.

Gabi's Story

"I don't think I'm going to be much help to you," said Gabi, a fifth-grade teacher in northern New Jersey. Like so many teachers I've interviewed, Gabi doesn't see body bullying or weight discrimination as a problem in her school—certainly not in her classroom. "I have a zero-tolerance policy," she told me. "The whole school does."

At 6-foot-2, Gabi had a commanding presence—tailored clothes, blunt-cut, "serious-looking" hair—yet her warm smile and freckled brown eyes seemed to soften her otherwise all-business demeanor. "We've moved from detention and writing 'I'm sorry' one hundred times to discussion and appropriate consequences," she told me proudly. Gabi explained that she had a "very diverse" classroom that consisted of kids from the surrounding upscale neighborhood as well as those who were bused in from "down the hill," so it was important that she remain vigilant regarding issues of discrimination. But when our conversation turned to specific methods used by her school, some cracks in the zero-tolerance policy began to emerge.

"Fourth and fifth graders are selected to be 'team mediators,' based on an essay they submit. They are actually encouraged to walk up to peers who are in conflict and ask if they can be helpful in orchestrating a compromise," Gabi said.

"Do students actually do this?" I asked. "That takes a lot of guts."

"At first they might, right after they get trained," she said. "But sometimes they're just role-playing, and it's not authentic. They try. But it wears off, and, in the end, they don't really do it on their own."

"So there is bullying at the school?"

"Well, if it's happening, it isn't happening in front of me, although I have to admit that, as a teacher, we don't always see what happens outside the classroom—that's when bullying is more likely to occur, since there is a lower likelihood of being caught. Actually, not too long ago, a parent came in to talk to me about her daughter who was having a horrible year. Two girls were picking on her during recess and telling everyone they would get fat if they played with her because 'fat' was contagious."

My first thought when Gabi said this was that if teachers know that this is an issue, they should be standing in their doorways in between classes and taking turns walking through the cafeteria or outside play areas during lunch. Or they should assign every teacher a day so that children don't feel so alone out there.

"What did you do?" I asked.

"I gave her an alternate recess option, to stay in if she was uncomfortable outside. I was surprised that this was happening to her, because she is such a quiet, low-key kind of girl." Gabi looked at me pointedly. "She wasn't a troublemaker."

Exactly. A girl who won't tell is an easy target. While giving her an alternative option for recess gives her a safe place to go, it doesn't address the issue of the bullies who are playing outside and are likely feeling very successful. All she's done, essentially, is punish the victim.

"You don't see what happens during recess?" I asked.

"No. So if the student or her parent doesn't come to me and tell me that it's happening, I will never know. And those people covering recess? Well, they don't give a damn." This was clearly a sore point for Gabi. "They get paid $5 an hour to listen to children yell for three hours in the cafeteria. Four lunchtimes. Five hundred kids. By the second lunch, they're done. All they do is yell. They're the lunch aides. If there's no blood, they don't want to know about it."

"So they don't have anyone to go to until they come back into the classroom?" I asked.

There was a pause, as if Gabi suddenly realized the flaws in the zero-tolerance system. "They can't tell then, either," she said finally. "When they come back into the classroom, the people who are victimizing the girl are watching."

"So how do you find out?" I asked.

"If I do, it's usually from a third party. A good kid will come to me and say, 'So-and-so was being mean to So-and-so.' And at a quiet time, I will talk to the bully."

"What would the school do, do you think, if a teacher was the one who was discriminating against the bigger girls in class?"

Gabi laughed. "That's a hard one. If you don't turn in your plan book on time, you get into trouble. But how is the school going to prove that a teacher is discriminating against certain kids?" She hemmed and hawed a bit. "To be honest, I don't think anything would happen. The complaint would have to come from more than one parent, and there would have to be more than one complaint. Then the principal would probably say to the teacher, 'I'm sure that this isn't true, but...' It wouldn't go further than that."

"Would you say something?" I asked.

"How could I? I'm her colleague. I can't go to her and say, 'I don't like what you're doing to that kid, just because she can't do jumping jacks the way you want her to.'" She said this as if it were not a hypothetical scenario but a real-life situation at her school that she didn't mention to anyone. "And I can't go to the principal, because that wouldn't be very good for the collegial relationship. I have to work with these people every day."

This is a jarring reality. We know that people don't like to rock the boat at work, but teachers are supposed to represent our children. I could feel my inner fifth grader stirring inside me. Now I was the one getting angry.

"So what you're telling me is that you teach peer mediation in which you encourage students to try to resolve conflict between peers before it escalates into something really hurtful, but in the real world among teachers, it's very hard to apply the same principle?"

"I'm Miss Nonconfrontational. I'm being honest now. I just wouldn't be able to say something."

Making the Grade

I always had a passion for theater—my mom used to joke that I would grow up to be a "singing doctor"—so when I graduated from Tufts University I got involved with the Randolph Community Theater in Massachusetts, which was putting on the musical *Cinderella*. The director, Connie, had all the girls audition for the lead role; no one, even if they'd wanted to, read for one of the "ugly stepsisters." When the play was cast, the lead role went to a twenty-two-year-old girl named Christyn, who didn't look at all like the traditional Cinderella—she was a dark-haired, plus-sized girl with an in-your-face attitude and a wicked sense of humor. People pulled me aside and said, "You should have landed that role!" I had gotten the role of Joy, one of the hilarious ugly stepsisters. But there was no denying that Christyn had the most melodic singing voice—the kind that gives you chills all the way down your neck.

"As you can see, I don't cast by physical type," Connie told the group on the first night of rehearsal. "Our Cinderella is not blond, but brunette, and a 'buxom beauty' like me, and our ugly stepsisters are anything but ugly." People seemed worried that Christyn wouldn't be able to pull it off. But on opening night, I saw scores of girls dressed in Cinderella dresses holding their wands and rushing the stage after we all bowed so they could take pictures with Christyn. They didn't care about her hair color or her waist size. To them, she was Cinderella. And that meant that no matter what they looked like, they could be Cinderella, too.

Connie opened up the minds of her actors and her audience by challenging established norms. Similarly, teachers challenge their students by speaking their minds, showing that they aren't afraid to take risks that get students, and other adults, to look within to change their current, often automatic actions and reactions. "Students who bully should be taken out of school until they see someone who can explain to them the consequences and conditions of their actions," said Ann Marie Perone, a health education teacher in a high school in Las Vegas, who takes a no-holds-barred approach to bullying in her classroom. "I do not tolerate my students making fun of others. When they do, I turn it around and say in front of the entire class, 'Now, tell me how you would feel if I called you that.' Then I also call home and explain to their parents that they have to understand that what their children do can affect others for their entire life."

Having been a person who was called "thunder thighs" and was mercilessly teased in school, Ann Marie is the kind of teacher who can talk about bullying and body image for hours and never tire of it. A girl who's right up my alley. "I had a student once who was told by a teacher that she did not match the weight chart that was posted in the classroom," said Ann Marie, who also founded Body Rocks, a positive image club. "The student came to me frantically crying because she didn't weigh 118 pounds. She was fourteen years old. Average girl, not overweight. I confronted the teacher, who was clueless as to how the information could have offended, embarrassed or upset the student. I told the administration that weight charts should be out of the classroom and that they can unintentionally become another form of bullying. After one year, there were no more weight charts in our school. She came back recently after graduating and told me that the day I stood up for her is a day she'll remember for the rest of her life. That's the kind of legacy I want to leave."

I believe it's time for educators to stand up for their female students. No more excuses. Here are some ideas on what teachers and school personnel can do, together, when there are concerns about a child being teased due to weight.

→ Use a "whole school approach." Get the administration, teachers and school counselors involved, and devise school policy and antibullying codes that apply to everyone. Integrate these lessons into the classroom and lace them into academic lesson plans for a seamless, schoolwide approach. For her high school's Body Image Awareness Week, Julia Taylor said the entire student population (2,275 students) watches special videos on bullying and body image awareness and participates in an assortment of related activities during their lunch periods.

→ Keep parents informed or involved. If a girl is being bullied and teased because of her weight, talk to her about including her parents in the conversation. Then go to the parents directly and address these concerns in private and in a respectful manner. Children should never be singled out in front of peers.

→ Work with parents, pediatricians and the child if there are legitimate, health-related concerns about weight. Together, you can devise an individual weight-control plan that is approved by the parents and feels comfortable for the child. The more a child is involved in devising such a plan, if it is warranted, the more agreeable she will be to the process. And it needs to be clear to school personnel that any weight-management plan is not being devised to segregate or punish the child in any way. Keep in mind, however, that if the parents or guardians are not in agreement with school involvement with regard to their child's weight, it is not the teacher's or school's place to move forward and circumvent the parents' decision. Only parents are legally permitted to make health decisions for their children. Only when school officials feel that the child's health and safety are at imminent risk, and the parents refuse to cooperate, should the school report the matter to the Department of Social Services.

→ The typical school curriculum should reflect relationship building and character development. Teaching students about powerful words such as *empathy, tolerance, impulse control, open-mindedness* and *anger management* is an important step toward creating a peaceful school built on principles of respect. They must be put into action in every class, authentically used and seriously adopted by everyone who makes up the school culture.

→ Schools should take a look at their own contributions to issues of weight and health issues. Serving peanut butter and fluff sandwiches for lunch, with a side of potato chips, isn't going to cut it. While some schools have "healthed up" their vending machines and lunches, others still have a long way to go. A specialty food program, such as the one instituted by renowned "Renegade Lunch Lady" Ann Cooper, is typically more expensive (about 20 percent more), but helps students make healthier choices. With First Lady Michelle Obama's "Let's Move" initiative to, in part, improve school breakfasts and lunches, even the federal government is getting in on the action. And network television has followed suit with programs such as *Jamie Oliver's Food Revolution*. Some schools are responding by creating "events," such as "Healthy Snack Fridays" or "Wear the Color of Your Favorite Fruit or Vegetable Day," as a fun way to drive home the message that our bodies deserve healthy foods and physical activity—and get the ball rolling in the right direction.

→ Insist on professional development for teachers to go over issues such as how to monitor, prevent, approach and deal with bullying of any kind. Teachers must step forward and say, "We want this" and "We need this" and commit to using what they learn in the classroom as well as in the halls, the lunchroom and recess areas. All staff should be involved—if they deal with the children, they need to be trained. Including lunch aides.

Deconstructing Media

Teachers must do more than teach core subjects—they must teach media literacy. The media have been criticized for glorifying "skinniness" and poor eating habits for years—decades—but it still astounds me that (1) it continues, (2) our girls still get sucked in by it all, and (3) very few seem to be doing much about it. Our girls need to know that runway models are 1 percent of the population and that most of them look nothing like the airbrushed aliens that grace magazine covers or the home pages of thousands of product-oriented websites. It's not a matter of simply understanding messages they get from "enjoyment" reading or when they are leisurely cybershopping, but rather how they interpret their everyday world, which is coming at them in "surround sound."

I have been working with Amy Jussel, the fearless leader of Shaping Youth, a nonprofit, nonpartisan consortium dealing with media and marketing's impact on kids, on ways that teachers can employ innovative programs that promote healthier values by understanding the use—and abuse—of media. Here are several strategies that we put into action in schools, share with parents and share with the girls with whom we coach outside of school.

DECONSTRUCT ADS

Look at and discuss the ads students see in magazines, on websites and on television. You don't even have to come up with the material yourself. Websites such as FatFoe (Federal Trade Commission) and organizations like the National Association of Media Literacy Education (NAMLE) teach young people to recognize the "too good to be true" red flags, bogus body claims and weasel words. This makes our daughters less susceptible to what I refer to as the "thinvertisers" who are out to convert them into diet-obsessed product buyers.

USE HANDS-ON DEMOS

Shaping Youth has found that kids "get it" much more quickly when they experience the "thinspiration" pitch firsthand and replicate it in some form of interactive lesson plan. I agree. In Sassy Sisterhood, girls became their own "editors" and created magazine covers in which they turned the tables on the image-obsessed glossies, using photographs and headlines based on what girls really want to hear—that they are good enough just the way they are.

MAKE THEIR VOICES HEARD

In 2009, readers of *Glamour* magazine praised its editors for including a plus-size model, twenty-year-old Lizzie Miller, size 12–14, in the September issue. Readers requested—demanded, actually—that they see more women like her in the traditionally supermodel-rich glossy. The editors, "blown away" by the response, committed to presenting a variety of body sizes in their magazine from that point onward. We must teach our girls that if they speak their mind, they can create the world they want to see.

It's easy to believe that what these girls are going through in school is just a rite of passage, something they need to "get through." Julia Taylor and I lamented how many teachers and parents have a tendency to tell girls who are bullied, "Just ignore it" or "What's it going to matter in twenty-five years?" Not only does that invalidate their feelings and shut them down emotionally, but it's also completely false. It matters. I'd know. I'm living proof.

BIQ:

Teachers of Habit: Are Your Daughter's Educators Head of the Class?

1. Does your daughter feel that her teachers adjust how they grade or who gets to participate in special activities depending on how students look?

A. Frequently. She feels that the thinner girls get special privileges in school.

B. Sometimes. When it comes to some things, the thinner girls tend to dominate.

C. Never. Teachers base grades and participation on pure performance and talent.

2. When it comes to girls bullying girls, the educators at your daughter's school:

A. Don't really see female relational aggression as a significant form of bullying.

B. Tend to act swiftly when they see female relational bullying get out of hand.

C. Have a clear policy that they follow each and every time they hear about incidents of any kind of bullying, be it relational aggression or physical bullying.

3. In gym class, my daughter would say:

A. The larger you are, the more harshly you are treated.

B. The best athletes, who also happen to be the thinnest and fittest kids, get picked first, but everyone is always included in the games.

C. The teacher makes gym fun for everyone.

4. When it comes to bullying programs that support respect, tolerance, confidence and positive relationships:

A. My daughter's school doesn't really have any of those.

B. We have an assembly each year about bullying or respect.

C. There are programs in place that provide regular open forums and discussion on such topics.

5. Weight, body size and diet plans:

A. Are often brought up by teachers at the school, whether it's regarding the students or the teachers themselves.

B. Are sometimes brought up by the teachers, usually in the context of being healthy.

C. Are just not something discussed between teachers and students unless there's a special body image program they're discussing in health class or a student brings up concerns privately with a teacher or coach.

Total number of:

As 1 point each	**Bs** 2 points each	**Cs** 3 points each	**Total** BIQ score for Chapter 5

Chapter 6

The School Fool, Part II:
Friends, Foes and Beaus

Mondays were "weigh-in" day, recalled Michelle, age twenty, a pouty-lipped towhead, whose friends were considered the pretty, popular girls at her prep school near Bridgeport, Connecticut. "We needed to record our weight in the L-WORD"—she said the last word dramatically, highlighting the name in quotes while rolling her eyes—"which stood for 'Lose Weight OR Die-ary.'" Michelle said her friends took to calling her "Shelly Belly" after she gained weight the summer before eighth grade.

"Cara kept a scale in her locker. She's the one who started it all. She'd take the scale out and make us get on. Cara's one of those girls—you don't know why, but you just listen to her," Michelle said. "My mother still jokes that Cara was the answer to the Brooklyn Bridge question. Yes, people would actually jump."

According to a recent study, the belief that "friends would like me more if I were thinner" was the strongest predictor of eating problems and body image concerns among nine- to eleven-year-olds. In older circles, thinness is more like a requirement for survival. "I would keep this little bag of garbage, like old banana peels and stuff, in a paper bag in my locker and smell it when I felt hungry," Michelle said. "Or I would eat a little of my dinner, and then pour some of my Diet Coke over the food so there would be no chance of me eating more. My mom always hated that, but you have to understand, my friends were, like, really tough on the fat girls. They acted like they didn't see them at all."

According to a 2003 survey of more than 17,500 thirteen- to eighteen-year-olds who were enrolled in the National Longitudinal Study of Adolescent Health (also called ADD Health):

→ Not only were teens considered overweight more likely to be socially marginalized than thinner girls, but they were more likely to be socially isolated.

→ When classmates were asked to write down the names of their friends, fat adolescents were about 70 percent less likely than thinner peers to be listed.

→ Adolescents who did write down the names of fat peers, and therefore considered them as friends, had fewer people recognize *them* as friends.

A 2008 study by Robert Crosnoe and colleagues, also based on a national study sample from ADD Health, analyzed friendship networks of adolescent students in sixteen schools and found that the social stigma of weight, along with the tendency for girls of similar body sizes to hang together—a mechanism called "homophily"—resulted in fewer friends for heavier girls. The phenomenon of rejecting someone whose physical appearance deviates from your own as a way to identify with and bolster your own "in-group" is referred to as "social identity theory"—the longer girls are with a group of like-minded people, the stronger their bias.

Perfectly decent, respectful girls can get easily swept up into a group that puts down heavier classmates. Many teens told me that some of their best friends suddenly became body bullies, either by donning a "split personality"—behaving like one person in school and another at home, away from watchful eyes—or by turning completely against them. "Over the summer, I'd gained weight—twenty pounds," said Theresa, age fifteen, a dramatic-looking girl with thick black hair and tight black jeans. "My best friend, Carley, actually laughed. My other friends, Katie, Andrea and Briah, looked at me with their eyes bugging out of their heads. It was the worst thing ever."

"So what happened?" I asked.

"I had a sinking feeling. Like I was being called into the principal's office. But this was worse. My friends met me at the mall. They asked me to sit down. One of them wouldn't even look at me. The other had a piece of computer paper in her hand. I could see something was typed on it. This had been planned. They had written something. It was like one of those college rejection letters my sister got from Vassar. You know, 'We regret to inform you that...' I barely know what it said, because I was so stunned. She was reading it to me—my ex–best friend. It said they didn't want to be friends anymore. That we had nothing in common."

"And you think it had something to do with your weight?"

"I know so. It's all about who you're with in school. I look back and I'm sure of it—they were cutting the fat, and the fat was me." Rachel Simmons, author of *Odd Girl Out,* calls this "clique expulsion": the equivalent of being voted off the island. Deject. Reject. Eject.

Cliques provide insulation and status, so most girls lack the guts and confidence to embrace unabashed individuality. They want to blend, but they want uniqueness within reason. I call this phenomenon "friend blending"—being just different enough to be admired and the same enough to be included. Blending is comfortable; even the popular kids only want to stand out so far. "There isn't a high social status group of girls that I've worked with who have had an overweight girl in their group," Rosalind Wiseman told me. "Not all overweight girls will be excluded, but if you are overweight, you'd better have a lot of other gifts to bring to the table."

However, many girls ignore those gifts; they see themselves as outliers on the normal bell curve of weight at their schools and obsess about their bodies. When these perceptions are temporary—like when a girl feels "bloated" and believes she looks fat (even when she doesn't) or thinks eating too much at lunch has marked her with pig ears that everyone sees growing out of her head—she has what psychologist Mary Pipher calls "Imaginary Audience Syndrome." She believes that her friends—everyone, really—are watching her all the time, rating her and calculating the rise and fall of her net worth based on how fat she looks, or at least how fat she feels.

"My friends never flat-out tell me I'm overweight or ugly," said Nikki, age fourteen, a stunning bombshell of a girl with long blond hair, long legs and a pearly white smile. "Some of them are the prettiest girls in our school. One, in particular, is my best friend and we do everything together. Including the beach. Walking next to her made me feel really self-conscious and fat. I feel like everyone's probably wondering how she can even be friends with me." It's not just about "being fat"; it's about "feeling fat" in comparison to someone else.

Ironically, feeling fat may lead to being fat: Research conducted at Harvard University and published in the *Archives of Pediatrics & Adolescent Medicine* shows that girls who just "think" they aren't popular are at a 70 percent higher risk for weight gain—over a two-year period, girls who thought they were low in the social pecking order averaged an eleven-pound gain, or a two-point increase in BMI scores. As one of the characters in Tina Fey's 2004 film *Mean Girls* says, "I don't hate you 'cause you're fat. You're fat because I hate you."

When Imaginary Audience Syndrome becomes a gaggle of bona fide spectators, overweight girls must cope with the social penalty, what I call the "fat tax"—they have to try harder than their thin counterparts to fit into the same circles or garner the same respect. "My friends used to take this big girl Stacey with them to the movies," twenty-three-year-old Jax told me. "They would have her do 'food runs' in the middle of the movie like to get someone a Diet Coke or a package of licorice. She would always do it."

"Were you there?"

"Um, yeah," she said with a glimmer of embarrassment.

"And?"

"Jujubes. I feel a little bad saying it now, but I asked for Jujubes. She never complained, though, so I thought maybe she didn't mind."

In Rosalind Wiseman's descriptions of "The Queen Bee and Her Court," Stacey straddles the "pleaser" and the "target" categories—she becomes a readily available punching bag who, essentially, is "adopted" by the more popular clique as a "pet"—in this case, a gopher. No doubt, she will be cast aside when the joke gets old, she complains or the clique wants to reinforce its "skinny" status. As Vicky, a target-pleaser at age fifteen, told me, "They can be really nice to me sometimes. People don't understand that, for me, sometimes is enough." Girls will do anything to fit in; standing out is for the hard-core courageous—or the rejected.

THE MANY FORMS OF A BODY BULLY

GOSSIP GIRL. She spreads rumors but seems innocent. By saying that "other girls" are making comments, the Gossip Girl doesn't have to take responsibility for her actions. This is passive-aggressive bullying. People keep her as a friend, so that they can stay in the know. "My best friend, Jen, was the gossip queen," said Dana, age sixteen. "Believe me, if anyone gained weight, she knew about it…and so did everyone else. When it was you—you kinda wished you never got out of bed."

THE BITCH. She says what's on her mind—the first thing that pops into her head. She calls your daughter names, makes jokes at her expense and loves to see the results of her verbal lashings. She seems cool, calm and calculated. "Sarah was so mean," Donna, a young twentysomething told me. "She would say things that no one would ever say, that were so shocking that you couldn't help but laugh, which only made her keep going. She would tell this one girl, who wasn't even fat, 'Do you have your period? Because you look really bloated today.' The girl's face was always priceless."

THE EXCLUDER. This is the bully I hear about most often from girls. She will take any friends who are meaningful to your daughter and make them pawns in pushing her out. People are drawn to her because she makes them feel important. Even if she has no real interest in them as friends, she will pal around with, tell secrets to and invite in those she wants to keep close to her and far away from her target.

THE BACKSTABBER. She legitimately is, or pretends to be, your daughter's close friend and confidant. Then, in order to move up the ranks at school and get in with the "in-crowd," she uses your daughter as a pawn or a stepping stone. She insults her publicly, reveals private information. I call this "friend bending" or "hooking"—using her current friend like a fishing hook to see what bigger fish she can catch. Unfortunately, girls who weigh more are often used as the sacrificial lamb. Maya, age eighteen, told me, "It happens all the time. It's not always that they don't like being with you. They just think that being with someone more popular would be better. More fun."

The Invisibles

Studies tell us that most girls who believe they are overweight have expectations of rejection and progressively with-draw, taking themselves out of the social networks that tend to characterize the preteen and teen years. Many girls have told me their goal in school is not to blend but

> ### "Overheard"
> *"If I think I've gained weight over the weekend, I throw up and tell my mom I'm sick so I can stay home from school."*
>
> Tara, age 14

to disappear—to be "invisible." They wear huge, oversized black T-shirts, don't do their hair or makeup and wear big, baggy jeans. They walk from class to class with their head down, hunched shoulders, an averted gaze; during social activities, their habitual self-placement is in the corner, against the wall. Their body language speaks loudly, even if they don't.

"I didn't exist in high school." Lori, age nineteen, spoke in short, choppy sentences and pulled at her shirt, which tended to ride up around her middle. "I just didn't care. Don't worry. Nobody missed me."

"What do you mean?"

"At graduation, this skinny girl, Tina, who always had,

like, a billion friends, walked up to me and asked, 'Do you have an extra graduation program?' I said, 'No, I just have mine.' She looked confused. 'Why do you need one?' she asked. 'Do you know someone who goes here?' She had no clue who I was! I sat in front of her every day in English class, and I even helped her with one of our assignments, but it was like she never met me. I didn't care anyway. I just…flowed, did my thing. Class. Home. Class. Home." While this routine insulated Lori, kept her "safe," she wasn't allowing herself to learn important friendship skills—nurturing others, being nurtured by others and creating connections that allow her to grow as a person.

Fitting in by Sticking Out

Then there are the girls who go the other way. "The 'hoochie mamas' wear what skinny girls would look good in if they were going out clubbing—clothes that are so tight and don't flatter at all," said Crystall, age nineteen. In an attempt to be accepted, Crystall said, she "tried the hoochie mama thing for a while—stuffed myself into this tiny shirt with all these tiny buttons down the front. It reminded me of a corset look. That's why I liked it, you know. Kinda old world-like."

"So it worked for you, then?" I asked.

"No. It didn't," Crystall said with a laugh. "I was in science class. Just sitting there. I made the mistake of stretching, and all those little buttons popped open. I spent the rest of the class with my notebook in front of my chest."

Clothing is a common complaint among my plus-size Sassy Girls. Many tell me it's hard to find "good clothes for girls who aren't tiny, like the models they see in the magazines." Of course. There is a sentiment out there that says if you don't fit the clothes, change your body, not the clothes. Although savvy retailers are beginning to cater to a fashion-forward plus-size clothing market (see Chapter 9), most girls still feel they only have two choices: Go invisible—the shapeless black look—or try to wear what everyone else is wearing, which was Crystall's choice. "If you dress like you don't care, now you're not only fat, but you're a mess," she said. "Nobody wants to be a fat mess."

Some girls take the "hoochie mama" sentiment to the nth degree. They come on strong, dress provocatively to make girls jealous and boys notice. And they do what they advertise; they're a sure thing. "I skipped the training bra and went straight to the B cup," said Marie, age twenty-one, who had crazy brown curly hair to go with her loud personality. She talked loudly and a lot. "Everything about me seemed bigger and just kept growing. So I figured, 'Go big or go home,' you know? I wasn't going to hide in the corner like some wallflower. I was going to come on strong. I would intimidate. Being on the heavier side, I always felt so much bigger than everyone else. I wanted boys to like me, though. I wanted to feel powerful. I made them like me by flaunting what I had. I was very sexual, talked in innuendos. Girls liked me because I was shocking and gutsier than they were. Boys liked me because they knew they could get it."

"Did that make you feel accepted?"

"In the beginning, yes, but after a while I realized that the boys didn't really like me at all. They just wanted to have sex."

In a world of girls, where everything is about comparisons, to be told by a boy or a popular girl, even just for a little while, that you matter can be intoxicating. Even if it feels a little uncomfortable and your stomach is doing flip-flops and your mind is shouting no, it's easy to get sucked into doing something to make yourself feel wanted. For girls who are continually evaluating themselves, sex can be one way that they can keep tabs on their ability to attract. According to a recent study conducted at the University of Pittsburgh, high school girls who are both sexually active and overweight, or who think they are overweight, are less likely to use condoms than normal-weight sexually active girls. When larger girls bring their people-pleasing skills to sexual relationships, they wind up risking their own sexual health and future.

PARENT ALERT: OVERT OR COVERT CUES

Your daughter may not be talking about the teasing going on at school, but that doesn't mean it's not happening. Look for these clues. She may be having a problem if she is...

1. Coming home with a minimally eaten or untouched lunch.

2. Suddenly complaining that her clothes make her look fat.

3. Withdrawing or losing friends, and staying in on the weekends instead of going out with peers.

4. Wearing big, baggy clothes or layers of clothes to school to hide her body.

5. Complaining of not getting into the school play or onto school teams or being given unfair grades due to her weight.

6. Refusing to go shopping for new school clothes until she loses weight.

7. Avoiding social situations with peers if they involve food or body-revealing activities like swimming.

8. Preoccupied with how other people look, both at school and in the media.

9. Obsessively weighing herself before and after school.

10. Insisting on packing her own lunch with no-calorie items like diet soda and gum, instead of substantive foods.

The Lowdown on Beaus

Anna, age nineteen, told her best friend, Lana, one evening, "I'm not going to school tomorrow. I ate too much tonight. Brian will think I look gross, and he'll break up with me. I need a day to drink water and eat nothing." At 5-foot-4 and 139 pounds, Anna could hardly be considered overweight, but it's easy to see why she feels she could be rejected over a few extra pounds. When

Michigan State University students were asked to rank potential marriage partners, 88 percent of young men were "extremely disinclined" to marry women who were obese—"More of these men were willing to marry cocaine users, ex–psychiatric patients, shoplifters, sexually promiscuous individuals, communists, blind and divorced women, atheists and marijuana users," according to the authors of the study. The University of North Carolina at Chapel Hill offers these recent findings:

→ For every point increase on the body mass index (BMI), the probability of having a romantic relationship decreased by a whopping 6 percent.

→ A girl who was 5-foot-3 and 126 pounds was only half as likely to get dates as a girl of the same height but 110 pounds or less.

→ Girls who were one standard deviation above the mean in body fat were three times as likely to have no dates as girls whose body fat was one standard deviation below the mean.

I recall one question on a popular blog: "Why don't you date fat girls?" The answer was, "While some guys are chubby chasers, the majority of guys feel fat girls are like motor scooters. They're fun to ride till your friends see you on one." Scott, age eighteen, spent one Saturday night frat party with Jenna, size 16, whom he really liked. However, Scott was reluctant to tell his frat brothers—most likely because thinness is associated with status. At the next fraternity meeting, Scott was rewarded for "pigging," the practice of picking up fat girls for a good time. "The pledge master and the president of the fraternity handed me a can of Spam and a pig nose

"Overheard"

"If you're whining about it, you're not just the one with the back fat—you're the bitch with the back fat or the crybaby with the back fat. You just need to let it go and, eventually, someone else will be the one talked about, and you'll be filed under 'been there, done that.'"

Jasmine, age 14

that I had to wear all day," he said. Scott never looked at Jenna again.

What's strange is that while thinness seems to be promoted by the media and fashion designers, guys like Scott might secretly prefer girls who are fleshier. Men's magazine *FHM* recently conducted an online survey asking whether its readers found a size 8, size 12 or size 14 model most attractive. The survey drew 60,000 responses—four-fifths said they were more attracted to the size 12 and 14 models than the size 8 model pictured. Most votes went to the size 12, with 41 percent of respondents saying she had the body shape of their "ideal girlfriend"; the size 8 came in a distant third with 20 percent. "Which proves one thing, ladies," *FHM* editor Ben Smithurst concluded. "Crack a beer, hoe into a hamburger and we'll love you just as much."

Still, women continue to believe that men value thinness. A 2003 study by Rochelle Bergstrom and colleagues at North Dakota State University found that women's inaccurate perceptions of what men want are associated with eating disorder symptomatology, which was exacerbated if their self-worth was tied closely to appearance standards. Similarly, a frequently cited 1985 study conducted by researchers at the University of Pennsylvania found that college women rate the "ideal weight" and "what men prefer" as being significantly thinner than "what men actually prefer."

"My boyfriend always compared me to other girls," Alexandra, age twenty-four, told me over the phone. "I'd be wearing these jeans and he'd be like, 'Dominique has those same jeans... but they don't look like that on her.'"

"So what did you think?"

"It wasn't about thinking. It was about knowing," Alexandra said. "He told me he was breaking up with me because I was obsessed with myself, but I don't believe it. I know why he doesn't want me. He's with a thinner girl now. I'm fat. I'm not perfect...like her."

Perfect Girls

An extension of Imaginary Audience Syndrome is the Perfect Girl Salute, silently admiring another girl, comparing yourself to her, making her out to be so flawless that no one could possibly measure up. I've heard comments ranging from longing ("I just want to be her") to disgust ("She thinks she's 'all that'") to anger ("I hate people like that") to total denial ("She's an idiot"). But at the end of the day, the comparison is a constant—something a girl just can't seem to get away from—and it erodes her self-worth.

Outside the locker room before track practice, I spoke to Jerri, age sixteen, a subtle beauty with long brown hair, olive skin, no makeup and no idea that she was at all attractive. "Everyone compares themselves to Tori Brady, the head cheerleader." She shook her head. "She's, like, the prettiest girl in the school. She's perfect. Perfect. Thin. Blond hair. Her legs are long, and I've got these stubby things." We started walking toward the track field. "It's like, if you're not Tori Brady, you might as well not exist."

"But you run track," I said. "Your legs must be pretty great to be able to do that."

"I guess," she said halfheartedly. "Oh, yeah, and she never had a pimple in, like, her whole life."

Jerri is a girl who has always been a straight-A student. She's in student government. She's received awards honoring her outstanding community service—she's raised thousands of dollars for abused girls. She does track, gymnastics, theater. And yet, she's not Tori Brady.

"Overheard"

"They called me 'thunder thighs' and 'fatso' in high school. They'd make pretend phone calls that they were at Dunkin' Donuts calling to tell me my credit card was past due. After I lost all my weight after high school, I ran into a guy who used to make fun of me. He was in the Wal-Mart parking lot. He said, 'Wow, Ann, is that you? You look so skinny! You look great!' I looked at him and said, 'Thanks, but I am still the same person, scumbag.'"

Ann, age 22

Jessica's Story

I met Jessica in high school. As far as I was concerned, she was perfect—a gorgeous redhead who stood about 5-foot-1 in her tallest shoes. Got the parts in the school play I was vying for. Dated the guys I liked. Was popular, smart and, ugh, even went to Princeton (undergrad) and Harvard (law school). Years later, I caught up with her on Facebook and learned what I should have known from talking to young girls—that even the "perfect girls" don't think they're such hot stuff.

"Each year, our middle school scheduled a few skiing trips to a local 'mountain,'" Jessica, now thirty-five, recalled. "My dad was often the chaperone, despite the fact that I didn't ski. I went on the trips just to sit in the lodge…and because, well, everyone went on the trips. The idea of staying home would have been just another strike against me in my attempt to be cool. Wearing ski clothes was the closest I was going to come to actually participating in the activity," she said with a laugh.

During one trip in her last year of middle school, Jessica was wearing a "cute" pink jacket with matching pink snowpants. "It didn't strike me as particularly scandalous at the time," she said. "I looked coordinated, I thought, but that was about it. But one night, when we were boarding the ski bus, one of the popular eighth graders from the baseball team said loudly, 'Hey, Mayer's got a nice ass.' Thankfully, my dad was not chaperoning that trip," Jessica said. "I was flattered and embarrassed. Then his buddies yelled out, 'Yeah, nice ass, Mayer!' By the time that bus rounded back into the school parking lot later that night, I had my first nickname: 'Cheeks.'"

Unlike the negative nicknames discussed in Chapter 1, when nicknames have a positive connotation, they can be worn proudly like a crown—elevating a girl's status. "Being anointed 'Cheeks' did wonders for my status at that middle school," Jessica said. "Overnight, I went from being someone who was only noticed during the school plays to someone who was getting noticed every time she walked down the hall. And, suddenly, the popular boys wanted to talk to me! One of the baseball players even invited me to be his date to the winter formal, and dammit, I went!"

Unfortunately, Jessica's reign at the top didn't last. One day the following spring, one of the "almost popular" boys made this announcement in the cafeteria: "You know, Mayer's ass isn't that great. In fact, it's kinda droopy."

And just like that, "Cheeks" became "Droopy." The middle school gods giveth; the middle school gods taketh away.

"My winter formal date continued to chat with me on occasion—in fact, to his credit, he's an active Facebook friend of mine to this day—but the rest of the baseball team forgot about me shortly after that," Jessica told me. "And who could blame them? Nobody wants to be seen with a girl who has a droopy bottom. Even now, years after, most of the time I look in the mirror and like what I see behind me, but every once in a while, I have to admit, it does look kinda droopy."

Six measly letters. One stinkin' word. Ugh. And Jessica's whole world changed. Whether in friendship circles or with boyfriends, girls must remain steadfast and confident. They can't let others define their identity. "My friend Alice says, 'No guys like me.' She'll take one comment and blow it up in her mind," Sam, age seventeen, told me. "She'll think, 'Another person must be talking about me, and another, and another.'" It creates more of a problem. I try to tell her that not everyone feels that way. That the entire public doesn't mean it. But it's already in the brain, and it's been happening so long, and her mind is stuck—it's tricking her and telling her that it's 'everyone,' that she's in a corner and can't get out."

This is a very common occurrence. Our girls must send out the right messages, that they're worthy or datable, because when they tell themselves they're not, they're probably right. To help your daughter get "unstuck" from this kind of negative feedback loop, tell her:

→ **Don't put words in the boys' mouths.** "I was ridiculed throughout my childhood because of my weight. Guys thought I was a joke," Rhonda, age seventeen, told me. "So when

I met Robert, I figured that since he was popular, he wouldn't want to go out with me. When he started to pursue me, I doubted his sincerity and said, 'You don't want me.' It took him five months to convince me that he was attracted to my laugh, my eyes, my long hair *and* my curves."

→ **Dress for the part you want.** "As soon as I started to dress in clothes that fit my size, I realized it wasn't that guys didn't want to date me because I was bigger but because I looked like I didn't care about myself," said Maggie, age fifteen.

→ **Personality does count.** Our mothers told us, and their mothers before them, but it bears repeating: A lot of boys don't know a size 4 from a size 14, but they do know the difference between a dull girl and one with a sense of humor and self-respect. "This one girl in my sorority—all she eats is ice cubes with salt on them. I never understood that," said Danielle. "My boyfriend always refuses to spend time with her—and definitely won't eat with her."

A Cyber Life

Interactions with peers and boyfriends have changed dramatically in the last few years as the online and "tech" lives of girls have become just as important as their in-person lives. A 2009 study of one thousand British teenagers showed that they spent an average of thirty-one hours a week, or over four hours a day, online doing everything from looking up cosmetic surgery procedures and investigating diets and weight loss to doing homework and chatting with friends. Although a 2009 Nielsen survey disputed that teens spent that much time online (they said it was about a third of that), its research suggested that cell phone use—texting—was taking up the majority of their tech time. Nielsen found that 77 percent of teens have their own cell phone and that these teens are sending and/or receiving a whopping 96 text messages a day, or nearly 2,900 a month, which is just about double the average number of text messages in 2008.

The increase in tech time goes hand in hand with the increase in irresponsible "faceless" interactions—incidents of cyberbullying are off the charts. According to a major survey of victimization in schools, half of all fourteen-year-olds are the victims of bullying, and cyberbullying is now one of the most common forms of abuse. Cyberbullying—by mobile phone, e-mail and on websites—is now as common as name-calling among teenagers, with another study by the National Institutes of Health suggesting that as many as one in ten students is affected by cyberbullying.

Body snarking, a term originally coined by journalist Hannah Seligson, and thrown around the blogosphere, refers to the "snarky," rude, off-the-cuff remarks about weight that have become the ever-present theme song for female-to-female interaction. But it's no longer only used to razz celebrities who've put on a few pounds; body snarking has hit Main Street. "Tech has ruined the world," said Kate, age seventeen, an athletically built girl. "Instant messenger. Hateful stuff. People unleash their true feelings online. In general, that's where a lot of stuff happens. People don't have the guts anymore to say what they want to say."

Body snarking has recently taken a turn for the worse. Formspring.me, a website that many parents may not have even heard of, has become an increasingly popular social networking site among teens. Opening an account is free, as it is with sites such as Facebook or Twitter, but the attraction of Formspring is its confidentiality—members are prompted to "ask anything," allowing them to pose questions and comment anonymously. While some interactions are innocuous, many teens confess to saying things on Formspring that they would never say in person—making it the newest, and perhaps most effective, delivery system for cruel covert communication and body bashing among classmates.

And it's not just talk, but images, too, that is part of the cyberbullying repertoire. Just like the celebrity magazines, teens are taking their digital cameras with them in order to snap the next hilarious, snark-inducing snapshot, which can be uploaded to the social networking sites in a matter of seconds and sent to everyone's friends and friends of friends. On the social networking sites, anyone can become an unwilling celebrity. "We don't really mean anything by it," Andrea, age sixteen, told me. "We're just having a little fun. Seriously. I mean, have a sense of humor."

Body snarking is easy, and the rewards are instant, gobbled up by an impulsive culture. People like Andrea are hailed as clever wordsmiths. I remember when I was asked for a quote from the *Washington Post*'s Celebritology section when Beyoncé's House of Deréon came out with its pimp-inspired clothing line for kids. I called it her "Sesame Street Walkers Collection." Moments later, people were making comments about my comment, cyberlaughing and giving me a digital thumbs-up. I hate to admit it, but it felt good. This goes the same way. If you say just the right thing, you'll be the hero for a day.

Beth's Story

"This is sooooo embarrassing," said Beth, age fourteen, a 5-foot-2, 144-pound devoted saxophone player who was very big on "stupid entertainment trivia." A friend of another girl I had interviewed, Beth contacted me because she "wanted to tell me that it could really happen."

"What could?"

"Facebook is evil," she said. "Actually, the girls on Facebook are evil. They're like a demented form of the paparazzi. I went on a camping trip with my seventh-grade class. I actually hate camping. It's so dirty, and everyone was looking pretty gross. I mean, who doesn't look gross when they're in the middle of the wilderness and the nearest bathroom is in a smelly box that's not even as clean as a muddy hole in the ground?

"So, there's this girl—her name is Hayley—who's like Little Miss High and Mighty, and she takes out this camera and is taking pictures of all of us. I was just doing my own thing. I mean, like, she barely pays attention to me most of the time but, I don't know, maybe I was delusional, but I was thinking that maybe she kind of actually liked me finally."

"What made you think she didn't?"

"Because she's evil! When she was taking those pictures, I had dropped the map I was looking at and picked it up. I didn't think much of it until after the trip when I was home, and I looked at my Facebook page and saw that I was tagged on a photo in Hayley's photo album on 'Seventh Grade Camping Trip.' There was the worst picture I've ever seen of myself. I was leaning down to pick up the map, and my pants were kind of pulled down a little for a second and you could see my underwear."

I was about to say something consoling when Beth stopped me. "That wasn't even the worst part! The caption, written by evil Hayley, said, 'MOOOOOn Over Moorestown.' And people were making comments, calling me 'blubber butt.'

"When I told my mom, she tried to be helpful and told me to pretend to have a sense of humor about it and say something like, 'Well, I know it's not my best side.' But I was really upset still. I was like, as much as I love Facebook most of the time, I wish I lived in the Dark Ages or at least when my mom was growing up."

"So what happened the next day?"

"The picture was taped to my locker and one guy, this idiot that people called "Caz," was wearing a T-shirt that he had his dorky ninth-grade brother make for him with the picture on it that said 'This Butt's for You.' Of course, the teachers made him take it off, but you know he was wearing it out, like, at the mall or at the parties. I wanted to die."

"What happened to the picture online?"

"The principal made them take that down. Hayley didn't really get in trouble, though. She was, like, in there, and she was supposed to apologize to me and instead she just was like, 'I thought you were, you know, doing it on purpose, mooning the camera! We were all kidding around. It was just supposed to be fun.' I'm like, 'Yeah, lots of fun for everyone.'" Beth's face was turning red. "And Hayley actually started to get mad like, 'I said I was kidding.' I'm like, 'Yeah, that makes it OK then, in your little evil world.' And then she started totally fake crying, like they do in beauty pageants. It was pathetic."

A truly frustrating situation. By saying "I thought you were doing it on purpose" and bringing everyone in with "We were all kidding around," Hayley doesn't have to take responsibility for her action. She is able to place the onus on Beth or on the class at large; she is merely the blamed messenger. Cyberspace provides a sort of digital code of protection. In *The Curse of the Good Girl,* Rachel Simmons says that phrases like "no offense" or "just kidding" are meant to erase the personal responsibility of the offender. Like a "get out of jail free" card, the line "If I didn't mean it, it didn't happen," or in this case, "If I say I didn't mean it, it didn't happen," lets the perpetrator off the hook. Of course, it did happen, and a young girl is still paying the consequences.

"Did the principal buy into that?"

Beth gritted her teeth. "He made us both apologize to each other. I was like, 'What am I apologizing for? I was the target!' And he was like, 'In every situation, both people contribute to the state of affairs.' I'm like, 'Huh?' But I just did it. I didn't see any other way out, even though it was so wrong."

"Did things change after that?"

"Not really. I mean, it was 'Hayley had to go to the principal's office.' 'Beth couldn't take a joke.' But I know it wasn't a joke, because I wasn't laughing."

Taking a Stand

Something's gotta change. While we can't eradicate bullies the way we exterminate bugs, we can lay the foundation for positive character in schools, as we discussed in Chapter 5, and we can also help our girls navigate their friendships with more confidence and better skills.

At sixteen, Sarah was sick of hearing her friends talk about not being thin enough. "I was ready to drop my friends altogether because it was getting boring listening to them. I'm not going to say that I didn't do it, too, sometimes, but it went too far. I could feel myself losing my appetite and picture myself throwing my lunch in the trash again. My thighs felt like they were getting bigger every minute."

"So how did you get it to stop?"

"We were at lunch. My friends were going on and on. Marley was too fat. April was going back on Weight Watchers. Marissa thought she looked disgusting. So I just got fed up. I was going to explode. I made an announcement. I was like, 'The next person who says she's too fat or needs to lose weight has to go somewhere else, because I can't stand hearing it.'"

"What did they say?"

"Believe it or not, my friends agreed with me. They were sick of it, too."

We must teach our girls to have these uncomfortable conversations, to endure rather than run, to talk face-to-face instead of backstabbing and gossiping. Here are some ideas to help them move into a better and more successful place.

→ **Bring it up.** By broaching the subject, even in a joking way, as Sarah did, girls might find that others want a change as well.

→ **Get involved with fun activities.** Adolescence is a time when many girls drop out of activities like sports. When girls can choose an activity that they can all do together, their discussions can turn from their bodies and what's wrong with them to the activity and their achievements.

→ **Organize a "pampering" day.** Many girls, regardless of weight, love to get their hair styled, nails done and clothes picked out. A pampering day can indirectly remind girls that they are "worth it" and deserve to be treated well.

→ **Let friends know what you like about them.** Honestly praising abilities, style and character can build self-worth and can take the focus off what girls wish they could change or fix. Praise, like fat talk, also has a way of being contagious. The entire climate of the peer group can be altered.

→ **Create a "grumble and groan" time limit.** Nonstop complaining is draining and unproductive. Have your daughter practice "clearing the air." She (and her friends) get a daily time limit for complaining—two minutes to gripe and whine about shortcomings or perceived problems, and that's it. After a while, girls will likely find that they don't even need the full two minutes.

→ **Add "in my head" to her evaluative statements.** People used to think it was funny to add "in bed" to the end of every Chinese fortune cookie fortune. This follows the same principle. Whenever girls say something like "I need to lose five pounds," "My thighs are so big" or "She has better legs than me," make a game by adding "in my head." It's important for girls—and women—to know that they are contributing to their own body image problems by allowing their perceptions to become reality.

Should Your Daughter Fire Her Friends?

Studies repeatedly show that girls who have friendships based on trust, communication and acceptance report high levels of self-worth and overall life satisfaction. They become less anxious about competition and more concerned with how they can help build each other up. "I was trying on bathing suits at the local mall, and just didn't like what I was seeing, so I turned to my best friend, Monica, and said, 'Please make me feel good about myself!'" Nicole, age sixteen, told me. "She took out a tube of red lipstick and wrote across the top of the dressing-room mirror, 'This is what gorgeous looks like.' She signed it with a heart and an arrow pointed down at my body. It was a turning point for me. Now every time either one of us looks in the mirror we say those words. It's our motto."

I've always told girls that when they find truly supportive friends, hold on to them. They are rare and precious. Studies agree that the key to happiness is strong social ties and a feeling of connection with others. In fact, studies show that if you have five or more friends with whom you can discuss important, meaningful topics, you are far more likely to describe yourself as "very happy" in comparison to those who have fewer such friends or no such friends at all. Close friendship cuts the risk of depression, makes you feel more joyful, boosts immunity and lengthens life. It's so important! How do you know when your daughter needs to fire her friends? Ask her:

→ Are these close, long-term relationships?

→ Can you see yourself being friends with these people for years to come?

→ Can you confide in these people without hesitation or fear of disclosure (and exposure)?

→ Do you feel that you belong?

→ Do you have an opportunity to get and give support to one another?

→ Do you feel that you can be yourself with these people?

→ If you think of your top three characteristics of a friend, do these people have those qualities?

In the words of Catherine Schuller, fashion consultant and plus-size icon, "Don't change the chicken, change the pot!" If girls are feeling bad about themselves every time they're with their friends, they should probably be spending time with more healthy-minded girls. Finding new friends is not always that easy, but you can encourage your daughter to explore different possibilities and even take the initiative to meet new friends outside of her current clique. Here's how:

→ **Volunteer.** Teens can be a big help at pet shelters, hospitals, museums and after-school programs. What interests her? By volunteering at places that she finds fascinating, she is likely to meet others who share her interest.

→ **Join an after-school program.** Cultural arts, scrapbooking, art—these programs draw participants from different towns and districts and open up your daughter's options to people who share a passion for her activity of choice.

→ **Join a club or support group.** Jess Weiner, Global Ambassador for the Dove Self-Esteem Fund, recalled in her book *A Very Hungry Girl* how at eighteen, after years of constant dieting, she went to a public bathroom to purge for the first time. "Inside the stall was a sign that said, 'Eating disorders can kill.' Below that, someone had written, 'I'm already dead.' And a second woman had scribbled, 'So am I.' I suddenly realized that I wasn't alone." Jess joined a therapy group where she could talk candidly with other girls her age. "The force of friendships can be quite powerful in recovery," she said, adding, "The healthier I got, the more healthy friends I attracted. The ones who treated their bodies well, however flawed, were my best role models."

Jenny, now twenty-two, has been an aspiring model and a plus-size girl for as long as she can remember. In both middle and high school, she was the captain of her cheerleading team and her school dance team. Jenny's best friend, also a bigger girl, co-captained the teams. They were both on the honor roll and had a lot of friends. "A lot of the other bigger girls would sink back and the other kids would make fun of them," she said. "My ability to participate and succeed was never about weight but about what I could do. I knew in my heart that no one could keep me from what I was destined to accomplish."

Of the many happy and successful plus-size girls I've spoken to, this sentiment is often repeated. In fact, I think it was best said when Eve, age eighteen, talked about a classmate, Ashley, whom she admired and befriended in high school. "I don't even know what size she is… It's far from the first thing I think of when I'm asked to describe her. So many other attributes would come way before that."

BIQ:
Your Daughter's School of Thought

1. Does your daughter say she's criticized or laughed at at school due to her weight?

A. Yes, frequently. It seems like every week there is somebody picking on her and making her feel inferior.

B. Sometimes, although she seems to handle it pretty well.

C. Not often. If my daughter were to get teased, I think she would nip it in the bud right away or let it roll off her shoulders.

2. Is your daughter careful about what she eats in front of her friends at school?

A. She barely eats in front of her friends. If she does, it is usually very low-calorie items or a very small amount of substantive food.

B. She modifies her food intake a bit, but she still eats enough to get her through the school day.

C. My daughter eats what she wants in front of her friends.

3. When your daughter walks into her classroom:

A. She worries that people will tease her or ignore her because of her appearance.

B. She thinks some people will be nice to her and some people will not because of how she looks.

C. She seems generally comfortable about how she looks and what people think of her.

4. When it comes to guys, your daughter:

A. Is self-conscious and thinks that no guy will ever like her because she is too fat.

B. Believes that the thinner girls have it easier than she does but knows that eventually she'll find the right guy who likes her for who she is.

C. Doesn't have much of a problem in that area. She feels comfortable and gets positive attention from guys.

5. Your daughter's peers tend to:

A. Make her feel ashamed, used, unsupported and alone.

B. Play the typical head games at times but all in all are pretty decent kids.

C. Rally around her, encourage her and bring out the best in her.

Total number of:

As 1 point each	Bs 2 points each	Cs 3 points each	Total BIQ score for Chapter 6

Chapter 7

Kiss My Assets:
The Secrets of Girls
Who Thrive at Every Size

We know it when we see it. Strength. Power. Self-assuredness. Guts. The wonder of assets in motion. Brought to life in a girl not only in the way she acts, but in the way she thinks and feels about herself and the world in which she lives. Studies of more than 2.2 million children and teens by the Search Institute, an organization that promotes healthy children, youth and communities, consistently show that the more assets young people have, the more successful they are and the less likely they are to engage in risky behaviors.

But it's more than just a list of competencies. Our children must have what researchers at Search call "spark"—an interest, talent, skill, asset or dream (academic, relational, athletic, artistic or intellectual) that excites them and enables them to discover their true passions, along with encouragement from trusted adults to nurture it. In my experience with girls, I have also seen "spark" further fueled when they have the "know-how," committed behaviors or "actions" behind those aspirations and defined reasons for pursuing their passion. Therefore, I've expanded the Search Institute term into the broader acronym SPARK:

→ **S**upport. Important mentors, most typically trusted adults, in different positions and places where girls work and socialize, who can guide, affirm, celebrate and encourage a child or teen to keep going.

→ **P**assion. The animated need, self-identified, and the interest to pursue this goal at this time.

→ **A**ction. The actual work that the child or teen commits to doing and does consistently without needing to be prodded or provoked.

→ **R**eason. The *why* that intrinsically motivates the child or teen to move forward and puts her in a state of flow.

→ **K**nowledge. The skills and capacity to actually tackle the goal.

SPARK takes our girls further away from the focus on "fat." When I was doing my research on aspiring and working plus-size models at Tufts, I was struck by the discrepancy between my findings and those in the published studies that affirm thinness as a precursor to success. In my research, plus-size models, who ranged in size from 12 to 22, saw themselves as *just as competent* as slimmer women and *much more competent* than women who were plus-size but not aspiring to become models—not just in appearance, but also in intelligence, romantic relationships, humor and global self-worth. My findings, contrary to most that are out there, suggest that some plus-size girls can succeed despite the powerful negative messages that tell them they can't, they shouldn't and they won't.

The Search Institute's list of assets, while dynamic, includes only forty items. They are not gender-specific. To me, because boys and girls are *not* the same, nor does society treat them the same way, the list is not complete. Girls have their own unique challenges and gifts, particularly with regard to body image and weight, and they need a belief system that allows them to put their assets into action and break free from those that tell them that if they are not thin, they are not valued. The following Ten Commandments—an amalgam of the assets set forth by Search, other research and my own—protect our girls and promote positive behaviors. They serve as reference points that can guide you in helping your daughter counter the negative body messages she receives while building up the positive assets within herself.

Commandment #1:
I know how I feel, and I can express my emotions in a healthy, productive way.
Assets: Emotional Intelligence, Assertiveness

I have the right to:
- Feel a full range of emotions, both positive and negative.
- Take care of myself and my emotional well-being.
- Express how I feel, even if the emotion is negative.
- Feel differently from others about the same experience.
- Change how I feel as I think, learn and grow from my experiences.

Emotional intelligence, a term that became widely popularized after the publication of Daniel Goleman's landmark book of the same name, refers to the ability to identify, express and accept one's emotions. It goes hand in hand with assertiveness—one manages the feelings; the other gives them wings. Girls who are assertive speak up for themselves and convey what they want, need and deserve in order to be successful, happy, safe and comfortable. I like to tell girls:

→ Say how you feel about the situation. "I feel hurt when you tell me I'm your best friend when we're alone but ignore me when we're in school."

→ Say how you feel when you are in the situation. "It makes me feel like you are embarrassed to be seen with me."

→ Say how you feel about the other person. "I care about you and respect you, so that's why I wanted to come to you directly."

→ Check in on how he or she is feeling. "How are you feeling about what I'm telling you?"

When emotional intelligence and assertiveness are successfully accessed and released, our girls can rescue themselves from the confines of hierarchy, status, rules and low expectations.

Like Mary.

On her Twitter page, Mary, age twenty-four, from Illinois, called herself an "activist, feminist, idealist...dork"—alongside a too-close-up photo of herself covered in face-painted flowers. I was immediately intrigued.

"I was told by my mother—a staunch feminist—that it was 'superficial' to care about my looks, that I was too 'smart' to fall for media messages and that the very notion of having a female body—fat or otherwise—put me at risk," Mary explained to me. "I was told the media was constantly trying to 'twist my perception,' and 'strange men' were out to get me. So when I noticed my body at all, I associated it most strongly with fear and pain. I even got stomachaches from thinking about it."

Mary hid her feelings of dissatisfaction so well that when she was diagnosed with an eating disorder just before her sixteenth birthday, the doctor was shocked to learn that her parents had never heard her express anything negative about her body or her weight. "It made perfect sense to me, however," she told me honestly. "I was as ashamed of caring about my body as I was of my body itself."

> ## "Overheard"
>
> *"I teach my daughters the same thing I live by myself; I set the bar low enough that I can see it but high enough that I have to stretch to reach it. Each time I grab hold of it, I move it up a notch and try again."*
>
> Gretchen Cawthon, mother of two, creator of Girls Can't What? website and clothing line

It wasn't until Mary was away from her mother's stringent rules of feminism that she was able to break free from the tight reins she kept on her emotions. "I went into residential treatment, and through that process, pretty much *everything*—including my sense of my body—improved dramatically," Mary said, her eyes getting wide and her shoulders rolling back just a bit. "The program

I was in included recreational therapy on a ropes course. Never having been an athlete, I grew to think of my body as 'strong' for the first time, and like many people beginning recovery, I learned how important it was to focus on what it could *do* rather than how it *looked*."

When I asked Mary how she would describe her appearance now, her weight was barely mentioned. "In a hard moment," she told me, "I guess the answer goes something like, 'I'm 5-foot-3, white-skinned, brown hair, brown eyes…and I haven't weighed myself in years, so I don't know.' In a good moment, it's, 'I'm 5-foot-3, I wear flip-flops even when I shouldn't, my hair changes constantly—blue or green or its current 'flapper' phase—I have rockin' thick-rimmed glasses and I smile like a little kid.'"

Mary's eyes gaze off for a moment, and she smiles absently. "I remember being in grade school, learning about eating disorders, and thinking how horrible they were and how I couldn't imagine anyone 'doing that.' Then I became a girl who had one," she said. "I was educated about the problems—the beauty myth, the thin ideal, violence against women—but I wasn't given any sense of my own power against these things. When I learned how to safely communicate those feelings to people who could be supportive and how to channel them into other avenues, like activism, I finally had some power in my own life."

Commandment #2:

I take healthy risks, and I am accountable for my actions.

Assets: Courage, Positive Risk-taking, Accountability

I have the right to:

- Take healthy risks.
- Fail without it crushing my self-esteem.
- Do something different than I've done before.
- Go against traditional "girl rules."
- Ask for support in taking my healthy risks.

ASSET-BUILDING BLOCK: HOW CAN I GET MY DAUGHTER TO SPEAK UP OR TRY SOMETHING NEW?

Getting girls to assert themselves involves an element of "risk." When I speak with girls, I discuss five areas, or "zones," that make up their continuum of risk:

1. **THE COMFORT ZONE.** Girls feel relaxed, calm and confident.

2. **THE CHALLENGE ZONE.** A zone just outside the comfort zone where girls need a little motivation and a strong desire to reach. This zone is divided into two categories—the "fly-solo" zone (girls go it alone) and the "wingman" zone (girls need some help or support).

3. **THE TARGET ZONE.** Where a girl is heading. The target zone coincides with her goals but takes more risk than she may be willing to accept at the present moment.

4. **THE DANGER ZONE.** An area of risk that a girl refuses to venture into because she believes the risks are unhealthy or counter-productive—drugs, eating disorders, walking alone at night, etc.

5. **THE WAR ZONE.** This zone travels throughout the other zones, depending on where the girl might encounter resistance, negative feedback or resentment from others. The benefit of anticipating the war zone is being able to prepare for it—mentally or by reaching for assistance, adjusting how you say something or doing something to ensure that you are being respectful of other people's feelings.

Example: Let's say your daughter, Jasmine, age fourteen, wants to run for a spot in student government but knows all the popular, thin girls are vying for the spots. You can take Jasmine through the Risk Zone exercise:

- Comfort Zone. "I don't run for a spot. I just go about my everyday life, bored but comfortable."

- Challenge Zone.

  SOLO. "I don't feel comfortable just walking into school and announcing that I'm running without a lot of help."

  WINGMAN/ASSISTED. "I would feel comfortable talking to my three closest friends and getting a campaign mapped out and then talking to my teacher, Mrs. Green, about it."

- Target Zone. "Running for student body president my senior year."

- Danger Zone. "Running against Cindy Meadows—I'd have to steer clear of her. She'd make my life a living hell."

- War Zone. "Running at all puts me in the war zone. Girls like me aren't supposed to do that. So I need to get as many of my friends to help me win as possible."

Through the Risk Zone exercise, Jasmine learns the possibilities beyond her comfort zone. She can try on each circumstance like a hat and see which one fits, which one she really wants and what she needs to get it.

Erika, age twenty-one, was a shy, chubby little girl who was "struggling to find herself and where she fit in this world," she told me. "At thirteen years old, I moved in with my stepmom, Debra—a gorgeous, thin, sweet, smart, generous, sexy woman who was a model and whose friends all looked like supermodels." She stopped and looked me in the eye. "I'm serious."

We were sitting in a Chinese restaurant in New York. Erika, a curvy and feisty size 10, was slouched back in her chair in a way that reminded me of an old Katharine Hepburn movie, as if she should be smoking a long cigarette with a holder. There was a sassiness about her, a quick wit. She had no qualms joking about her appearance or her weight—in fact, the zingers just kept on coming. "I've slept in the most uncomfortable positions, because I think they make me look skinny."

Ba dum bum.

"Muffin tops might be great for breakfast, but nobody wants them for dessert!"

The humor seemed effortless. But Erika didn't come upon her love of comedy in the typical way. She wasn't the class clown, didn't crave the center of attention. Erika lived on the Upper East Side of Manhattan, where girls came in only two sizes: "small and extra small." "The average woman is a size 2," she said. "So that's the size I thought I needed to be. Growing up, I could count on three fingers how many women I saw who were my size. Given all that I had been through already, you'd think weight was at the bottom of the totem pole, but all I had to do was take one look at my stepmom, and I thought, 'Now, there's a mold I'll never fit.'"

Erika recalled scores of times that she went shopping with her stepmom—"I loved spending time with her"—but suddenly feeling uncomfortable the moment they walked into a clothing store. "The only sizes they'd put out were 0 to 6," she said, "and the saleswomen would always have to bring out the 'embarrassing sizes' from the back when I wanted to try something on. They would scream in front of everyone, 'I need a 10!' I wanted to die."

Erika decided there was no way she could fit in on these

terms and needed to do something that challenged and fulfilled her. "I tried as many things as possible to see what would stick," Erika said. She started a magazine. Became a party planner. Acting. Singing. Cooking. Nothing stuck. "I thought it was because of my weight," she told me. "Then I became destructive." Dieting. Overeating. Drugs. "When you don't like who you are, because you can't be 'that,' you are naturally going to be destructive to your self and others. Everything was failing. I was failing. My dad and Debra took me aside and told me, 'You've got to stop this and get back on track.' I knew they were right."

> ## "Overheard"
>
> *"Meeting people is one thing. Connecting in a trusting, soul-satisfying way is unquestionably better."*
>
> Holly Getty, member, Women on Fire, a support and inspiration organization for women

Not knowing what else to do, Erika started a blog—writing about herself, her experiences—as a way to take responsibility for her life. "I started putting my everyday thoughts out there for the whole world to read. I just never thought anyone would actually read them," she said. "But all of a sudden, people would come up to me and say, 'Hey, you're Erika, right? I read your blog, and you're hilarious!'" Then one day, Erika was asked to perform stand-up comedy for a charity event. Leaning in for emphasis, her voice getting slightly louder, Erika said, "I told them, 'But I don't do comedy.' They said, 'Have you read your blog?'"

Two weeks later, Erika was onstage. Terrified. "At first, I thought I was just going to read an entry from my blog, but then I decided, why not really go for it? I created a set, walked out there and just told people my story. I was completely myself, and all of a sudden I was at peace. They were laughing. I saw my dad and Debra. They were laughing. I was having a blast. It was that day I knew it...I had found my size 2!"

ASSET-BUILDING BLOCK: BTF

I used BTF, one of my most popular courage-building exercises, to help a teen named Caitlyn overcome her fears of going through a haunted house on *The Tyra Show* last year. BTF stands for two concepts that work together: "Beat The Fear" and "Body, Thoughts and Feelings." Have your daughter try this exercise when she is nervous about taking a healthy but challenging risk.

BODY. Stand (or sit) tall, shoulders back, head held high, as a physical reminder that there is confidence and courage inside you.

THOUGHTS. Think about the benefits that will come with this healthy risk. Use positive self-talk (your "power voice") to remind yourself of what you want.

FEELINGS. Think about where you are and what you are doing when you feel the most courageous and confident. Call up those feelings.

Example: "I'm scared to ask Jason to come with me to the prom, because I think he'll laugh at me and make me feel like a fat loser."

- Body. "When I'm confident about talking to a guy, I look directly at him and have a smile on my face. I walk right up to him without hesitation."

- Thoughts. "I think to myself, 'Of course, he'll want to talk to me. I'm a lot of fun!' I think of the great time we have when we hang out and the great time we will have if we hang out some more."

- Feelings. "I have energy in my arms and legs, but I feel comfortable and relaxed at the same time."

All systems go! Body. Thoughts. Feelings. Put yourself in that space of success and all you need to do is follow the path that you, yourself, have set before you.

Commandment #3:

I set and go after goals to create the future I want.

Assets: Goal-setting, Expectations, Initiative, a Positive View of the Future

I have the right to:

- Dream big and make plans for a successful future.
- Challenge myself to do something I've never done before.
- Set a challenging yet realistic timeline.
- Ask for support and assistance to reach my goals.
- Fail, then revise my plan with my newfound knowledge or skill.

As a sophomore in high school, Lynae Tucker, the 2009 Miss Plus Teen USA, witnessed the gut-wrenching disappointment of friends who couldn't afford to attend their school prom. "It just didn't seem right," said Lynae, age seventeen. Compelled to help, Lynae created Operation Dream Come True for juniors and seniors who had a C average or better and whose parents made less than $20,000 a year.

"I approach all my goals the same way," she said. At 5-foot-4, Lynae was poised, confident and astoundingly articulate—not a single "errr," "um" or "you know" ever came out of her mouth in the hour we spent talking. "First, I ask myself, 'What is the problem? And what do I want it to look like at the end?' If you're not clear about the problem, how can you fix it? I envisioned a dream prom for every girl no matter what her financial situation."

Lynae made a list of the top three things she needed to make her goal a reality. "Number one, dress donations. Number two, hair and makeup donations. And number three, a venue donation," she said, emphatically enumerating each point. "Next it was time to pound the pavement. I made up 150 flyers and handed them out around town. I introduced myself, talked about my mission and what we needed from others. I received commitments from five dress stores, three salons and one venue. I knew of a modeling instructor who wanted to find more girls for her agency. Together, she got her girls and, using her contacts, I got my venue."

I don't come across this type of maturity and determination often, even among adults. It's not the scope of the goal that matters: Goals that our girls pursue with such fervor during their teen years lay the groundwork for them to achieve the broader, long-term goals of adulthood.

"Many adults don't give teens credit, but we have passion, we have drive and we have goals," Lynae said, as if reading my mind. Research actually tells us that only a minority of teens experience an abundance of support across all parts of their lives—between 67 percent and 95 percent feel that key adults and authority figures think negatively of them. "You just have to do it," she said.

Lynae is now channeling her energies into contacting radio stations and presenting to women's groups about the need to get more supportive adults in the lives of teenage girls. "Every girl, no matter what her size, deserves to feel valued and beautiful— she needs to hear that message from strong adult women in the community," she told me. And what about the future? "I know this sounds clichéd coming from a beauty queen, but I've been touched by cancer in my life—my father and grandfather had it. I want to make it my goal to find the funds, help the researchers, be the spokesperson and help the children who are suffering with it today and in the future. I know we can do it."

With past successes to draw on, a host of assets to rely on and the drive to propel them into action, I have no doubt: There will be no stopping her.

It's the final day of one of our Sassy Sisterhood sessions, and we are all in a ceremonial mood. Soft music is playing. Candles are lit. The girls are quiet and thoughtful. As each girl comes up to me privately, I ask her, "What will you take from this experience?" This is what I hear:

→ "I will remember that I am beautiful the way I am."

→ "I am more than just my body."

→ "I now know that what I see isn't always the truth."

→ "I have the ability to speak out and speak up for myself."

→ "There are no limits to what I can do."

Commandment #4:
I see my body and myself in a positive light, and I speak to myself accordingly.

Assets: Body Image, Self-esteem, Positive Self-talk

I have the right to:
- Be happy with what I see in the mirror, even if there are things I want to improve.
- See a reflection that is real and true, not shrouded by perceived outside opinions and demands.
- Have a realistic perception of what a girl's body can look like and still be considered beautiful and healthy.
- Know that how my body looks is not a reflection of its worth or capabilities.
- Refrain from obsessing about what others think about my appearance.

Then, as a final parting gesture, each girl walks under a "support bridge" that all the girls have formed with their hands, a visual and positive representation of the feedback loop we've discussed throughout this book:

Body positive thoughts → Encouraging, affirmative people → Increased body positive thoughts

"My defining moment came when my mom and I went for a special girls' day to a local spa at the mall," said Sarah, an athletic seventeen-year-old girl with a pixie haircut and a bright white smile. "We had a woman, a personal shopper, with us who was supposed to show us our 'best look.' We got our nails done, our hair done, makeup and I put on a new outfit. When I saw the total effect, I said to the woman, 'It's amazing. I never look like this. I usually feel like a sausage or a cow when I get dressed. You know, my thighs stick out. My butt looks enormous, and I figure I need to lose at least fifteen pounds. But now I look good.' The stylist turned me toward the mirror and said, 'Sarah, I didn't change your body. I changed your clothes. You didn't have the wrong body. You had the wrong clothes. This is exactly the way you look.' I thought to myself, 'I really am beautiful. Just as I am.'"

Toccara's Story

Walking around New York City with Toccara Jones, who came in seventh on the third season of *America's Next Top Model (ANTM)*, was an experience. At 5-foot-9 and a size 14, Toccara was hard to miss, especially when she was walking around with 5-foot-3 me. People stopped, stared, took photos and asked for autographs. They oohed and aahed. Some people just cried. Toccara was very gracious, smiling sweetly through it all, as if she were in one of those animated musicals with the birds chirping happily around her head.

"People tell me I'm attractive, but I just don't pay attention to looks," she told me at 7:00 a.m., the time she picked to rise, shine and do our interview. It was a funny thing for a top model to say, especially with the amount of publicity she gets for that very thing. "When I'm at home in LA, I'll pass a mirror and surprise myself and think, 'Hey! You're kind of pretty!' That's how I talk to myself. Never in the negative." While many girls have told me in the course of researching and writing this book that when they gain weight, they don't "feel" like themselves, Toccara was quick to say, "I've always felt like 'me' no matter what my size. I've been a size 4 and a size 14. I think I was too involved with things like theater classes and after-school programs to ever have a problem with my body image."

Toccara was "completely into theater" and wanted to be an actress when she was a little girl. She did everything she could to express her talents—music, dance, singing. ("I couldn't sing a lick, but I tried," she laughed.) She took violin, was in the chess club, played sports—activities that provided her with opportunities to grow, develop her passions and meet all kinds of people. "God has always sent me teachers," she said. "When I was about nine years old, I met a stunning, vivacious model named Jamaica from Dayton, Ohio. She was all I wanted to be," Toccara said of the woman who remains her mentor to this day. "She was my celebrity. She was, and is, a beautiful woman. She never treated me like a child. She helped make me feel like I was competent."

ASSET-BUILDING BLOCK: FAT "TALKING TRASH" CAN

As part of the Sassy Sisterhood ceremony on the last day, I ask my Sassy Girls what they "plan to throw away"—what negative belief, thought or lie they refuse to keep in their lives. They take out a piece of paper and then jot down whatever comes to mind: "I hate my thighs." "My stomach isn't flat enough." "I'm not *her*." Some choose to read theirs to the group, some don't, but they all crumple up the pieces of paper and throw them in the trash can. Parents can have their daughters try this exercise at home and ask them:

> Where do these thoughts come from?
> Whose voice is telling you these limiting thoughts?

If she doesn't want to read them out loud, don't pressure her; rather, encourage her to keep her thoughts in a diary where, again, she can counter the thoughts with affirmations and realizations about what makes her worthy.

The final step in this exercise is a letter of apology to the body part she has been bashing. A sample letter might sound like this:

Dear Legs,

I'm sorry for insulting you. You aren't ugly. You aren't useless. You allow me to kick soccer balls into goals and help win the game. Go, Tigers! You allow me to go walking with my mother and coach Special Olympics. Without you, I wouldn't be able to do the things that make me happy.

xoxo, Melanie

Raised by her grandmother, Toccara said she suffered from the same worries as any other developing girl. "I wanted breasts!" she said with a laugh. "I used to stuff my bra. But I didn't think to myself, 'I need to lose weight.' I was a size 14. I went online, knowing I wanted to model, and I researched it. I didn't even know about plus-size modeling. But when I found it, I just decided, that's what I'm going to do. I just kept moving."

Imagine being surrounded by thin, beautiful women, when you outweigh them by more than fifty, sixty or seventy pounds and not only feeling as secure but more secure than they do. "I felt sorry for what the girls on *ANTM* felt was necessary to do to themselves," Toccara said. "They were a size 2 or a 0, and they were always complaining about their hips, booties, pouches. They were dieting, bulimic, throwing up. They worked out in the middle of the night to maintain this image. I was the happiest girl in the house, and all the other girls were thinner."

Commandment #5:

I surround myself with and am surrounded
by positive, encouraging, supportive adults
who serve as role models and peers
who share my values.

Assets: Positive, Supportive Adults; Role Models; Positive Peer Groups

I have the right to:

- Feel supported by the adults in my life.
- Engage in positive communication with the adults and peers in my life.
- Seek out supportive environments in which I can be encouraged.
- Seek out adults who will inspire and guide me.
- Surround myself with friends who support me for who I am today.

With a sense of humor, a healthy dose of perspective and a contagious acceptance for a wide array of body types, Toccara inspires girls and women to embrace themselves. "I like my butt, my breasts, my shape, even though they're not perfect. Don't get me wrong. There are days when I get up and I feel bloated or I feel like my face looks round, but then I know that the next day I'll be back to myself. Most girls start in a place of 'hate.' I've learned that you have to start in a place of 'like.' You need to say, 'I like my arms, I just want them to be more toned.' As women, we need to see ourselves as good and getting better."

Talking with Connie Lindsey was like listening to a book on tape—engaging and engrossing. I found it hard to believe that a woman who was so painfully shy as a girl would one day grow up to inspire more than 3 million Girl Scouts as the president of the board of directors for the Girl Scouts of America and the organization's highest-ranking volunteer.

Connie's Girl Scout experience spans decades and began at age eleven when she first became a member. It was a big deal to a young girl living in public housing on the "wrong side" of Milwaukee, Wisconsin. She grew up in a broken home, with a single mother who worked hard but didn't make much money. "People had already predetermined how my life was supposed to be based on a zip code and how I looked," she told me. "I barely spoke."

However, Connie was blessed with a rich support network that helped her find her voice:

On her very first day of scouting, Connie, wearing a Girl Scout uniform bought for her by the women of her church, listened closely as her troop leader looked at each girl and told her these words: *"You matter. And don't let anyone tell you different."*

And the volume of Connie's voice got a little bit louder.

At home, her supportive mother would tell her, *"You are a beautiful girl. What you need to do is to be smarter than the meanest kid in your class—because twenty years from now, doll baby, they won't be anywhere near where you'll be."*

And the volume of Connie's voice got a little bit louder.

In church on Sunday, her pastor, who had marched with Martin Luther King, Jr., told his congregation, *"You have worth. Who you are in God's eyes is far more important to how you will turn out than the physical side of you."*

And the volume of Connie's voice got a little bit louder.

But it was her choir director, Gloria Wright, who fully uncovered that voice from within. Knowing that Connie was a fiercely intelligent girl who loved and mastered reading from a very young age, she said to Connie, *"You have a wonderful vocabulary, and words can either bless a person or curse a person. I know that you will use your words to bless. You have a gift. Use it!"*

Connie realized that it wasn't only the great authors whose words could change views and opinions, but her words could have impact, too. "I tell Gloria that she wrote things on the tablet of my heart," she told me. "And I would watch her and think to myself, 'When I grow up, I want to have that kind of positive effect on people.'"

Studies continue to show that the number and quality of fulfilling, supportive relationships in a child's life—across all gender, racial, ethnic and social class lines—are seen as the most critical predictor of health, resilience and well-being. The 2003 Commission on Children at Risk, a group of leading physicians, researchers and youth-serving professionals, was so adamant about the need of supportive relationships in the lives of children and teens that it identified a lack of connectedness as a major contributor to deteriorating behavioral and mental health among young people in the United States.

Today, Connie teaches members of the Girl Scout organization everything she was taught. "Love and accept your bodies," she said. "Lean on those around you. Speak up, and we will listen. Show your gifts, because we will nurture them. Your voice has meaning, and it will be heard."

ASSET-BUILDING BLOCK:
ACCOUNTABILITY PARTNER (AP)

Support isn't always about telling a girl that everything she is doing is OK. My experience has shown me that girls are much more apt to achieve their goals when they have someone to check in with and keep them on task. I often advise my coaching clients to name and establish a supportive accountability partner (AP)—a person (friend, parent, teacher, coach) who allows them to stay true to the dreams, plans and healthy risks that they've laid out for themselves. An AP is the person who helps keep our daughters on track and honest with themselves about their goals and timeline.

Teach your daughter to ask herself these four key questions:

1. What am I going to do?

2. What is my date for completing it?

3. Who is my agreed-upon accountability partner (AP)? (Keep in mind that your daughter's AP serves no good purpose if he or she is wishy-washy.)

4. How will I inform my AP that I've completed my task?

If the task is not completed, all is not lost. It simply means that the accountability plan needs to be revisited and tweaked.

Meghan, age thirteen, was a thoughtful, quiet member of my Sassy group who hung back from discussions and only spoke when she really had something to say. Today, to the surprise of the group, she raised her hand.

"You mean, we've all been wanting to look like the girl on the cover of one of those magazines, and what you're saying is… the girl on the cover doesn't even really look like the girl on the cover?"

At that moment the veil was lifted. Meghan knew the truth.

Commandment #6:

I am aware and critical of the messages I receive about thinness and keep a healthy perspective on how I fit within those parameters.

Assets: Media Literacy and Perspective

I have the right to:
- Learn the tricks that the media use to persuade me to feel a certain way about myself.
- Dissect and be critical of what I see and read.
- Expand my opinion of what it means to be beautiful.
- Discuss what I see in the media and how I feel about it with people I trust.

Asset Girls are savvy media critics; they don't allow themselves to become objects or pawns but rather actively evaluate the marketing messages assaulting them and look for the hidden meanings and ruses. Even when they temporarily get swept away by what they see, they are able to step back to gain perspective to ensure that they haven't been unfairly persuaded. Like looking at a magic trick, but knowing how it's done, media literacy takes the impact out of the countless messages that tell our girls that their bodies are not right and that they will never be right until they buy a certain product, undergo a certain procedure or lose weight.

Tiffany's Story

This time, you can believe the hype: Tiffany Braxton, a beautiful plus-size model with dark, laughing eyes, *is* the girl in the magazine—and more.

Tiffany participated in my dissertation study through Tufts University. We met up a few years later in preparation for this book, as she was an example of a woman who defied the odds with a staggering amount of personal power to make a change despite a family legacy of body bashing and bad self-talk.

Tiffany's mother, like her grandmother before her, was an overweight child. Tiffany recalled with sensitivity the stories her mother and grandmother would tell her about having to wear adult-size clothing, because the children's clothes were too small, and how they were often teased by their classmates. These memories became etched into her grandmother's mind, and then her mother's, a fate they wanted Tiffany to avoid.

Little by little, her mother's emotional scars were revealed as she monitored what Tiffany ate and called attention to any pound gained. While Tiffany wasn't considered an overweight kid and lived far from a sedentary lifestyle—she did cheer, played tennis and ran track—Tiffany's mom felt the need to head off any signs that she might be following in the footsteps of the other women in her family. "I can remember one day, when I was a teenager, I poured a bowl of cereal and milk to eat," Tiffany said. "My mom insisted that she did not want me to eat the cereal, because I was gaining weight, and she thought I didn't need it. Anyone who knows my mom knows that she wasn't 'suggesting' I didn't eat it. She was *telling* me not to eat it."

Another time, when Tiffany's boyfriend broke up with her, Tiffany's mother said to her "in all sincerity" that it happened "because my friend was thinner than me, and it would continue to happen if I didn't lose weight." At the time, Tiffany was a size 12.

Because Tiffany was privy to the legacy that her mom was trying to protect her from, she never faulted her mom for her obsession with weight, dieting and body image. She rose above it. Ironically, it was her mother's obsession with weight that propelled Tiffany to pursue modeling and pageantry and start a mentoring program. "I believe that understanding my mother's pain as an overweight child has helped me become steadfast in my advocacy for empowering plus-size girls and women," she told me. Tiffany was determined to break the cycle and channel her desire for positive body esteem into helping girls learn that all sizes are beautiful and worthy, including her own. "The first time she saw me modeling was on a television series more than a year after I started," Tiffany recalled. "I was standing on the beach in a white bra and panties at 270 pounds. I was more nervous about how she would feel about it than doing the actual job. The first words out of her mouth were, 'Oh my goodness, you looked so beautiful.'"

Tiffany, her voice quickening, told me about the pride her mother, a teacher, felt the very first time she picked up a copy of a magazine that Tiffany was featured in. "She takes every opportunity she can to show her colleagues and students the work that I do," she said. "Often, she tells me that she admires my confidence and my ability to be a role model for young girls and women. I'm grateful that I was able to recognize that the things my mom said when I was growing up weren't to hurt me and that it was just her way of keeping other people from hurting me. I was able to stop the cycle of emotional scars."

Commandment #7:

I use my time constructively and participate in activities that contribute to my mental and physical well-being and/or the well-being of others.

Assets: Constructive Use of Time, Sports, Alternative Activities for Girls, Volunteerism/Contribution to Community

I have the right to:
- Spend time developing my skills and interests.
- Develop mature peer relationships based on commonalities, rather than school "rules" and clique mandates.
- Try new things that challenge me.
- Expose myself to new opportunities.
- Have a home away from home.

Drama. Scouting. Sports. Volunteering. When Asset Girls participate in activities that build on their passion, or "SPARK," it opens up their world and their sense of themselves. Many sports-related activities, due to their countercultural nature, are especially meaningful to girls as they challenge and build a sense of independence, strength, competitive spirit and clear, direct communication skills.

After dabbling in soccer, basketball and other "traditional" sports as an "avid benchwarmer," Lizzie Hickey, age eighteen, a "bit of a hippie" girl with a strong, muscular body, found the perfect fit with lacrosse. "Everyone started on the same level, and whoever worked the hardest got the best results," she said. "I used to go home from practice and throw the ball against a wall for hours, just catching and throwing. I gained confidence in my play, came out as one of the lead scorers my senior year and got lacrosse MVP and most improved player."

In particular, activities typically seen as "boy sports," such as lacrosse, basketball, soccer and martial arts, can bring out the best in girls of any size. Why?

→ **The uniform.** Basketball and martial arts uniforms, no matter what their school color, are typically loose-fitting and practical, rather than revealing and tight, and they look the same regardless of the child's gender.

→ **Judgment.** High scores are based on technical points and domination. Winners can be tall and thin or short and stout.

→ **Ranking.** The martial arts ranking system is typically unrelated to competition or winning. Everyone can be "tied for first" in that no one has to lose in order for a girl to win. Girls can achieve black belt status (and beyond) even if they're not "perfect."

→ **Physical confidence.** There's nothing particularly "ladylike" about martial arts, lacrosse, kicking a ball or dribbling down the court. These activities give girls permission to be powerful, to exert dominance, to sweat and even to release aggression.

→ **Character education.** At a time when many school systems are having to cut out moral education from their lesson plans and families with two working parents barely have time to ensure that dinner's on the table, some activities, like martial arts, are picking up the slack. Conversations with instructors or coaches give girls the opportunity to speak up, speak their mind and connect with different adults.

For Lindsey Adelstein, age sixteen, it wasn't just the physicality of her athletic outlet that inspired her to feel valuable and constructive. As part of the requirements for her black belt in martial arts, Lindsey was asked to lead a community service project—a lesson that being a black belt meant much more than achieving physically. Lindsey organized a contingent of twenty people and "cleaned up" a public area—planting flowers, placing pumpkins, cornstalks and haystacks and disposing of litter. "I was very nervous about the project," said Lindsey, who says she still feels the same "rush" of energy practicing martial arts as when she first began. "But when we were finished, I beamed with pride."

> ## "Overheard"
>
> *"There's something very comforting about your daughter being so skilled in martial arts that she can put a 200-pound man on his butt."*
>
> Ruth, mother of Abby, age fourteen, both martial artists

At the tender age of sixteen, Lexi Lorch was telling me how much she's "grown over the last few years" and how she's "happy with who she is now" with a maturity that most people lack when they enter their thirties. Although her voice was unmistakably young and high-pitched, she spoke in the experienced tones of a sage: "Every girl goes through a tough time where they ask themselves, 'Do I like who I am?' I went through that. Over time, I learned to look at everything as a gift."

With a mom in a nontraditional role as a firefighter and a father who was diagnosed thirteen years ago with multiple sclerosis (MS), Lexi's idea of body expectations and limitations were flipped on their ear. "My mom always tells my sister and me that we can move mountains, and I believe her—you don't see many 5-foot-1 female firefighters, but she can do it, and it lets me know that I can, too," Lexi said. "And my dad was a huge cyclist before he had MS. He used to ride a tandem with a man who was blind and needed someone to lead him. I think that provided inspiration for me. Whenever my dad is going through a hard time with his MS, and he can't ride a bike like he used to, I think, 'I'm gonna ride the bike...for him.' I thought of that idea and ran with it."

Commandment #8:
I believe in my own power to affect my world and take action on something that is important.

Assets: Personal Power, Sense of Purpose and Initiative

I have the right to:
- My own opinion.
- Make my own choices.
- Stand up for what I believe.
- Dream, hope and plan.
- Believe that I can make a difference.

Two summers ago, Lexi "rode her bike for MS." I was picturing a big bike ride with hundreds of people. Nope. Just Lexi and one of her best friends, Hannah. She came home one day and just "decided" to organize a thirteen-day bike ride around Indiana to raise money for MS. "I wanted to do one day for every year since my father had been diagnosed with MS," she said.

Lexi and her younger sister, Kenzie, mapped out thirteen towns in which various MS patients lived who would allow her to camp in their backyards overnight. "The whole idea behind it was to connect all of these people to show that we are stronger and bigger than this disease," she said. "For each family I stayed with, I tried to do something to help them out, whether it be cleaning, pulling weeds or whatever, and then interviewed them on their life with MS—when they were diagnosed, what therapies they were on, how they live with it every day."

On the seventh day, the girls camped in the backyard of Lexi's house. Lexi split the backyard into even squares and "sold" each plot to families who wanted to join her on her crusade and camp with her that night to promote a sense of solidarity; more than 150 people camped out in her backyard. They decorated their tents, each with a different theme: Hawaiian, carnival. They set up a campfire, talked, laughed and sang.

"It sounds lovely," I said, imagining the camaraderie among all the participants.

"It was, but the next three days proved the toughest of all. By then, I was mentally and physically exhausted," she said. "By day 10, I was just like, 'Is this really helping anyone? Or am I just camping every night and riding seven hundred miles just for myself?' But I didn't give up, and we raised $7,000 for the National MS Society."

Lexi plans to write a book about her experience, based on the interviews she conducted, that "will go in doctors' offices and other places for people who are newly diagnosed for them to read and learn about MS," she said. She's already spoken in front of hundreds of adults and children as part of the MS Society's National Conference and Tour of Champions—teaching others how to take the initiative to raise money for a cause they all hold so dear. "It may sound funny, because I'm sixteen and I'm not, like, Oprah, but you don't have to feed all of Africa to change the world. You can change the life of one person, and that person can help the next and the next, like a chain. We all have the ability to change the world. It just depends on what we choose to act on and how we choose to act on it."

"I knew I could do the dance."

Kacie had taken dance lessons for thirteen years and was preparing a group hip-hop routine when her teacher called a meeting with her and her mother. "My teacher said she 'loved' me, but that I shouldn't do the competition, because 'I think you'll get hurt.' I was in shock," Kacie said. "The costumes had already been ordered. I had been practicing with everyone else. I had my part. I had worked hard. I think she was just making excuses, because she wanted a gold medal and apparently my presence would prevent her from getting it. Well, that was when my mom had it. She said, 'That's discrimination!' Things suddenly changed when my mom said that word. Then my teacher said I could do it...if I promised to lose weight."

These are the kinds of situations that "break" girls and their spirits. But not Kacie.

"I didn't lose weight. I danced in the competition, and I would be lying if I said my determination wasn't driven partly by spite," Kacie said. "This had nothing to do with dancing skill. There was never a situation that I felt that I wouldn't do my best.

ASSET-BUILDING BLOCK: THE 5 WHYS

I did this exercise with Lexi. It explores the real purpose behind one's actions. Compare your daughter's answers to Lexi's and those of another girl I interviewed, Marla, whose "desperate purpose" was to lose weight.

Question: "Lexi, why did you do the thirteen-day bike challenge?"

WHY 1: "Because it's a challenge for myself, and I wanted to do something that other people can't do that can help other people."

WHY 2: "Because there's just something in me that makes me want to help others."

WHY 3: "Because if you have the ability to do something, you should do it."

WHY 4: "Because it makes people happy when you can help them and it makes me feel happy inside, too."

WHY 5: "Because we were all put on this earth to help each other, and I need to do my part."

Conclusion: With each progressive "why," Lexi shows a deeper and deeper sense of purpose that drives her behavior. Motivated by a strong sense of community, a positive view of the future, a staggering amount of personal power and inspiring adult mentors, she, herself, became an inspiration.

Question: "Marla, why do you want to lose weight?"

WHY 1: "Because I want to be thinner."

WHY 2: "Because I think I'll look hotter."

WHY 3: "Because nobody likes extra flab on them."

WHY 4: "Because fat is ugly."

WHY 5: "Because it looks bad and makes people think you're lazy and stupid, even if you're not."

Conclusion: For Marla, each progressive "why" is simply another opportunity for destructive body bashing. She is concerned only with the way she looks and what other people think. No purpose. No personal power. Just disgust.

Commandment #9:

I believe in my competencies and self-worth, and refuse to allow negative feedback to derail me.

Assets: Competencies (physical, cognitive, social), Positive Attitude, Self-worth, Leadership

I have the right to:
- Build and refine my skills to make myself stronger mentally and physically.
- Stake more importance on my skills than on my appearance.
- Disallow anyone to define me by my weight.
- Share my many gifts with the world.
- Step up and take leadership positions in the areas in which I'm skilled.

Yes, I couldn't do a split, but neither could the tiniest girl. I needed to eliminate any doubt by going out on that stage and performing the dance and proving my capabilities."

"How were you able to do that?" I asked, baffled at her ability to regroup and rise to the occasion.

"Because I've made it a point to never allow anyone to put up a wall so high that I can't get over it."

Meet Kacie Conlon. Age eighteen. Size 18. President of her student body. Popular. By her own definition: "Loud. Outgoing. Open-minded. Driven. Motivated. Fun." We met at a restaurant near her home in a suburb outside of Boston. When she arrived, I recognized her immediately from her Facebook photos: brown medium-length hair, round face, kind eyes, a dimple in her right cheek, a girl who was front and center in pictures from the senior prom—thirty friends all smooshed together, including her date.

"I am outrageously outgoing," Kacie said as she smiled widely. "If someone decides to limit her interactions with me because of my physical appearance, I don't need her friendship. I don't like shallow people. It's an awful quality in a person. They truly are doing me a favor by not bringing that unnecessary drama into my life."

It would be inaccurate to say that Kacie's parents and friends are not worried about her weight—there is a history of heart-related illness in her family (her uncle died of heart failure), but they address it as only one aspect of any otherwise extraordinary girl. "I want Kacie to lose weight, but not because I am embarrassed by her, or anything like that," Kacie's best friend, Lizzie, told me. "I want Kacie to lose weight to be healthier. I love and care for her so much, and I worry about the complications that come with how big she is. She is a beautiful person, and I want to keep her that way."

"I can try to change my physical appearance as much as I want, but I still feel that who I am and what I accomplish are something to be proud of," Kacie said. "I don't need to focus on my imperfections but on how I can help others. I know that I go above and beyond in everything I do. It's just something inside of me. I see myself differently than other people when they look at me. But who cares? Project yourself as you want others to see you, and project that inward, so that you believe it, too."

Commandment #10:

I allow my positive values to guide my thoughts and behavior, rather than doing what's popular or easy.

Assets: Values, Authenticity, Caring, Character

I have the right to:
- Brainstorm.
- Make decisions based on my values.
- Think for myself, without the influence of others.
- Remain true to what is meaningful to me.
- Guard myself against those who try to compromise my values.

"This is definitely a sore subject for me."

Cati Grant, a 5-foot-9½-inch junior in high school, spent most of her life as a competitive cheerleader, so body image was perpetually at the forefront of her mind. "People said it all the time—nobody likes a fat cheerleader," she said convincingly.

By "people," she actually meant "person," one person—a "former friend" and cheerleader who, in sixth grade, accused Cati of stealing a portable gaming system. "I never did steal it, but she would never let it go," Cati told me. She called Cati a thief. A snitch. The bullying escalated to cyberbullying, attacks on her appearance, even death threats:

> UR KINDA UGLY AS F***. GROW SOME BOOBS. U SHOULD PRETTY MUCH DIE. NO ONE WOULD CARE OR MISS U. FUGLYASSBITCHH

"It was like an avalanche," Cati said. "It changed my life forever."

The following year, as the girls moved into middle school, the bully kept it up, despite warnings from the school administration, and the bullying continued for the next several years, into Cati's first year of high school. "I was sick and tired of being bullied and treated badly for nothing I did wrong—and for my body type was even worse," Cati said.

For her fifteenth birthday, Cati asked her parents to fund a website to start a movement of teens caring, and CatiCares.com was born. "Being authentic definitely does not make for being popular in middle school or early in my high school career," said Cati. "But I am who I am, and I have become confident about being me, my size and my values."

CatiCares.com educates teens about bullying and cyberbullying in an effort to prevent it from happening to anyone else. To help spread the word, she even convinced her parents to spend a summer vacation touring America—fifty cities in eight days. "One of my favorite sayings is 'Handle with care,'" said Cati, who was named a Teen Ambassador for Love Our Children USA's STOMP Out Bullying campaign and was a featured teen speaker at Kids Are Heroes Day in Maryland, based on the caliber of her work. "What if we started our day with that saying? What if we handled everything with care? What a different kind of day most of us would have."

ASSET-BUILDING BLOCK:
THE GIRL I REALLY AM

A favorite among my Sassy Sisterhood groups, "The Girl I Really Am" is inspired by an exercise mentioned in facilitator training for Girls Circle, a leading provider of gender-specific, research-based programs for girls, some mask-making tips from community artist Maggie Sherman and my own research on authenticity. It is quite simple and fun and can be a shared activity among family members and friends.

Supplies:

→ A mask (some years we made them out of plaster of paris; other years I bought plain white masks from a craft store)

→ Paints, feathers, ribbons, glitter glue, buttons, patches, alphabet stickers and other scrapbook supplies in an assortment of colors

To start, ask your daughter to paint and decorate the outside of the mask as the face she shows to others, using the following color chart:

→ **Red:** danger, boldness, excitement, strength, desire, courage
→ **Orange:** cheerfulness, enthusiasm, creativity
→ **Yellow:** cowardliness, hunger
→ **Green:** reliability, optimism, calm
→ **Blue:** loyalty, honor, trust
→ **Purple:** power, elegance, sophistication
→ **Gray:** dull, uninteresting
→ **Brown:** confident, casual, earthy, genuine
→ **Black:** power, strength
→ **White:** cleanliness, purity, innocence

Once that dries, have her paint and decorate the inside of the mask in a way that represents the girl she "really" is. Afterward, discuss the end result:

→ What does the outside of the mask say about who you show to the world?

→ What does the inside of the mask tell you about who you really are?

→ How much overlap is there between the inside and the outside of the mask?

→ What blocks you from showing these parts of yourself to others?

→ How can we become more authentic?

Seeing the congruency of the inside and outside masks is a commentary on the girls' ability to be authentic.

As your daughter learns to follow these commandments as well as others that are most important to her and your family, understand that she may waver at times. Fat talk can sometimes overtake positive self-talk. Predictable friendship scripts can counter assertiveness. Goal-setting and risk-taking can be precluded by self-doubt. You, however, must be consistent. The key to an authentic life is a process, not a prescription. Every misstep, every hesitation, represents a chance for her to grow and move forward.

Assets at a Glance

Commandment #1: She knows how she feels and can express her emotions in a healthy, productive way.

Assets: Emotional Intelligence and Assertiveness

Commandment #2: She takes healthy risks and is accountable for her actions.

Assets: Courage, Positive Risk-taking and Accountability

Commandment #3: She sets and pursues goals to create the future she wants.

Assets: Goal-setting, Expectations, Initiative and a Positive View of the Future

Commandment #4: She sees her body and herself in a positive light and speaks to herself accordingly.

Assets: Body Image, Self-esteem, Positive Self-talk

Commandment #5: She surrounds herself with and is surrounded by positive, encouraging, supportive adults who serve as role models and peers who share her values.

Assets: Positive, Supportive Adults; Role Models; Positive Peer Groups

Commandment #6: She is aware and critical of the messages she receives about thinness and keeps a healthy perspective on how she fits within those parameters.

Assets: Media Literacy and Perspective

Commandment #7: She uses her time constructively and participates in activities that contribute to her mental and physical well-being and/or the well-being of others.

Assets: Constructive Use of Time, Sports, Alternative Activities for Girls, Volunteerism/Contribution to Community

Commandment #8: She believes in her own power to affect her world and takes action on something that is important.

Assets: Personal Power, Sense of Purpose and Initiative

Commandment #9: She believes in her competencies and self-worth and refuses to allow negative feedback to derail her.

Assets: Competencies (physical, cognitive, social), Positive Attitude, Self-worth, Leadership

Commandment #10: She allows her positive values to guide her thoughts and behavior, rather than doing what's popular or easy.

Assets: Values, Authenticity, Caring, Character

BIQ:
Is Your Daughter an Asset Girl?

Check "yes" or "no," depending on which describes your daughter most of the time.

Commandment #1: She knows how she feels and can express her emotions in a healthy, productive way.

Yes: ___ **No:** ___

Commandment #2: She takes healthy risks and is accountable for her actions.

Yes: ___ **No:** ___

Commandment #3: She sets and pursues goals to create the future she wants.

Yes: ___ **No:** ___

Commandment #4: She sees her body and herself in a positive light and speaks to herself accordingly.

Yes: ___ **No:** ___

Commandment #5: She surrounds herself with and is surrounded by positive, encouraging, supportive adults who serve as role models and peers who share her values.

Yes: ___ **No:** ___

Commandment #6: She is aware and critical of the messages she receives about thinness and keeps a healthy perspective on how she fits within those parameters.

Yes: ___ **No:** ___

Commandment #7: She uses her time constructively and participates in activities that contribute to her mental and physical well-being and/or the well-being of others.

Yes: ___ **No:** ___

Commandment #8: She believes in her own power to affect her world and takes action on something that is important.

Yes: ___ **No:** ___

Commandment #9: She believes in her competencies and self-worth and refuses to allow negative feedback to derail her.

Yes: ___ **No:** ___

Commandment #10: She allows her positive values to guide her thoughts and behavior, rather than doing what's popular or easy.

Yes: ___ **No:** ___

Total number of:

YES's 1 point each	**NO's** 2 points each	**Total** BIQ score for Chapter 7

Chapter 8

Your Daughter's BIQ
(Body Image Quotient):
What's Her Total?

Throughout this book, you have answered questions about your daughter based on your knowledge and experience as her parent/guardian. Before we move on to the final chapter, let's total up her score and find out where she stands:

Totals:

Chapter 1: _____

Chapter 2: _____

Chapter 3: _____

Chapter 4: _____

Chapter 5: _____

Chapter 6: _____

Chapter 7: _____

Total BIQ Score: _____

Body Confident: 81–100 Points

Congratulations! Your daughter is confident in her appearance and body size. When she looks in the mirror, she is complimentary about herself. She's not afraid to stand up for herself. Her friends are not obsessive about weight, she feels her teachers treat her fairly and she feels that her family is supportive and responsive.

Your daughter has a healthy skepticism about the thin ideal she sees on TV, in magazines and in the electronic media. She has a wide-ranging definition of beauty and believes that people should not use weight loss or surgery as a way to ensure happiness.

When you look at the commandments and list of assets in Chapter 7 that help girls thrive, she has many of them. She is courageous, confident and connected. She not only has "SPARK" but has put that passion into action and has the support and encouragement she needs to nurture it. Even on days when things are not "perfect," she has an inner calm and truly seems to be fulfilled.

Your goal for her is to maintain her healthy body image, even if you see her as "overweight," and you need to help her stay balanced and levelheaded. It's normal to want her to make improvements in herself and become more skillful in certain areas, so that she may achieve her dreams. Allow her to challenge herself by trying out various ways to express and address different assets that lead to an even stronger expression of the Asset Girl commandments. She may make mistakes along the way, but since she's already proven that she has the inner resources to take healthy risks and bounce back from negative feedback, you can rest assured that she will eventually succeed with perseverance. And, with you as her primary support, she has a safe place to fall, rest and regroup if and when she needs it. Then, she's sure to be well on her way, stronger and more powerful than ever.

Body Moderate: 51–80 Points

Your daughter is generally happy about her body. Occasionally, she may adjust her eating habits in order to make herself feel more attractive—she might even catch herself being a body bully—but, on most days, she does not tend to overfocus on her flaws.

Neither your daughter nor most of her friends tend to obsess about their appearance, although they may occasionally compare themselves to others and wish their bodies looked different. Your daughter feels that people may judge her unfairly sometimes, but she knows she has good friends who will value and like her for who she is.

When you gauge her assets, you see that there are some gaps that need attention—areas that may be completely lacking or are simply underdeveloped, such as social support, identity development or the way she spends her time. These are all issues that can be addressed with some persistence and consistency.

Your daughter may be getting some negative messages from you, other family members or friends about the importance of appearance over character, and she, like many girls, may be vulnerable to society's pressures. Use the Asset-Building Block Exercise at the end of this chapter to help her build on her strengths rather than her flaws.

Body Insecure: 30–50 Points

Your daughter seems to suffer from a negative body image and possibly low self-worth. She compares herself to others and feels that she comes up short. As her own body bully, she's often upset by what she sees in the mirror. Skinny celebrities, friends and peers make her feel inadequate, and she believes that being thin would make her happier. When she enters a room, she often worries that she will be teased about or judged on her appearance. She changes the way she eats around certain people, because she feels uncomfortable. She socializes with friends who also obsess about their weight and body size.

Your daughter may perceive you, the parent/guardian, as someone who feels that dieting is necessary to be beautiful. In looking at the assets we've discussed, you notice that she needs support and development in many or most areas. You see glimmers of strength, but they are often tainted with self-doubt and body-bashing thoughts.

The good news is that it's never too late for your daughter to hone her Ten Commandments and become an Asset Girl. She has great potential, and now's the time to set her on a healthy course. Poor body image can put your daughter at risk for a host of problems, including eating disorders and depression. If you believe that she may be at risk, seek medical assistance from a qualified psychologist, coach or specialist.

As parents/guardians, we need to take some purposeful steps to ensure the health and well-being of our daughters. We can't just hope for the best. Read through your scores, and take note of the influencers and issues that need your attention. What adjustments must be made? What strengths, skills or support systems does your daughter need to develop? Then take a cue from our previous chapters, and plan a course of action and accountability that not only reduces your daughter's exposure to deficit-inducing body bullies and negative messages but also builds on her assets.

Asset-Building Block: Asset Girls for Life

Make a list of any areas you want to address with your daughter and the skills or assets that she is lacking (keep in mind that you may need to work on or change some of these areas in yourself, too). For each area of concern or asset that needs support, go through this series of self-questioning:

> **Target issue/area of concern.**
> **Target commandment(s).**
> **Target asset/strength/skill.**
> → What are you going to do?
> → When are you going to do it?
> → Who will be the accountability partner (AP)?
> → How will you inform the AP that you've completed your task?

For example:

> **Target issue/area of concern:** My daughter lacks confidence and doesn't fight back when her friends pick on her.
> **Target commandment(s):** #1, #2, #10.
> **Target asset/strength/skill:** Self-esteem, personal power, courage, assertiveness.
> → What are you going to do? Talk to my daughter about signing up for martial arts or another sport that can serve as a physical outlet, social

opportunity and confidence skill-building activity, and then sign her up once a decision is made.

→ When are you going to do it? By the end of breakfast tomorrow, I will have an answer from her, and we will sign her up together after school.

→ Who will be her AP? My best friend, Cheryl, who is currently looking over my shoulder as I write this.

→ How will you inform her? I will text her after breakfast and follow up again after we sign my daughter up after school.

I would also like to offer myself as an accountability partner. Write to me on my website, DrRobynSilverman.com, and while you're there, download a free digital discussion guide, titled "Dr. Robyn's Body Image Conversation Starters," which provides specific questions and exercises to get you and your girls talking.

Feel free to also contact me through any of the following social networks:

- Facebook.com/DrRobynSilverman
- Twitter.com/DrRobyn
- YouTube.com/DrRobynSilverman
- LinkedIn.com/in/DrRobyn

Tell me your accountability plan and how you've followed through with it. Or ask me how to get started. I'm rooting for you, and other parents you'll meet through one of my coaching or online groups are rooting for you, too. We're all in this together.

Chapter 9

Goodbye, Good Girl.
Hello, Asset Girl!

I wish I could say there's a secret formula to raising a girl with a healthy attitude. I can't. But what I can say is that those girls who see themselves in terms of strengths, who feel supported by those they love and have come to a place of acceptance about their bodies, are the ones who flourish. Their "SPARK" takes on a life of its own.

I feel privileged to have seen this happen, to watch girls break free of the confines of "good" and claim the boundless opportunities afforded by their personal power. At first, my Sassy Girls are timid when it comes to sharing, are reluctant to take risks, have trouble opening up. As the weeks and months pass, lightbulbs go off. Postures straighten. Laughs get louder. Emotions swell from contained, awkward giggles to passionate, lively shouts: "Her legs were 'shopped'!" "Nobody's body looks like that!" "My mom was wrong!" "My mom was right!" And, to my greatest satisfaction, "I am beautiful just the way I am!" Within

> ## "Overheard"
>
> *"When I look in the mirror now, I see a girl who is going places. When you finally see all the great stuff other people see—not what you think they should see, but what they really see—you realize, 'Who am I to say no?' You realize, 'I can be anything, so I might as well be the best version of me there is.'"*
>
> Dominique Delprete, an original Sassy Girl

a safe, supportive haven that challenges what limits them, these girls suddenly have trouble "shutting up." They are fiery, alive—some of them for the first time in their lives.

The way I see it, you have a choice. You can jump on society's bandwagon and tell your daughter that she needs to lose weight to be acceptable, successful, happy, loved and "good." Or you can focus on her strengths and surround her with people who do the same thing. That means shoving aside your feelings about weight and helping your daughter feel healthy, beautiful and full of potential, no matter what her size. She needs you to be her positive power voice until she can find her own.

While this book has come to an end, our time together is just beginning. I anticipate working with many of you in coaching groups, mother–daughter days, father–daughter days, teleseminars, blog debates and webinars on DrRobynSilverman.com as we figure out how all this information relates to you and the girls in your life.

You're not alone. Help is all around you. Following this parting note, I've included my "Big Black Book," my personal resource list of companies, organizations, websites and more that promote positive, healthy, powerful living in girls. These links, along with many others, exist on a special "asset-building" resource center on my website as well. There are many amazing people working on behalf of your daughter and her well-being who would be excited to be a part of your support team.

As we charge forward, get your daughter out there—doing, becoming, *being*—in whatever way you can. Together, we can inspire her to develop her assets. Together, we can help her thrive. And, if we choose to pay attention, she'll surely teach us a thing or two about what's really beautiful.

Dr. Robyn's Big Black Book of Asset Builders

Best Blogs/Communities for Raising Confident Girls

5 Resolutions: 5resolutions.blogspot.com

DadsandDaughters.com

Daughters.com

DrRobynSilverman.com

TheGirlRevolution.com

HangProud.com

JessWeiner.com

KathleenHassan.com

TheMother-DaughterProject.com

RachelSimmons.com

Raising Smart Girls: Raisingsmartgirls.wordpress.com

RealBeautyIs.com

RespectRx.com

RosalindWiseman.com

ShapingYouth.org

Smart Girls Fun: Smartgirlsfun.blogspot.com/

SmartGirlsKnow.com

We Are the Real Deal: Watrd.wordpress.com

WhatAboutOurDaughters.com

Girls as Change Agents and "Cyclebreakers"

4GGL.org

AAUW.org (formerly known as the American Association of
   University Women)

BodyImageProject.com

CampaignForRealBeauty.com

TheGirlEffect.org

GirlsForAChange.org

Girls Helping Girls: Empoweragirl.org

GirlsLeadershipInstitute.org

GirlsLeadNow.org

Nike GameChangers: Nike.com/gamechangers/

OperationBeautiful.com

RadicalParenting.com

WhatAboutOurDaughters.com

WomenTalkSports.com

Girls' Workshops/Programs/Curriculum

About-Face.org

Any-Body.org

Dove Self-Esteem Workshops: Dove.com

The F Word: The-f-word.org/blog

Full of Ourselves: Amazon.com & CatherineSteinerAdair.com

G.E.M.S.: Gemsgirl.com

Genaustin.org

GirlsEmpowered.com

HeyUgly.org

JEWELS: Jewelsgirl.com

JustThink.org

Opheliaproject.com

Owning Up: RosalindWiseman.com

ParentingTeenGirls.com

RespectRx.com

Salvaging Sisterhood: Amazon.com

Sassy Sisterhood: DrRobynSilverman.com

Step Up Women: suwn.org

Transforming Girls & Women into Powerful Actionists: DrRobynSilverman.com

TrueChild.org

Uniquely Me: GirlScouts.org (a Girl Scouts/Dove Self-Esteem Fund joint program)

Books That Give Girls a Jolt of Inspiration

The 7 Habits of Highly Effective Teens by Steven Covey

113 Things to Do by 13 by Brittany and Terri MacLeod

All Made Up: A Girl's Guide to Seeing Through Celebrity Hype to Celebrate Real Beauty by Audrey Brashich

Feel Good, Girl! by Felicia Richardson-Battle

Girls Inc. Presents You're Amazing: A No-Pressure Guide to Being Your Best Self by Claire Mysko

GirlWise: How to Be Confident, Capable, Cool, and in Control by Julia DeVillers

Girl Zines: Making Media, Doing Feminism by Alison Piepmeier

How I Look Journal by Molly and Nan Dellheim

Kiss My Math: Showing Pre-Algebra Who's Boss by Danica McKellar

Math Doesn't Suck: How to Survive Middle School Math Without Losing Your Mind or Breaking a Nail by Danica McKellar

Rock 'n' Roll Camp for Girls, The Book: How to Start a Band, Write Songs, Record an Album, and Rock Out! edited by Marisa Anderson

Strong, Beautiful Girls series (Abdo Publishing)

By Girls for Girls (online communities/e-zines)

General

AGirlsWorld.com

AllyKatzz.com

ChicaCircle.com

GirlsAllowed.org

New Moon Girls: NewMoon.com

TeenInk.com

TeenLit.com

TeenVoices.com

Specific

EngineerYourLife.org

Girls@Play: Caaws.ca/girlsatplay/

GirlsHorseClub.com

GirlsMakeMedia.org

GirlsWriteNow.org

GoGirlsMusic.com

IndieGrrl.com

Nerdgirls.com

ReaderGirlz.com

Reelgrrls.org

WomenTalkSports.com

WriteGirl.org

Encouraging Science, Technology, Engineering and Math (STEM) Competencies

Girls

BinaryGirl.com

BrainCake.org

DigiGirlz: Microsoft.com/about/diversity/programs/digigirlz/
default.aspx

Digital-Sistas.org

EngineerGirl.org

GirlGeeks.org

GirlsAreIt.org

GirlsInTech.net

GirlsGoTech.org

GirlStart.org

MathDoesntSuck.com

ZoeysRoom.com

Women

Center for Women and Information Technology: Umbc.edu/cwit/

FemaleScienceProfessor: http://science-professor.blogspot.com/

IEEE Women in Engineering (WIE): Ieee.org/web/membership/
women/index.html

Inspirational Women from WISE: http://www.wisecampaign.org.uk

Junkfood Science: http://junkfoodscience.blogspot.com

NASA Quest: Women of NASA: Quest.nasa.gov/women/WON.html

Women's Work: Wwork.com

Positive Movies and Media for Girls and Teen Girls

Akeelah and the Bee (2006)

An American Girl: Chrissa Stands Strong (2009) (and other
American Girl movies)

Anne of Green Gables (1985)

Bend It Like Beckham (2002)

Circle of Friends (1995)

Fly Away Home (1996)

Girls Rock! The Movie: girlsrockmovie.com

Gracie (2007)

Hairspray (2007)

A League of Their Own (1992)

Little Women (1949, 1994)

Mean Girls (2004)

Million Dollar Baby (2004)

Mona Lisa Smile (2003)

Odd Girl Out (Lifetime, 2005)

Real Women Have Curves (2002)

The Sisterhood of the Traveling Pants (2005)

The Sisterhood of the Traveling Pants 2 (2008)

Steel Magnolias (1989)

Thelma & Louise (1991)

Best Bet Positive-Message Clothes/Products for Girls

Products

Beaconstreetgirls.com (books/products)

Girls Are Not Chicks coloring book: GirlsNotChicks.com

GirlTech.com (8–12/tween products via Mattel)

NewLeafTouchStone.com (bracelets/inspiration)

Self-Esteem Passport: Odt.org/SelfEsteemPassport.htm

SmartGirlsRock.com

StickerSisters.com

Ugogrl.com (trading cards)

Clothing

AvasCloset.net

Design-It.com

EmotionalArmor.com

GirlMogul.com

Girls Can: Printfection.com/GirlsCan

GirlsCantWhat.com

Gis4Girl.com

JordannsPositive.com

MindCandyClothing.com

OneAngryGirl.net

OneBrownGirl.com

PigtailPals.com

PinkStinks.co.uk

Girl Specific: Advocacy Orgs/Empowerment
Big and Bold
GirlsCircle.com

GirlScouts.org

GirlsInc.org

GirlsHealth.gov

Go Girls: Nationaleatingdisorders.org

National Coalition of Girls Schools: Ncgs.org/

National Council for Research on Women: Ncrw.org

ParentingPink.com

TitleIX.info

TheWhiteHouseProject.org

WomensSportsFoundation.org/GoGirlGo

Small and Mighty
BodyImageHealth.org

Daughters.com

EducatingJane.com

EmpowerGirls.com

Hardy Girls, Healthy Women: Hghw.org/

In Her Image: Juliabarry.com/inherimage/

Girls Helping Girls: EmpoweraGirl.org

GirlsInTech.net

GirlsLeadershipInstitute.org

GirlsMatter.com

GirlsOnTheRun.org

GirlStart.org

GirlZone.com

Gurl.com

HelpingOurTeenGirls.org (HOTGIRLS)

Opheliasvoice.org

PlusTeenUSA.com

RespectRx.com

The Role Model Project: Womenswork.org/girls/index.html

SallyRideScience.com

Sassy Sisterhood: DrRobynSilverman.com

SeeJaneWin.com

Best Bet Stores for Plus-Size Girls

Ashley Stewart

Avenue

ElegantPlus.com

Fashion Bug

Forever 21

Hot Topic

Kohl's

MarieDenee.com

Maurice

Old Navy

Rainbow

Target

Torrid

Wal-Mart

> ## "Overheard"
>
> *"Keep an eye out in your local paper for Fashion Bug, Lane Bryant, Ashley Stewart, Torrid and Avenue, all of which have fashion shows from time to time that use volunteer models from the community, especially around the back-to-school and holiday season."*
>
> Thea Politis, *Elegant Plus* magazine

Best Bet Plus-Size Fashion in Magazines

Bombshell

Bust

Elegant Plus

Figure

Glamour

Phatabulous

Plus Model

Skorch

> ## "Overheard"
>
> *"Help your daughter identify what kind of style she wants to embrace. Is she romantic? Modern? Country? Call stores, and have them pull some outfits in her size that capture her style of interest."*
>
> Catherine Schuller, plus-size stylist and former plus-size model

Great Books about "Growing Up Girl"

12 Going on 29 by Silvana and Sondra Clark

101 Ways to Help Your Daughter Love Her Body by Brenda Lane Richardson and Elane Rehr

Between Fathers and Daughters by Linda Nielsen

Body Drama: Real Girls, Real Bodies, Real Issues, Real Answers by Nancy Redd

Body Outlaws (Ophira Edut; anthology via AdiosBarbie.com creators)

The Curse of the Good Girl by Rachel Simmons

Dealing with the Stuff That Makes Life Tough: The 10 Things That Stress Teen Girls Out and How to Cope with Them by Jill Zimmerman Rutledge

Fat Talk by Mimi Nichter

Father Hunger by Margo Maine

Girlfighting by Lyn Mikel Brown

Girl in the Mirror by Dr. Nancy Snyderman

Lessons from the Fat-o-Sphere: Quit Dieting and Declare a Truce with Your Body by Kate Harding and Marianne Kirby

Life Doesn't Begin 5 Pounds from Now by Jessica Weiner

Life Without Ed by Jenni Schaefer

My Sister, My Self by Vikki Stark

No Body's Perfect by Kimberly Kirberger

Odd Girl Out by Rachel Simmons

Packaging Girlhood by Lyn Mikel Brown and Sharon Lamb

Perfect Girls, Starving Daughters by Courtney Martin

Queen Bees & Wannabes by Rosalind Wiseman

Raising Our Athletic Daughters: How Sports Can Build Self-Esteem and Save Girls' Lives by Jean Zimmerman

Real Gorgeous by Kaz Cooke

Reviving Ophelia by Mary Pipher

Schoolgirls by Peggy Orenstein

So Sexy So Soon: The New Sexualized Childhood and What Parents Can Do to Protect Their Kids by Diane E. Levin and Jean Kilbourne

Supergirls Speak Out by Liz Funk

You'd Be So Pretty If... by Dara Chadwick

Other Helpful Parenting Books:

The 7 Habits of Highly Effective Families by Stephen Covey

12 Simple Secrets Real Moms Know: Getting Back to Basics and Raising Happy Kids by Michele Borba

"Overheard"

"Diversity makes the world go round, and when it comes to our bodies, there's no question that the world is full of different shapes and sizes. The key is to accept your shape and learn to work it to your advantage. Very few people can wear every style, so don't get discouraged! Find clothes that feel good, are comfortable and are made with fabrics that embrace your curves."

Betsy McLaughlin, CEO, Hot Topic and Torrid

The Big Book of Parenting Solutions by Michele Borba

Confident Parents, Exceptional Teens by Ted Haggard and John Bolin

The Good Teen by Richard Lerner

Launching Your Teen into Adulthood: Parenting Through the Transition by Patricia Hoolihan

Live-Away Dads by William Klatte

Parenting Apart by Christina McGhee

Parenting Preteens with a Purpose by Kate Thomsen

Sparks by Peter Benson

Wit's End by Sue Scheff

Best Bet Children's Books on Body Image, Being Yourself

Belinda's Bouquet by Leslea Newman

Don't Pop My Bubble by Kimber Bishop Yanke

Feel Good, Girl! by Felicia Richardson-Battle

The Hundred Dresses by Eleanor Estes

I'm Gonna Like Me by Jamie Lee Curtis

Incredible Me! by Kathi Appelt

Perfectly You by Julia V. Taylor

Proud to Be You by Pamela Espeland and Elizabeth Verdick

Shapesville by Andy Mills, Becky Osborn and Erica Neitz

Square Peg, Round Hole by Kathleen Hassan and Dr. Robyn Silverman

Stand Tall, Molly Lou Melon by Patty Lovell

Teen Lit on Weight, Body Image and Eating Disorders

All About Vee by C. Leigh Purtill

Bathing Ugly by Rebecca Busselle

Beacon Hills High: A Novel by Mo'Nique and Sherri McGee McCovey

Beacon Street Girls: Lake Rescue by Annie Bryant

Fat Chance by Lesléa Newman

The Fat Girl by Marilyn Sachs

Fat Hoochie Prom Queen by Nico Medina

I Am an Artichoke by Lucy Frank

I Was a 15-Year-Old Blimp by Patti Stren

Life in the Fat Lane by Cherie Bennett

Looks by Madeleine George

Models Don't Eat Chocolate Cookies by Erin Dionne

My Big Fat Manifesto by Susan Vaught

One Fat Summer by Robert Lipsyte

Second Star to the Right by Deborah Hautzig

Secrets of Truth and Beauty by Megan Frazer

The Sisterhood of the Traveling Pants by Ann Brashares

Stick Figure: A Diary of My Former Self by Lori Gottlieb

This Book Isn't Fat, It's Fabulous by Nina Beck

Best Bet Magazines/Publications for Girls

GirlChildPress.com

Girls Can Do Anything: gcdamagazine.com

Justine

Latinitas: latinitasmagazine.org

New Moon

Teen Ink: TeenInk.com

Helpful Websites for Girls

CatiCares.com

Fem2pt0.com

HealthyWeight.net

HonorTheGirl.me

InsideBeauty.org

KidsAreHeroes.com

LoveYourBody.org

SmartGirl.org

StompOutBullying.org

TeensTurningGreen.org

WomensHealth.gov

Helpful Websites for Parents

AAP.org

American Library Association (ALA)/Young Adult Library
   Services Association (YALSA): http://ALA.org/ala/mgrps/divs/
   yalsa/yalsa.cfm

BAM! Body and Mind (Centers for Disease Control and
   Prevention [CDC]): bam.gov

Bullying.org

ChildhoodMatters.org

Eating Disorder Referral and Information Center:
   Edreferral.com

KidsHealth.org

MicheleBorba.com

NAAFA.org

NationalEatingDisorders.org

OurBodiesOurselves.org

PBS.org

Parents.com

ParentsJournal.com

SueScheff.com

UniteForChange.com

WomensHealth.gov

Best Bet Media Literacy Resources/Programs

AboutFace.org

Campaign for a Commercial Free Childhood:
  CommercialExploitation.org

ChildrenNow.org

CommonSenseMedia.org

FrankW.Baker.com

Geena Davis Institute on Gender in Media:
  thegeenadavisinstitute.org

Media Awareness Network: media-awareness.ca

MindOnTheMedia.org

MyPopStudio.com

ProjectGirl.org

ShapingYouth.org

TrueChild.org

WIMNonline.org

YouthMediaReporter.org

Youth Research

APA Taskforce/study: Apa.org/pi/wpo/sexualization.html

Gamine Expedition: Gamineexpedition.blogspot.com

MobileYouth.org

ReachStudents.co.uk

Search-Institute.org

Ypulse Research: research.ypulse.com/

Films, Documentaries, Books and Other Teaching Tools to Uncork Body Chats

America the Beautiful: http://americathebeautifuldoc.com

The Beauty Myth: How Images of Beauty Are Used Against Women by Naomi Wolf

The Body Project: An Intimate History of American Girls by Joan
Jacobs Brumberg

Cover Girl Culture: CoverGirlCulture.com

Dove videos: *Evolution, Onslaught, True Colors, Daughters*

Killing Us Softly (*1, 2, & 3*) series of films

Lauren Greenfield's faculty guide to *Girl Culture:*
CreativePhotography.org

Playing Unfair: The Media Image of the Female Athlete

Slim Hopes: Advertising & the Obsession with Thinness

This Is Who I Am: Our Beauty in All Shapes and Sizes by
Rosanne Olson

Tri Delta video: *Fat Talk Free Week*

Just for Mom (Support, Insight)

TheDreamingYou.com

FemaleScienceProfessor: Science-professor.blogspot.com/

Inspirational Women from WISE: Wisecampaign.org.uk

NASA Quest: Women of NASA: Quest.nasa.gov/women/WON.
html

NOW.org (National Organization for Women)

Revolution of Real Women: Revolutionofrealwomen.blogspot.com

Wise-Women.org

WomenInEngineering.org

Women on Fire: Beawomanonfire.com/

Women's Work: Wwork.com

References

Introduction

GirlGuiding Results. "19 out of 20 Young Women 'Would Change Bodies.'" *The Independent,* http://www.independent.co.uk/lifestyle/health-and-families/health-news/19-out-of-20-young-women-would-change-bodies-1813551.html (accessed November 3, 2009).

Girls Circle. http://www.girlscircle.com. (Note: The format of Sassy Sisterhood is partially based on Girls Circle, a well-researched program model for girls that has been shown to increase girls' self-efficacy, body image and social support.)

Puhl, R., and K. D. Brownell. "Bias, Discrimination and Obesity." *Obesity Research* 9 (2001): 788–805.

Schoenberg, Judy, ed., et al. Girl Scout Research Institute. *The New Normal? What Girls Say About Healthy Living.* New York: Girl Scouts of the USA, 2006.

Note: Since 2003, I've seen other "weight rules" developed for the purposes of discussion, including "The Thin Commandments" by Carolyn Costin, MA, MEd, MFT, clinical director of the Eating Disorder Center of the Monte Nido Treatment Center in California. "The Thin Commandments" have unfortunately been wrongly adopted by many "pro-ana" and "pro-mia" websites.

Chapter 1

ABC News. "Lawmakers Study Steroid Use Among Young Women," http://www.abcnews.go.com/GMA/story?id=850725&page=1&CMP=OTC-RSSFeeds0312 (accessed August 5, 2006).

Albright, J. M. "Impossible Bodies: TV Viewing Habits, Body Image and Plastic Surgery Attitudes among College Students in Los Angeles and Buffalo." *Configurations* 15 (2007): 103–23.

Altabe, M., and K. N. O'Garo. "Hispanic Body Images." In *Body Image: A Handbook of Theory, Research and Clinical Practice*. Edited by T. F. Cash and T. Pruzinsky. New York: Guilford Press, 2002.

American Association of University Women (AAUW). *Shortchanging Girls, Shortchanging America: A Call to Action.* Washington, D.C.: AAUW, 1991.

The American Society for Aesthetic Plastic Surgery. "Cosmetic Surgery National Data Bank Statistics (2009)," http://www.surgery.org

Associated Newspapers Ltd. "Schools Health Education Unit Survey." *Mail Online,* http://www.dailymail.co.uk/news/article-1219960/The-girls-living-just-meal-day-Teens-risk-health-copy-stick-celebrities-eating-disorder-anorexia-bulimia.html#ixzz0ZKOOPfS9 (accessed October 13, 2009).

Berning, J. M., K. J. Adams, and B. A. Stamford. "Anabolic Steroid Usage in Athletics: Facts, Fiction, and Public Relations." *Journal of Strength Conditioning Research* 18 (2004): 908–17.

Brown, L. M., and C. Gilligan. *Meeting at the Crossroads: Women's Psychology and Girls' Development.* Cambridge, Mass.: Harvard University Press, 1992.

Caldwell, M. B., K. D. Brownell, and D. E. Wilfley. "Relationship of Weight, Body Dissatisfaction and Self-esteem in African American and White Female Dieters." *International Journal of Eating Disorders* 22 (1997): 127–30.

Celio, A. A., M. F. Zabinski, and D. E. Wilfley. "African American Body Images," in *Body Image: A Handbook of Theory, Research and Clinical Practice.* Edited by T. F. Cash and T. Pruzinsky. New York: Guilford Press, 2002.

Centers for Disease Control and Prevention. "Cigarette Smoking Among Adults—United States, 2004." *Morbidity and Mortality Weekly Report* 54(44) (2005): 1121–24.

Dalley, S. E., and A. P. Buunk. "Thinspiration vs. Fear of Fat." *Appetite* 52 (2009): 217–21.

Ditteich, E. A. "Socio-cultural Factors That Influence Body Image Satisfaction in Women." *Dissertation Abstracts International,* http://www.about-face.org (accessed October 20, 2000).

Elliot, D. L., et al. "Cross-sectional Study of Female Students Reporting Anabolic Steroid Use." *Archives of Pediatrics & Adolescent Medicine* 161(6) (2007): 572–77.

Filozof, C., M. C. Fernandez Pinilla, and A. Fernandez-Cruz. "Smoking Cessation and Weight Gain." *Obesity Reviews* 5 (2004): 95–103.

Grabe, S., L. M. Ward, and J. S. Hyde. "The Role of the Media in Body Image Concerns Among Women: A Meta-Analysis of Experimental and Correlational Studies." *Psychological Bulletin* 134(3) (2008): 460–76.

Granberg, Ellen M., et al. "The Relationship between Body Size and Depressed Mood: Findings from a Sample of African American Middle School Girls." *Youth & Society* 39(3) (2008): 294–315.

Gruber, A. J., and H. G. Pope, Jr. "Psychiatric and Medical Effects of Anabolic-Androgenic Steroid Use in Women." *Psychotherapy Psychosomatics* 69 (2000): 19–26.

Hayes, S., and S. Tantleff-Dunn. "Am I Too Fat to Be a Princess? Examining the Effects of Popular Children's Media on Young Girls' Body Image." *British Journal of Developmental Psychology* 28 (2010): 413–26.

Jarry, J. L., et al. "Weight Gain after Smoking Cessation in Women: The Impact of Dieting Status." *International Journal of Eating Disorders* 24 (1998): 53–64.

Jeffery, R. W., et al. "Smoking-Specific Weight Gain Concerns and Smoking Cessation in a Working Population." *Health Psychology* 16 (1997): 487–89.

Mackey, E. R., and A. M. La Greca. "Does This Make Me Look Fat? Peer Crowd and Peer Contributions to Adolescent Girls' Weight Control Behaviors." *Journal of Youth and Adolescence* 37(9) (2008): 1097–110.

Malarkey, W. B., et al. "Endocrine Effects in Female Weight Lifters Who Self-Administer Testosterone and Anabolic Steroids." *American Journal Obstetric Gynecology* 165 (1991): 1385–390.

McCabe, M. P., et al. "Where Is All the Pressure Coming From? Messages from Mothers and Teachers about Preschool Children's Appearance, Diet and Exercise." *European Eating Disorders Review: The Journal of the Eating Disorders Association* 15(3) (2007): 221–30.

Neumark-Sztainer, D., et al. "Does Body Satisfaction Matter? Five-Year Longitudinal Associations between Body Satisfaction and Health Behaviors in Adolescent Females and Males." *Journal of Adolescent Health* 39 (2006): 244–51.

O'Loughlin, J., et al. "Does Cigarette Use Influence Adiposity or Height in Adolescence?" *Annals of Epidemiology* 18(5) (2008): 395–402.

Pangea Media, LLC. "Are You Resolving to Lose Weight This Year?" *Quibblo,* http://www.quibblo.com/quiz/3fbWQX1/Are-You-Resolving-to-Lose-Weight-this-Year (accessed January 8, 2009).

Parker Pope, Tara. "Spending Less on Plastic Surgery." *New York Times,* http://well.blogs.nytimes.com/2010/03/09/sagging-interest-in-plastic surgery.

Peng, Tina. "Out of the Shadows." *Newsweek,* http://www. newsweek.com/id/170528 (accessed November 23, 2008).

Pipher, Mary. *Reviving Ophelia: Saving the Selves of Adolescent Girls.* New York: Ballantine Books, 1995.

Robinson, T. N., et al. "Ethnicity and Body Dissatisfaction: Are Hispanic and Asian Girls at Increased Risk for Eating Disorders?" *Journal of Adolescent Health* 19 (1996): 384–93.

Schools Health Education Unit. "Young People into 2008." Chapter 1: Food Choices and Weight Control, page 4. http://www. sheu.org.uk/publications/yp08docs/chp1.pdf (accessed April 15, 2009).

ScienceDaily. "New Study Shows Teenage Girls' Use of Diet Pills Doubles Over Five-Year Span," http://www.sciencedaily.com/ releases/2006/10/061030143332.htm (accessed December 13, 2008).

Silverman, Robyn J. A. "Body Size, Society Views of." *Encyclopedia of Applied Developmental Science* 1 (2005): 160–64.

Simmons, Rachel. *The Curse of the Good Girl: Raising Authentic Girls with Courage and Confidence.* New York: Penguin Press, 2009.

———. *Odd Girl Out: The Hidden Culture of Aggression in Girls.* New York: Harcourt Inc., 2002.

Strauss, R. H., M. T. Liggett, and R. R. Lanese. "Anabolic Steroid Use and Perceived Effects in Ten Weight-Trained Women Athletes." *JAMA* 253 (1985): 2871–73.

Striegel-Moore, R. H., and L. Smolak. "The Influence of Ethnicity on Eating Disorders in Women." In *Handbook of Gender, Culture, and Health.* Edited by R. M. Eisler and M. Hersen. Mahwah, N.J.: Lawrence Erlbaum Associates, 2000.

Swahn, Monica H., et al. "Perceived Overweight, BMI, and Risk for Suicide Attempts: Findings from the 2007 Youth Risk Behavior Survey." *Journal of Adolescent Health: Official Publication of the Society for Adolescent Medicine* 45(3) (2009): 292–95.

Sweeney, C. "Seeking Self-Esteem through Surgery." *New York Times,* http://www.nytimes.com/2009/01/15/fashion/15skin.html (accessed January 14, 2009).

Viladrich, A., et al. "Do Real Women Have Curves? Paradoxical Body Images Among Latinas in New York City." *Journal of Immigrant Minority Health* 11 (2009): 20–28.

Williamson, D. F., et al. "Smoking Cessation and Severity of Weight Gain in a National Cohort." *New England Journal of Medicine* 324 (1991): 739–45.

Wiseman, Rosalind. *Queen Bees & Wannabes: Helping Your Daughter Survive Cliques, Gossip, Boyfriends & Other Realities of Adolescence.* New York: Crown Publishers, 2002.

"Young People's Food Choices: Attitudes to Healthy Eating and Weight Control," 1983–2007, http://www.sheu.org.uk/publications/trendsfoodchoices.htm (accessed April 15, 2009).

Chapter 2

Chadwick, Dara. *You'd Be So Pretty If…: Teaching Our Daughters to Love Their Bodies—Even When We Don't Love Our Own.* Cambridge, Mass.: Da Capo Press, 2009.

Cooley, E., et al. "Maternal Effects on Daughters' Eating Pathology and Body Image." *Eating Behaviors* 9 (2007): 52–61.

Ellin, A. "What's Eating Our Kids? Fears About Bad Foods." *New York Times,* http://www.nytimes.com/2009/02/26/health/nutrition/26food.html (accessed February 25, 2009).

Forbes, G. B., et al. "Body Dissatisfaction in College Women and Their Mothers: Cohort Effects, Developmental Effects, and the Influence of Body Size, Sexism, and the Thin Body Ideal." *Sex Roles: A Journal of Research* 53 (2005): 281–98.

Gustafson-Larson, A. M., and R. D. Terry. "Weight-Related Behaviors and Concerns of Fourth-Grade Children." *Journal of the American Dietetic Association* 92(7) (1992): 818–22.

Haines, J., et al. "Child versus Parent Report of Parental Influences on Children's Weight-Related Attitudes and Behaviors." *Journal of Pediatric Psychology* 33(7) (2008): 783–88.

Harding, K. "Don't You Realize Fat Is Unhealthy?" http://kateharding.net/faq/but-don't-you-realize-fat-is-unhealthy/ (accessed June 25, 2007).

Jaffe, K., and J. Worobey. "Mothers' Attitude towards Fat, Weight, and Dieting in Themselves and their Children." *Body Image* 3 (2006): 113–20.

McCabe, M. P., and L. A. Ricciardelli. "A Prospective Study of Pressures from Parents, Peers, and Media on Extreme Weight Change Behaviors among Adolescent Boys and Girls." *Behaviour Research and Therapy* 43 (2006): 653–68.

McCabe, M. P., et al. "Where Is All the Pressure Coming From? Messages from Mothers and Teachers about Preschool Children's Appearance, Diet and Exercise." *European Eating Disorders Review* 15(3) (2007): 221–30.

McGhee, Christina. *Parenting Apart: How Separated and Divorced Parents Raise Happy and Secure Kids.* New York: Berkley Publishing Group, 2010.

Musher-Eizenman, D. R., et al. "The Narrow Range of Acceptable Body Types of Preschoolers and Their Mothers." *Journal of Applied Developmental Psychology* 25 (2003): 541–53.

Nasser, M., and M. Katzman. "Eating Disorders: Transcultural Perspectives Inform Prevention." In *Preventing Eating Disorders: A Handbook of Interventions and Special Challenges.* Edited by N. Piran, M. P. Levine, and C. Adair Steiner. Philadelphia: Brunner/Mazel, 1999.

New York–Presbyterian Hospital Website. "Anorexia Nervosa," http://nyp.org/health/mentalhealth-edanorex.html (accessed December 1, 2008).

Pike, K. M., and J. Rodin. "Mothers, Daughters, and Disordered Eating." *Journal of Abnormal Psychology* 100(2) (1991): 198–204.

Salkeld, Luke. "Mothers Who Diet Are 'Twice as Likely' to Have Daughters with Eating Disorders," http://www.dailymail.co.uk/news/article-1223641/Mothers-diet-twice-likely-daughters-eating-disorders.html (accessed October 29, 2009).

Scaglioni, S., M. Salvioni, and C. Galimberti. "Influence of Parental Attitudes in the Development of Children Eating Behaviours." *British Journal of Nutrition* 99 (2008): S22–S25.

Taylor, C. B., et al. "The Adverse Effect of Negative Comments about Weight and Shape from Family and Siblings on Women at High Risk for Eating Disorders." *Pediatrics* 118(2) (2006): 731–38.

Chapter 3

Adecco USA. "Would Working Dads Take a Pass on Paternity Leave?" http://www.adeccousa.com/articles/Would-working-dads-take-a-pass-at-paternity-leave.html?id=28&url=/pressroom/pressreleases/pages/forms/allitems.aspx&templateurl=/AboutUs/pressroom/Pages/Press-release.aspx (accessed June 4, 2007).

Agras, S. W., et al. "Childhood Risk Factors for Thin Body Preoccupation and Social Pressure to Be Thin." *Journal of the American Academy of Child & Adolescent Psychiatry* 46 (2007): 171–78.

Al Sabbah, H., et al. "Body Weight Dissatisfaction and Communication with Parents among Adolescents in 24 Countries: International Cross-sectional Survey." *BMC Public Health* 9 (2009): 52.

Barras, J. *Whatever Happened to Daddy's Little Girl?* New York: Ballantine, 2000.

Bengtson, V. B. T., and R. Roberts. *How Families Still Matter.* New York: Cambridge University Press, 2002.

Bonney, J. F., M. L. Kelley, and R. F. Levant. "A Model of Fathers' Behavioral Involvement in Child Care in Dual-Earner Families." *Journal of Family Psychology* 13 (1999): 401–15.

Botta, R., and R. Dumlao. "Communication Patterns between Fathers and Daughters and Eating Disorders." *Health Communication* 14 (2002): 199–219.

Brayfield, A. "Juggling Jobs and Kids." *Journal of Marriage and the Family* 57 (2003): 321–32.

Coley, R. "Daughter-Father Relationships and Psychosocial Functioning." *Journal of Marriage and the Family* 65 (2004): 865–75.

Coley, R. L., E. Votruba-Drzal, and H. Schindler. "Fathers' and Mothers' Parenting Predicting and Responding to Adolescent Sexual Risk Behaviors." *Child Development* 80 (2009): 808–27.

Crouter, A. C., et al. "Implications of Overwork and Overload for the Quality of Men's Family Relationships." *Journal of Marriage and the Family* 63 (2001): 404–16.

Dixon, R. S., J. M. W. Gill, and V. A. Adair. "Exploring Paternal Influences on the Dieting Behaviors of Adolescent Girls." *Eating Disorders* 11 (2003): 39–50.

Erickson, B. *Longing for Dad.* Deerfield Beach, Fla.: Health Communications, 1998.

"Financial Incentives for Weight Loss." *ABC: The Health Report.* http://www.abc.net.au/rn/healthreport/stories/2009/2478259.htm (accessed February 2, 2009).

Flouri, E. *Fathering and Child Outcomes.* Chichester, UK: John Wiley, 2005.

Funk, L. *Supergirls Speak Out: Inside the Secret Crisis of Overachieving Girls.* New York: Simon & Schuster, 2009.

Galinsky, Ellen. *Ask the Children: What America's Children Really Think about Working Parents.* New York: William Morrow, 1999.

———. "Findings from Ask the Children with Implications for Early Childhood Professionals." *Young Children* 55(3) (2000): 64–68.

Gayles, G. *Father Songs.* Boston: Beacon Press, 1997.

Hosley, C., and R. Montemayor. "Fathers and Adolescents." In *The Role of the Father in Child Development.* Edited by M. Lamb. New York: Wiley, 1997.

Kast, V. *Father-Daughter, Mother-Son.* Rockport, Mass.: Element, 1997.

Kelly, J. *Dads and Daughters: How to Inspire, Understand, and Support Your Daughter When She's Growing Up So Fast.* New York: Broadway Books, 2002.

Klatte, W. *Live-Away Dads: Staying a Part of Your Children's Lives When They Aren't a Part of Your Home.* New York: Penguin Books, 1999.

Larson, R., and M. Richards. *Divergent Realities: Emotional Lives of Mothers, Fathers and Adolescents.* New York: Basic Books, 1994.

Leonard, L. *The Wounded Woman: Healing the Father-Daughter Wound.* Boston: Shambhala, 1998.

Maine, M. D. *Father Hunger: Fathers, Daughters, and the Pursuit of Thinness.* 2nd ed. New York: Gürze Books, 2004.

McBride, B. A., et al. "The Differential Impact of Early Father and Mother Involvement on Later Student Achievement." *Journal of Educational Psychology* 101(2) (2009): 498–508.

Meeker, M. *Strong Dads, Strong Daughters: 10 Secrets Every Father Should Know.* New York: Ballantine Books, 2006.

Morgan, J., and A. Wilcoxon. "Fathers and Daughters." *Family Therapy* 25 (1998): 73–84.

Nielsen, Linda. *Adolescence: A Contemporary View.* Fort Worth: Harcourt Brace, 1996.

———. *Between Fathers and Daughters: Enriching or Rebuilding Your Adult Relationship.* Nashville, Tenn.: Cumberland House Press, 2008.

———. "College Daughters' Relationships with Their Fathers: A 15 Year Study." *College Student Journal,* 2007, http://findarticles.com/p/articles/mi_m0FCR/is_1_41/ai_n18791246/ (accessed May 20, 2009).

———. "Demeaning, Demoralizing and Disenfranchising Divorced Dads." *Journal of Divorce & Remarriage* 31 (1999): 139–77.

———. *Embracing Your Father: How to Build the Relationship You've Always Wanted with Your Dad.* New York: McGraw Hill, 2004.

———. "Father-Daughter Relationships: A Needed Course in Family Studies." *Marriage and Family Review* 38(3) (2006): 1–13.

———. "Fathers and Daughters: Why a Course for College Students?" *College Student Journal* 35 (2001): 280–316.

———. "Strengthening Father-Daughter Relationships in Our Schools." In *Our Children*. Washington, D.C.: Parent Teacher Association of America, March 2–5, 2005.

Perkins, R. "Father-Daughter Relationships and Family Interactions." *College Student Journal* 35 (2001): 616–26.

Phares, V. *Poppa Psychology*. Westport, Conn.: Praeger, 1999.

Pleck, J. "Paternal Involvement: Levels, Origins, and Consequences." In *The Role of the Father in Child Development*. 3rd ed. Edited by M. Lamb. New York: Wiley, 1997.

Roper Poll. *Dads Talk about Their Daughters*. New York: United Business Media, 2004.

Shulman, S., and I. Krenke. *Fathers and Adolescents*. New York: Routledge, 1996.

Snarey, J. *How Fathers Care for the Next Generation*. Cambridge, Mass.: Harvard University, 1993.

"The Supergirl Dilemma: Girls Grapple with the Mounting Pressure of Expectations." Commissioned by Girls Inc. and conducted online by Harris Interactive, http://www.girlsinc.org/supergirldilemma/ (accessed January 17, 2007).

Tannen, D. *You Just Don't Understand: Women and Men in Conversation*. New York: Ballantine Books, 1991.

Taylor, K. *Black Fathers*. New York: Doubleday, 2003.

Updegraff, K., et al. "Parents' Involvement in Adolescent Peer Relationships." *Journal of Marriage and the Family* 63 (2001): 655–68.

Volpp, K. G., et al. "Financial Incentive-Based Approaches for Weight Loss: A Randomized Trial." *JAMA* 300(22) (2008): 2631–37.

Weiler Grayson, Pamela. "Dieting? Put Your Money Where Your Mouth Is." *New York Times,* http://www.nytimes.com/2009/02/05/health/nutrition/05fitness.html (accessed February 4, 2009).

Chapter 4

Attar-Schwartz, Shalhevet, et al. "Grandparenting and Adolescent Adjustment in Two-Parent Biological, Lone-Parent, and Step-Families." *Journal of Family Psychology* 23(1) (2009): 67–75.

Benson, P. *All Kids Are Our Kids: What Communities Must Do to Raise Caring and Responsible Children and Adolescents.* 2nd ed. New York: John Wiley and Sons, 2006.

Bernat, D. H., and M. D. Resnick. "Healthy Youth Development: Science and Strategies." *Journal of Public Health Management and Practice Supplement* 6 (2006): S10–S16.

Brown and Gilligan. *Meeting at the Crossroads.*

Canetti, L., et al. "Anorexia Nervosa and Parental Bonding: The Contribution of Parent-Grandparent Relationships to Eating Disorder Psychopathology." *Journal of Clinical Psychology* 64(6) (2008): 703–16.

Coomber, K., and R. M. King. "The Role of Sisters in Body Image Dissatisfaction and Disordered Eating." *Sex Roles* 59 (2008): 81–93.

Gross, R. M., and E. S. Nelson. "Perceptions of Parental Messages Regarding Eating and Weight and Their Impact on Disordered Eating." *Journal of College Student Psychotherapy* 15 (2000): 57–78.

Holm-Denoma, J. M., et al. "Parents' Reports of the Body Shape and Feeding Habits of 36-Month-Old Children: An Investigation of Gender Differences." *International Journal of Eating Disorders* 38(3) (2005): 228–35.

Kichler, Jessica C., and Janis H. Crowther. "Young Girls' Eating Attitudes and Body Image Dissatisfaction: Associations with Communication and Modeling." *Journal of Early Adolescence* 29 (2009): 212–32.

Kim, Ji-Yeon, et al. "Longitudinal Course and Family Correlates of Sibling Relationships from Childhood through Adolescence." *Child Development* 77 (2006): 1387–1402.

Kostanski, M., and E. Gullone. "The Impact of Teasing on Children's Body Image." *Journal of Child and Family Studies* 16(3) (2006): 307–19.

McHale, S. M., et al. "When Does Parents' Differential Treatment Have Negative Implications for Siblings?" *Social Development* 9 (2000): 149–72.

O'Connell, Claire. "Friends Influence Body Image." *Irish Times* (2009), http://www.irishtimes.com/newspaper/health/2009/0317/1224242942776.html (accessed March 17, 2009).

Rhodes, J. E., L. Ebert, and K. Fischer. "Natural Mentors: An Overlooked Resource in the Social Networks of Young, African American Mothers." *American Journal of Community Psychology* 20 (1992): 445–61.

Rieves, L., and T. F. Cash. "Reported Social Developmental Factors Associated with Women's Body-Image Attitudes." *Journal of Social Behavior and Personality* 11 (1996): 63–78.

Stark, Vicki. *My Sister, My Self: Understanding the Sibling Relationships That Shapes Our Lives, Our Loves, and Ourselves.* New York: McGraw-Hill, 2006.

Tannen. *You Just Don't Understand.*

Wiseman. *Queen Bees & Wannabes.*

Zimmerman, M. A., J. B. Bingenheimer, and P. C. Notaro. "Natural Mentors and Adolescent Resiliency: A Study with Urban Youth." *American Journal of Community Psychology* 30(2) (2002): 221–43.

Chapter 5

Chambliss, H. O., C. E. Finley, and S. N. Blair. "Attitudes toward Obese Individuals among Exercise Science Students." *Medicine & Science in Sports & Exercise* 36 (2004): 468–74.

Crandall, Christian S. "Prejudice against Fat People: Ideology and Self-Interest." *Journal of Personality and Social Psychology* 66(5) (1994): 882–94.

Crosnoe, R. "Gender, Obesity, and Education." *Sociology of Education* 80 (2007): 241–60.

Crosnoe, R., and C. Muller. "Body Mass Index, Academic Achievement, and School Context: Examining the Educational Experiences of Adolescent at Risk of Obesity." *Journal of Health and Social Behavior* 45 (2004): 393–407.

Davison, K. K., M. B. Earnest, and L. L. Birch. "Participation in Aesthetic Sports and Girls' Weight Concerns at Ages 5 and 7 Years." *International Journal of Eating Disorders* 31 (2002): 312–17.

Dokoupil, T. "Classroom Bullies." *Newsweek* (2009), http://www.newsweek.com/id/215997 (accessed September 30, 2009).

Greenleaf, C., and K. Weiller. "Perceptions of Youth Obesity among Physical Educators." *Social Psychology of Education* 8(4) (2005): 407–23.

Martin, C. E. *Perfect Girls, Starving Daughters: The Frightening New Normalcy of Hating Your Body.* New York: Free Press, 2007.

Neumark-Sztainer, D., M. Story, and T. Harris. "Beliefs and Attitudes about Obesity among Teachers and School Health Care Providers Working with Adolescents." *Journal of Nutrition Education* 31 (1999): 3–9.

O'Brien, K. S., J. A. Hunter, and M. Banks. "Implicit Anti-Fat Bias in Physical Educators: Physical Attributes, Ideology and Socialization." *International Journal of Obesity* 31 (2007): 308–14.

O'Dea, J., and S. F. Abraham. "Knowledge, Beliefs, Attitudes and Behaviors Related to Weight Control, Eating Disorders, and Body Image in Australian Trainee Home Economics and Physical Education Teachers." *Journal of Nutrition Education* 33 (2001): 332–40.

"Report on Size Discrimination." Prepared for the NEA Executive Committee's consideration by NEA Human and Civil Rights, pursuant to the following motion adopted by the NEA Board of Directors at its meeting, December 10–11, 1993. http://www.lectlaw.com/files/con28.htm (accessed January 4, 2000).

Scales, P. C., and N. Leffert. *Developmental Assets: A Synthesis of the Scientific Research on Adolescent Development.* 2nd ed. Minneapolis: Search Institute, 2004.

Schoenberg, ed., et al. *The New Normal? What Girls Say About Healthy Living.*

Science Daily. "Negative Phys Ed Teacher Can Cause a Lifetime of Inactivity." Research conducted by University of Alberta. Retrieved May 20, 2010, http://www.sciencedaily.com/releases/2010/01/100106193328.htm.

Silverman, Robyn J. A. "Body Size and Image, Female Attitudes and Perceptions About." *Encyclopedia of Applied Developmental Science* 1 (2005): 155–60.

———. "Body Types, Appraisals of." *Encyclopedia of Applied Developmental Science* 1 (2005): 164–69.

"The Supergirl Dilemma: Girls Grapple with the Mounting Pressure of Expectations," http://www.girlsinc.org/supergirldilemma/ (accessed January 17, 2007).

Szwarc, S. "Clueless Parents? Not Necessarily." *Junkfood Science,* http://junkfoodscience.blogspot.com/2008/10/clueless-parents-not-necessarily.html (accessed October 21, 2008).

———. "Remember the BMI Report Card Debate?" *Junkfood Science,* http://junkfoodscience.blogspot.com/2008/09/remember-bmi-report-card-debate.html (accessed September 27, 2008).

———. "School Childhood Obesity and BMI Screening Legislation Update." *Junkfood Science Blog,* http://junkfoodscience.blogspot.com/2008/03/school-childhood-obesity-and-bmi.html (accessed March 10, 2008).

Weisberg, Daniel, et al. "The Widget Effect: Our National Failure to Acknowledge and Act on Differences in Teacher Effectiveness." *The New Teacher Project,* http://widgeteffect.org/ (accessed June 1, 2009).

Yager, Z., and J. O'Dea. "Body Image, Dieting and Disordered Eating and Activity Practices among Teacher Trainees:

Implications for School-Based Health Education and Obesity Prevention Programs." *Health Education Research* 24(3) (2009): 472–83.

Chapter 6

Akers, A. Y., et al. "Exploring the Relationship among Weight, Race, and Sexual Behaviors among Girls." *Pediatrics* 124(5) (2009): e913–e920.

American Association of University Women (AAUW). *Shortchanging Girls, Shortchanging America: A Call to Action.*

Bergstrom, R., C. Neighbors, and M. A. Lewis. "Do Men Find 'Bony' Women Attractive?: Consequences of Misperceiving Opposite Sex Perceptions of Attractive Body Image." *Body Image* 1 (2003): 183–91.

Cawley, J., K. Joyner, and J. Sobal. "Size Matters: The Correlation of Adolescents' Height and Weight with Dating, Sex, Condom Use, and Pregnancy Rationality and Society." *Rationality and Society* 18(1) (2006): 67–94.

Crosnoe, R., K. Frank, and A. S. Mueller. "Gender, Body Size and Social Relations in American High Schools." *Social Forces* 86(3) (2008): 1189–1216.

Douvan, E., and J. Adelson. *The Adolescent Experience.* New York: Wiley, 1966.

Eisenberg, M. E., et al. "The Role of Social Norms and Friends' Influences on Unhealthy Weight-Control Behaviors among Adolescent Girls." *Social Science & Medicine* 60(6) (2004): 1165–73.

Fallon, A. E., and P. Rozin. "Sex Differences in Perceptions of Desirable Body Shape." *Journal of Abnormal Psychology* 94 (1985): 102–5.

FHM. "What Men Want: Thin's Not In." *Brisbane Times,* http://www.brisbanetimes.com.au/news/life-and-style/what-men-want-thins-not-in/2008/04/05/1207420346331.html (accessed April 8, 2008).

Gerner, B., and P. Wilson. "The Relationship between Friendship Factors and Adolescent Girls' Body Image Concern, Body Satisfaction, and Restrained Eating." *International Journal of Eating Disorders* 37 (2005): 313–20.

Halpern, C. T., et al. "Effects of Body Fat on Weight Concerns, Dating, and Sexual Activity: A Longitudinal Analysis of Black and White Adolescent Females." *Developmental Psychology* 35 (1999): 721–36.

Holub, S. C. "Individual Differences in the Anti-Fat Attitudes of Preschool Children: The Importance of Perceived Body Size." *Body Image* 5 (2008): 317–21.

"How Teens Use Media." *NielsonWire,* http://blog.nielsen.com/nielsenwire/consumer/teens-more-normal-than-you-think-regarding-media-usage/ (accessed June 25, 2009).

Hutchinson, D., and R. Rapee. "Do Friends Share Similar Body Image and Eating Problems? The Role of Social Networks and Peer Influences in Early Adolescence." *Behaviour Research and Therapy* 45(7) (2007): 1557–77.

Lemeshow, S. M., et al. "Subjective Social Status in the School and Change in Adiposity in Female Adolescents." *Archives of Pediatric Adolescent Medicine* 162(1) (2008): 23–28.

Levine, M. P., and L. Smolak. "Toward a Model of Developmental Psychopathology of Eating Disorders: The Example of Early Adolescence." In *The Etiology of Bulimia Nervosa: The Individual and Familial Context.* Edited by J. Crowther, et al. Washington, D.C.: Hemisphere, 1992.

MacDonald Clarke, Paige, Sarah K. Murnen, and L. Smolak. "Development and Psychometric Evaluation of a Quantitative Measure of 'Fat Talk.'" *Body Image,* in press.

Mackey, E. R., and A. M. La Greca. "Does This Make Me Look Fat? Peer Crowd and Peer Contributions to Adolescent Girls' Weight Control Behaviors." *Journal of Youth and Adolescence* 37(9) (2008): 1097–1110.

Nichter, Mimi. *Fat Talk: What Girls and Their Parents Say about Dieting.* Cambridge, Mass.: Harvard University Press, 2000.

Paxton, S. "Friendship, Body Image and Dieting in Teenage Girls: A Research Report." National Eating Disorder Information Centre. Toronto, Ontario, 1996, http://www.nedic.ca (accessed October 7, 2000).

Paxton, S. J., et al. "Friendship Clique and Peer Influences on Body Image Concerns, Dietary Restraint, Extreme Weight-loss Behaviors, and Binge Eating in Adolescent Girls." *Journal of Abnormal Psychology* 108 (1999): 255–66.

Pipher. *Reviving Ophelia.*

Schutz, H. K., and S. J. Paxton. "Friendship Quality, Body Dissatisfaction, Dieting and Disordered Eating in Adolescent Girls." *British Journal of Clinical Psychology* 46 (2007): 67–83.

Schutz, H. K., S. J. Paxton, and E. H. Wertheim. "Investigation of Body Comparison among Adolescent Girls." *Journal of Applied Social Psychology* 32 (2002): 1906–37.

Simmons. *Odd Girl Out.*

Sobal, J. "Social Consequences of Weight Bias by Partners, Friends, and Strangers." In *Weight Bias: Nature, Consequences and Remedies.* Edited by K. D. Brownell, et al. New York: Guilford Press, 2005.

Strauss, R. S., and H. A. Pollack. "Social Marginalization of Overweight Adolescents." *Archives of Pediatric and Adolescent Medicine* 157(8) (2003): 746–52.

The Telegraph. "Teenagers 'Spend an Average of 31 Hours Online.'" Research conducted by CyberSentinel.co.uk, http://www.telegraph.co.uk/technology/4574792/Teenagers-spend-an-average-of-31-hours-online.html (accessed February 10, 2009).

Tompkins, K. B., et al. "Social Likeability, Conformity, and Body Talk: Does Fat Talk Have a Normative Rival in Female Body Image Conversations?" *Body Image* 6(4) (2009): 292–98.

Townsend, J. M. *What Women Want—What Men Want: Why the Sexes Still See Love and Commitment So Differently.* Oxford, UK: Oxford University Press, 1998.

Tucker, K. L., et al. "Examining 'Fat Talk' Experimentally in a Female Dyad: How Are Women Influenced by Another Woman's Body Presentation Style?" *Body Image: An International Journal of Research* 4 (2007): 157–74.

Vener, A. M., L. R. Krupka, and R. J. Gerard. "Overweight/Obese Patients: An Overview." *Practitioner* 226 (1982): 1102–9.

Wiseman. *Queen Bees & Wannabes.*

Chapter 7

Benson. *All Kids Are Our Kids: What Communities Must Do to Raise Caring and Responsible Children and Adolescents.*

———. *Sparks: How Parents Can Help Ignite the Hidden Strengths of Teenagers.* San Francisco: Jossey-Bass, 2008.

Benson, P. L., and P. C. Scales. "The Definition and Preliminary Measurement of Thriving in Adolescence." *Journal of Positive Psychology* 4(1) (2009): 85–104.

Benson, P. L., et al. "Executive Summary: Successful Young Adult Development," a report submitted to the Bill & Melinda Gates Foundation (2004), http://www.search-institute.org (accessed January 12, 2005).

Bernat, D. H., and M. D. Resnick. "Connectedness in the Lives of Adolescents." In *Adolescent Health: Understanding and Preventing Risk Behaviors.* Edited by R. J. DiClemente, J. S. Santelli, and R. A. Crosby. San Francisco: Jossey-Bass, 2009.

Bradberry, Travis, and Jean Greaves. *Emotional Intelligence 2.0.* San Francisco: Publishers Group West, 2009.

Commission on Children at Risk. *Hardwired to Connect: The New Scientific Case for Authoritative Communities.* New York: Institute for American Values, 2003.

French, S. A., et al. "Adolescent Binge/Purge and Weight Loss Behaviors: Associations with Developmental Assets." *Journal of Adolescent Health* 28(3) (2001): 211–21.

Goleman, D. *Emotional Intelligence: Why It Can Matter More Than IQ.* New York: Bantam Books, 1995.

Lerner, R. M., and P. L. Benson, eds. *Developmental Assets and Asset-Building Communities: Implications for Research, Policy, and Practice.* Norwell, Mass.: Kluwer Academic Publishers, 2002.

Moninger, Jeanette. "Kick Together! Family Martial Arts Classes Boost Confidence, Improve Fitness, and Cement Family Bonds." *Prevention* (January 2007): 135–38.

Scales, P. C., and N. Leffert. *Developmental Assets: A Synthesis of the Scientific Research on Adolescent Development.* 2nd ed. Minneapolis: Search Institute, 2004.

Silverman, Robyn J. A. "Fitting into America: The Status of Developmental Assets and Sources of Positive Youth Development among Young Adult Plus Size Models." UMI Dissertation Services, 2004.

———. "Hang Up the Pink Tights: Why Martial Arts Is Great for Girls." *MA Success* (August 2008).

———. "Powerful Words Character Development," http://www.powerfulwords.com (accessed September 15, 2005).

Stice, E., and K. Whitenton. "Risk Factors for Body Dissatisfaction in Adolescent Girls: A Longitudinal Investigation." *Developmental Psychology* 38 (2002): 669–78.

Thomsen, K. *Parenting Preteens with a Purpose: Navigating the Middle Years.* Minneapolis: Search Institute Press, 2008.

Ungar, M. "The Importance of Parents and Other Caregivers to the Resilience of High-Risk Adolescents." *Family Process* 43(1) (2004): 23–41.

Van den Berg, P., and D. Neumark-Sztainer. "Fat 'n' Happy 5 Years Later: Is It Bad for Overweight Girls to Like Their Bodies?" *Journal of Adolescent Health* 41 (2007): 415–17.

Note: Maggie Sherman is a community artist who runs Hand On Productions. She graciously took me through the mask-making process in 2006.

Index

E

F

About the Author

Gary Goodman

DR. ROBYN J. A. SILVERMAN is an internationally recognized speaker, author, success coach and educator. A body image and teen development expert for dozens of books, she serves as an Advisory Board Member for *Shaping Youth,* a consortium of professionals concerned about harmful messages to children. She created *Powerful Words Character Development,* a character education and leadership development program that runs in ten countries. Known for her no-nonsense yet positive approach, Dr. Silverman also provides popular teleseminars and coaching opportunities to parents and families. As a way to interact with girls personally, she founded *The Sassy Sisterhood Girls Circle,* a program for young teen girls that is designed to foster self-awareness, challenge stereotypes and counter trends toward self-doubt.

Dr. Silverman keeps in touch with parents, educators and fans through her active Twitter and Facebook pages as well as through her blog.

Follow Dr. Robyn on:

www.drrobynsilverman.com
Twitter: twitter.com/drrobyn
Facebook: facebook.com/drrobynsilverman
YouTube: youtube.com/drrobynsilverman